Quotes

&

National Proverbs

Coloring Book

Quotes

&

National Proverbs

Coloring Book

Quotes

&

National Proverbs

Coloring Book

Silhouette Leah

Copyright:

Quotes & National Proverbs Coloring Book
Copyright © 2021
By Silhouette Leah

All Rights Reserved. Without prior written permission from the author, no segment, including rights of reproduction in any form (electronic version /soft copy or paper version/hard copy), of this book may be used in part or whole, except a brief portion by a reviewer for review purposes.

Printed in the United States of America

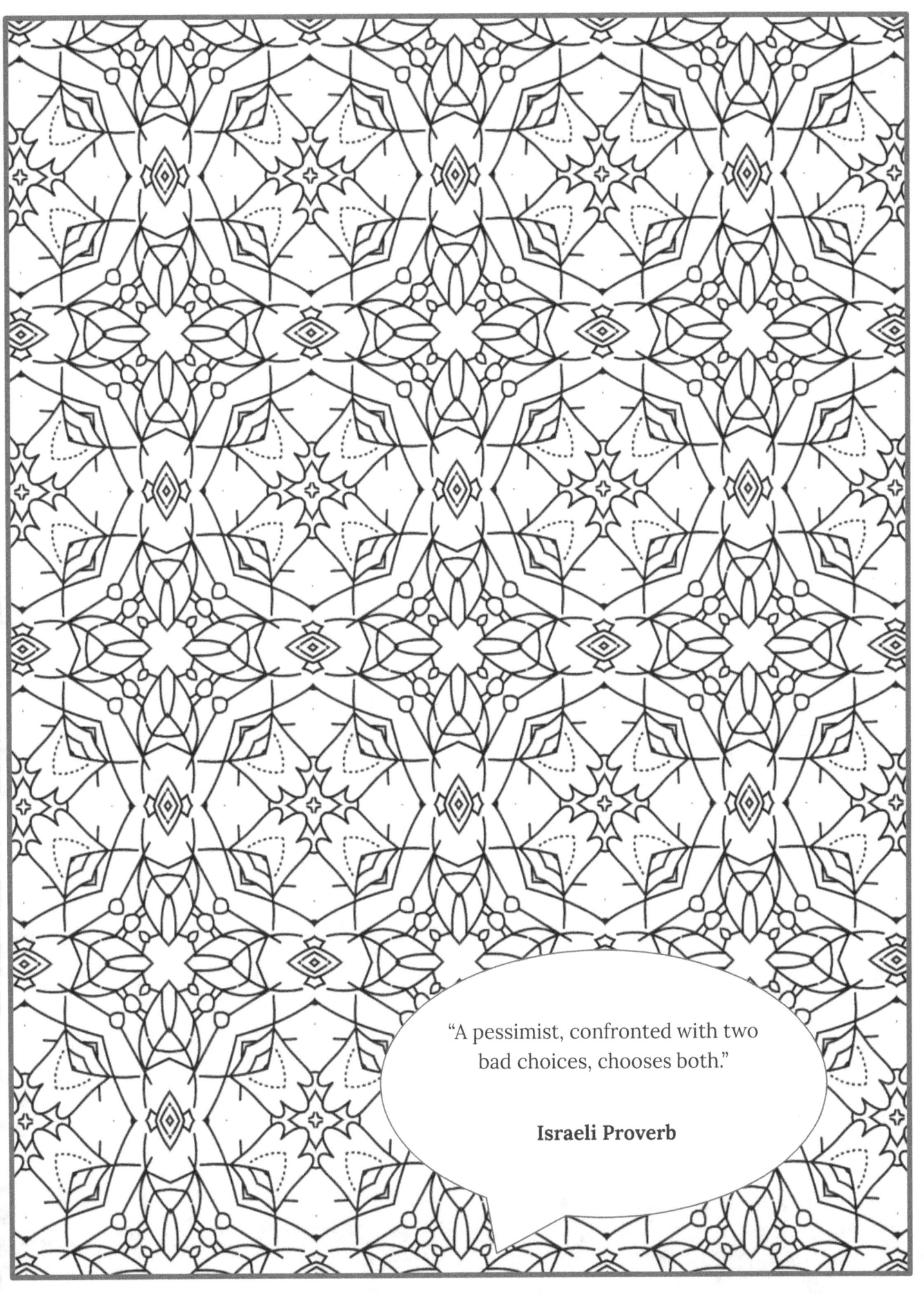

"A pessimist, confronted with two bad choices, chooses both."

Israeli Proverb

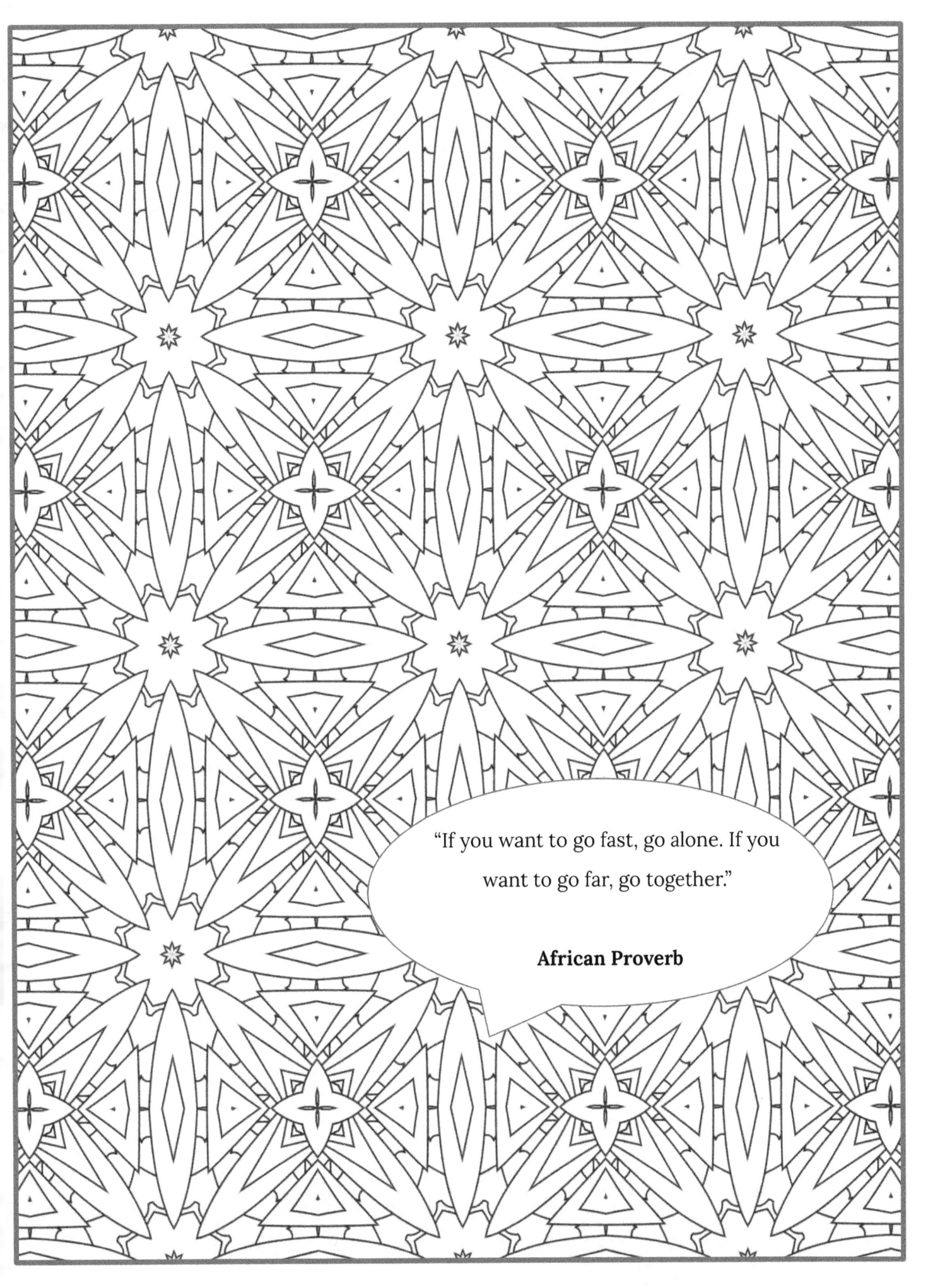

"If you want to go fast, go alone. If you want to go far, go together."

African Proverb

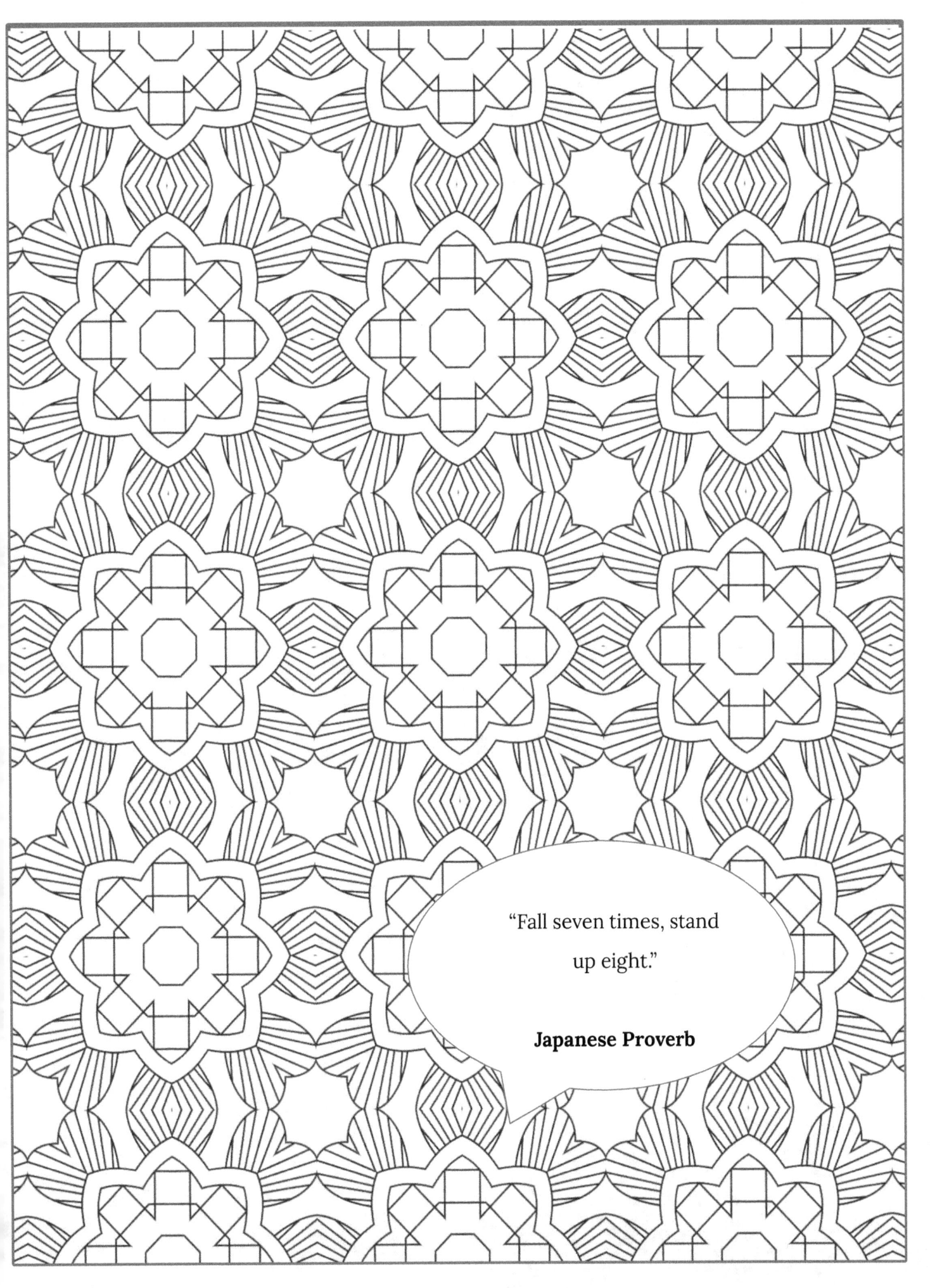

"Fall seven times, stand up eight."

Japanese Proverb

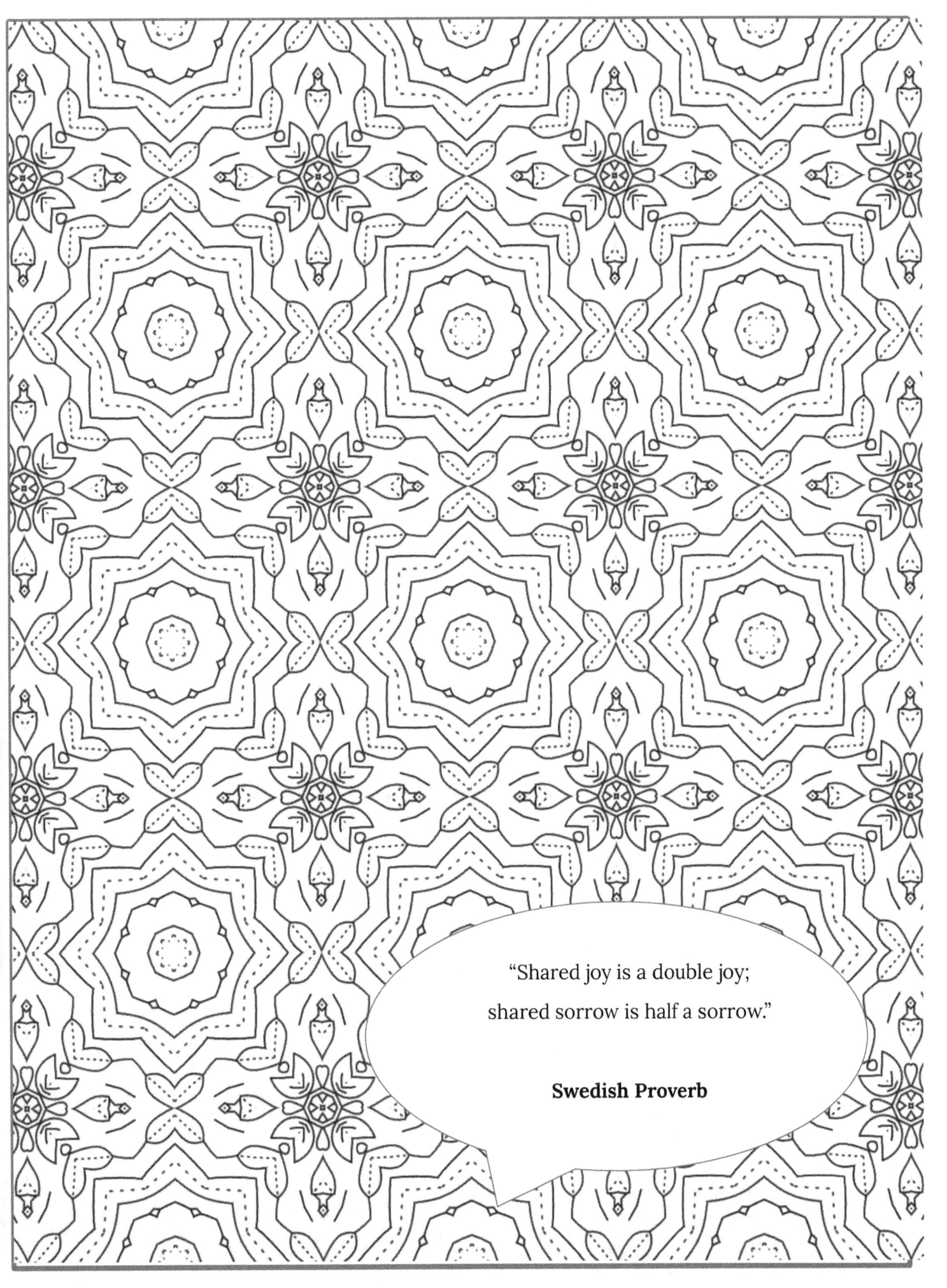

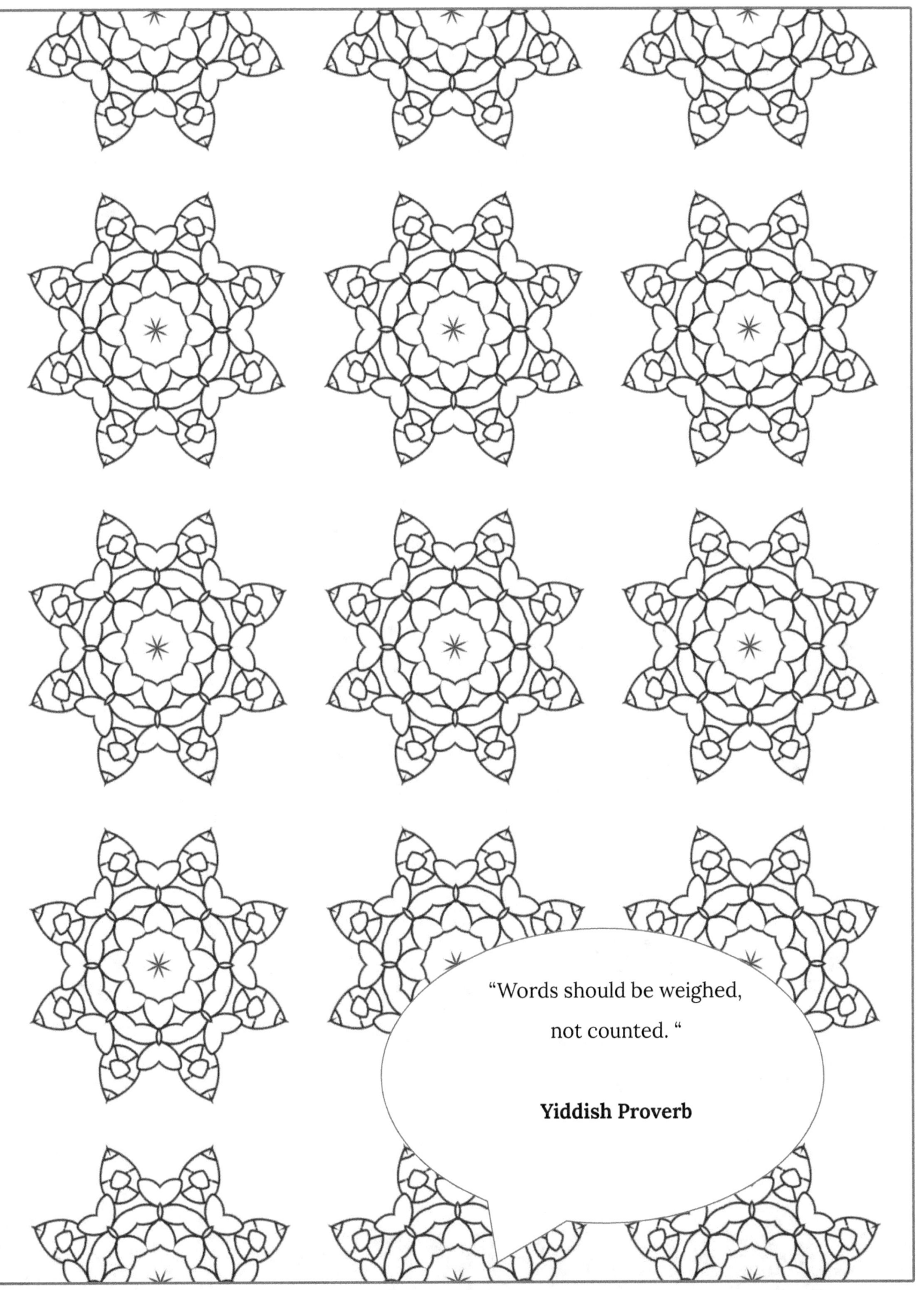

"Words should be weighed, not counted."

Yiddish Proverb

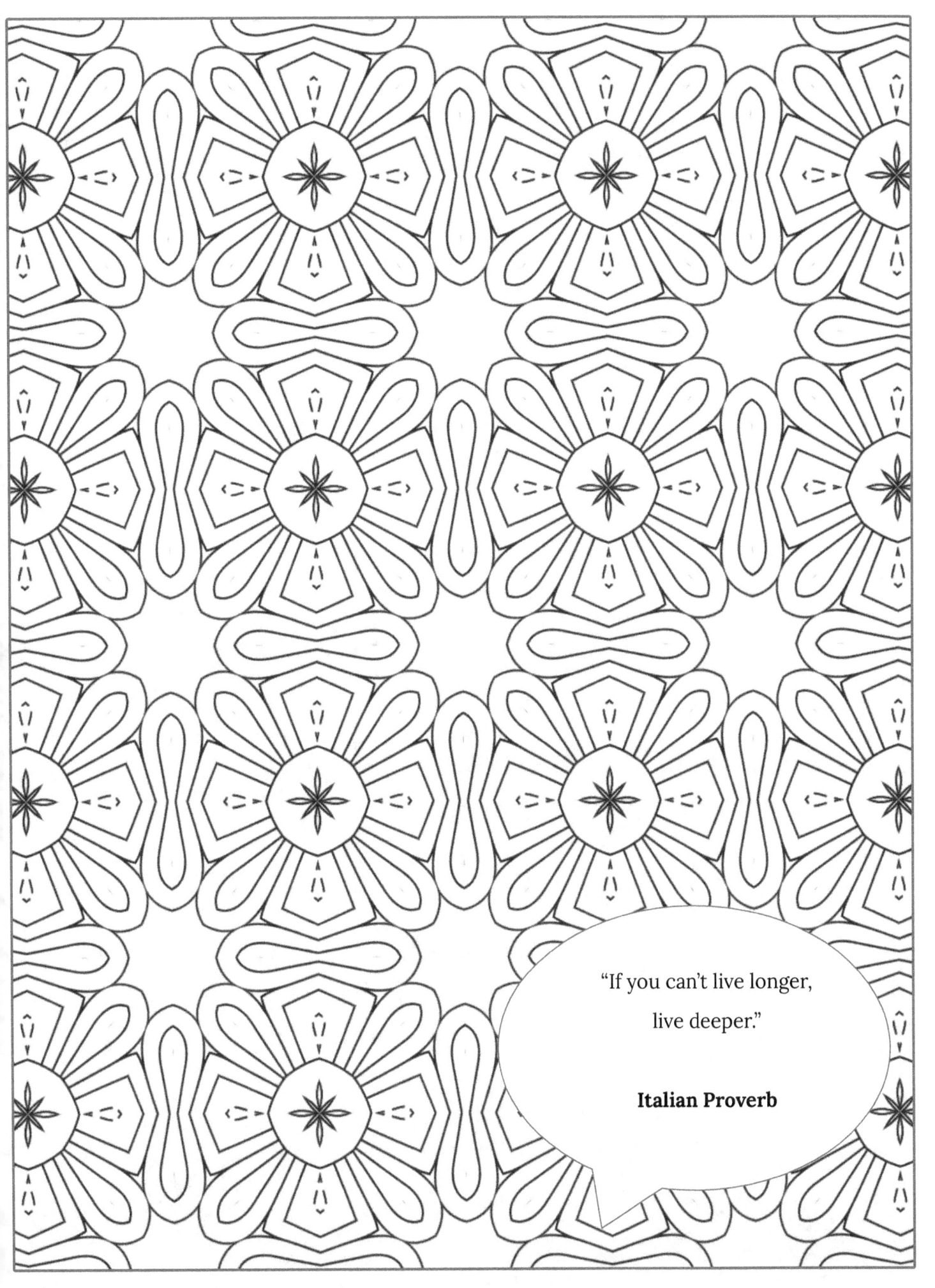

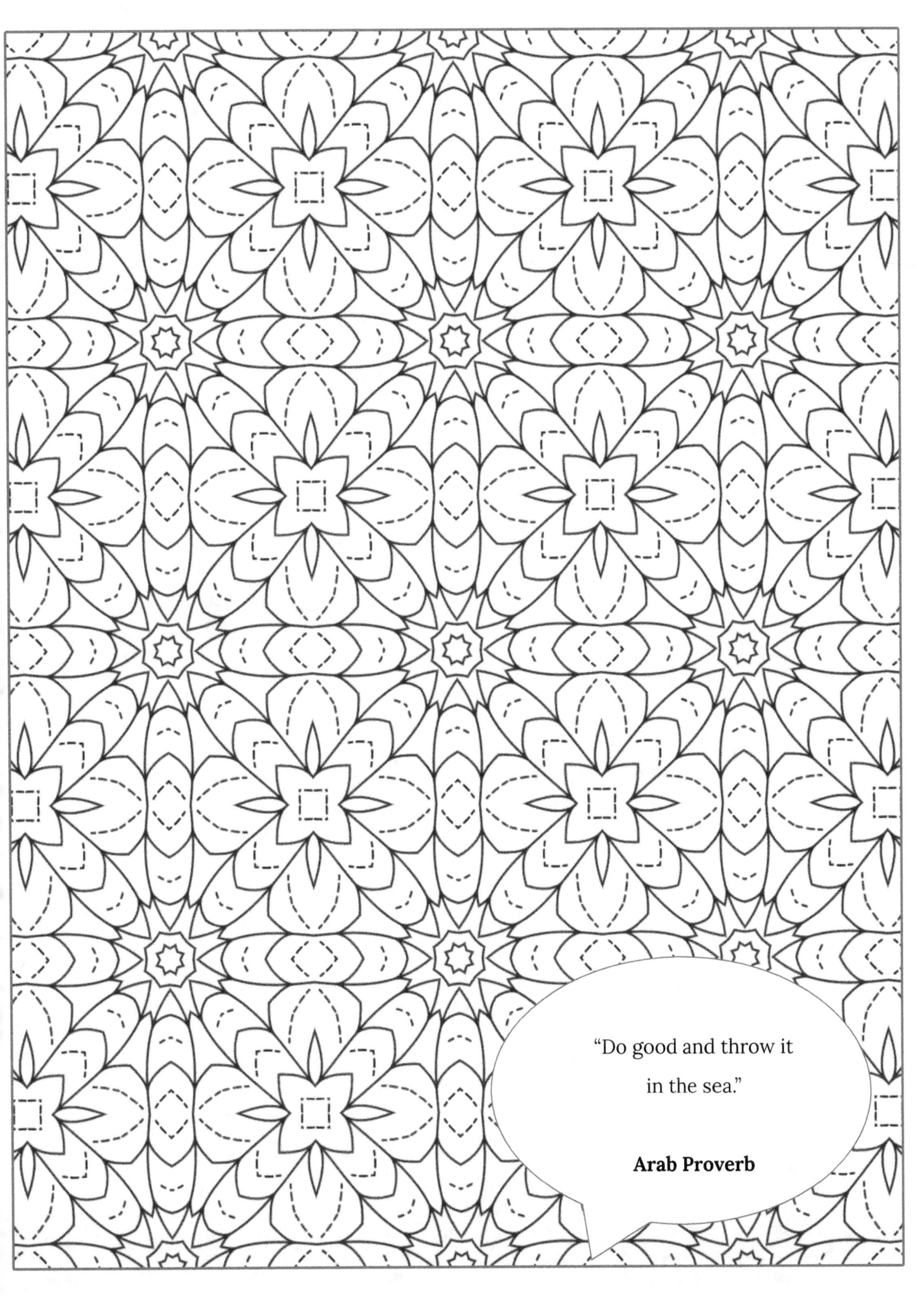

"Do good and throw it in the sea."

Arab Proverb

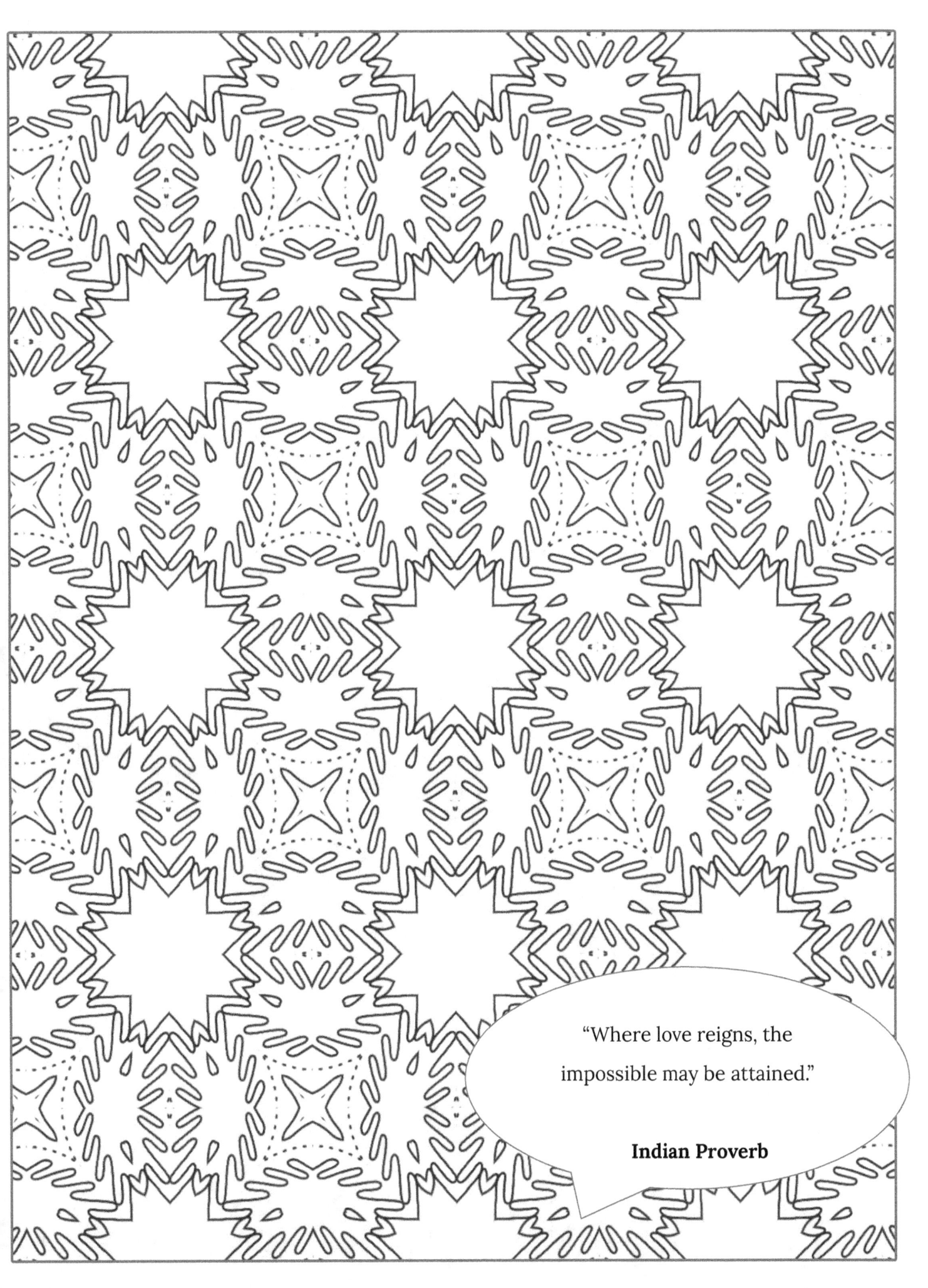

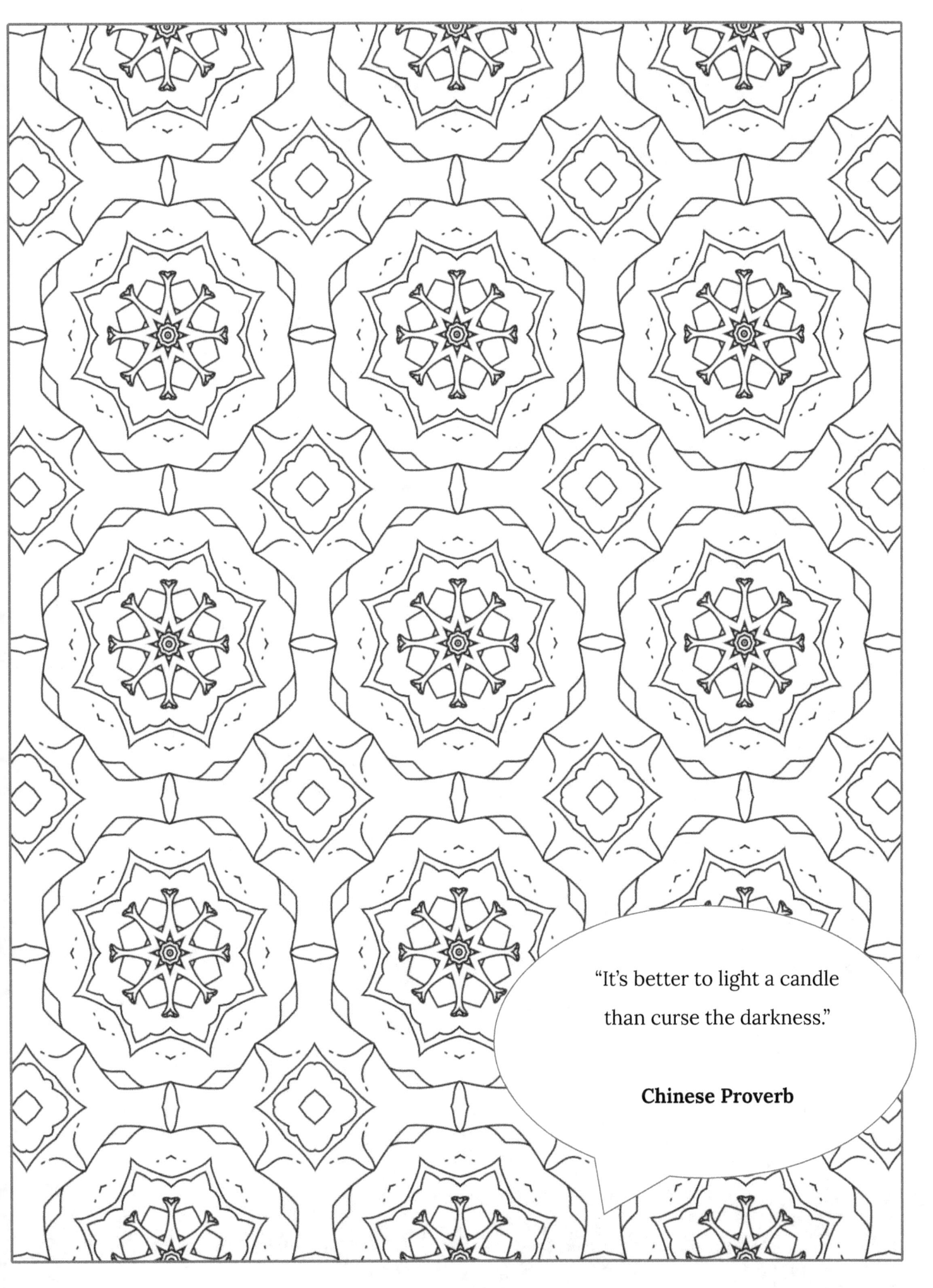

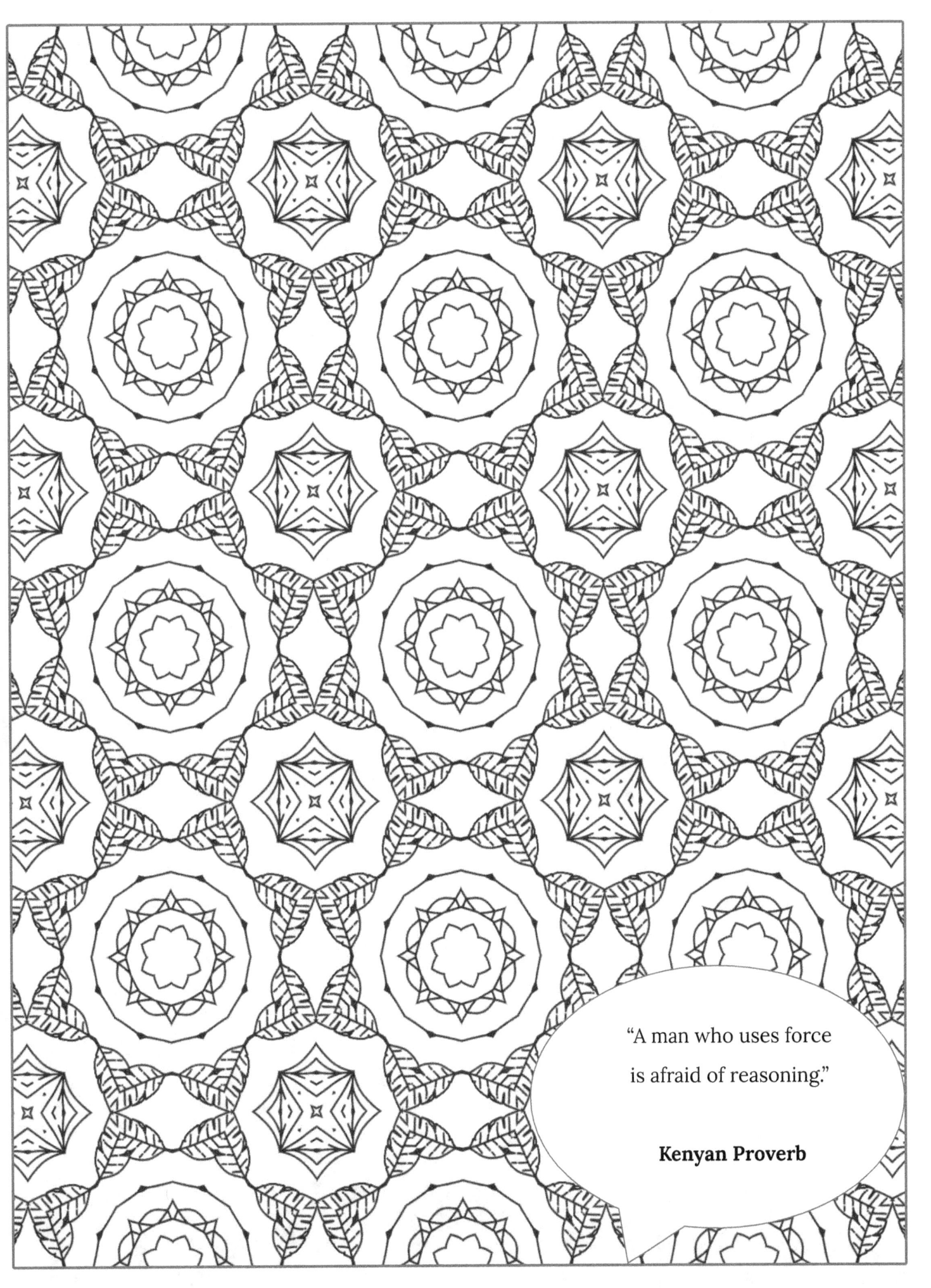

"A man who uses force is afraid of reasoning."

Kenyan Proverb

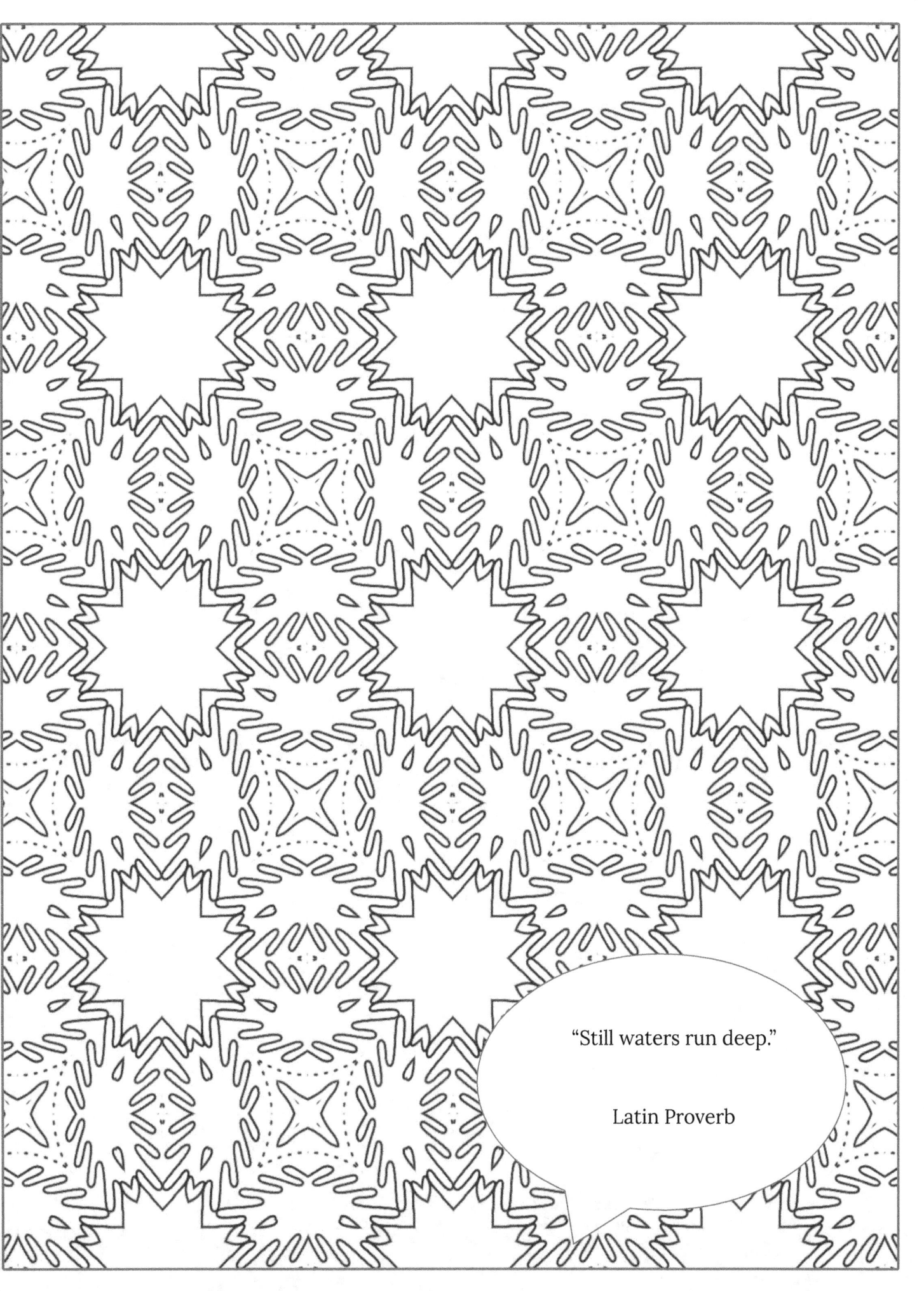

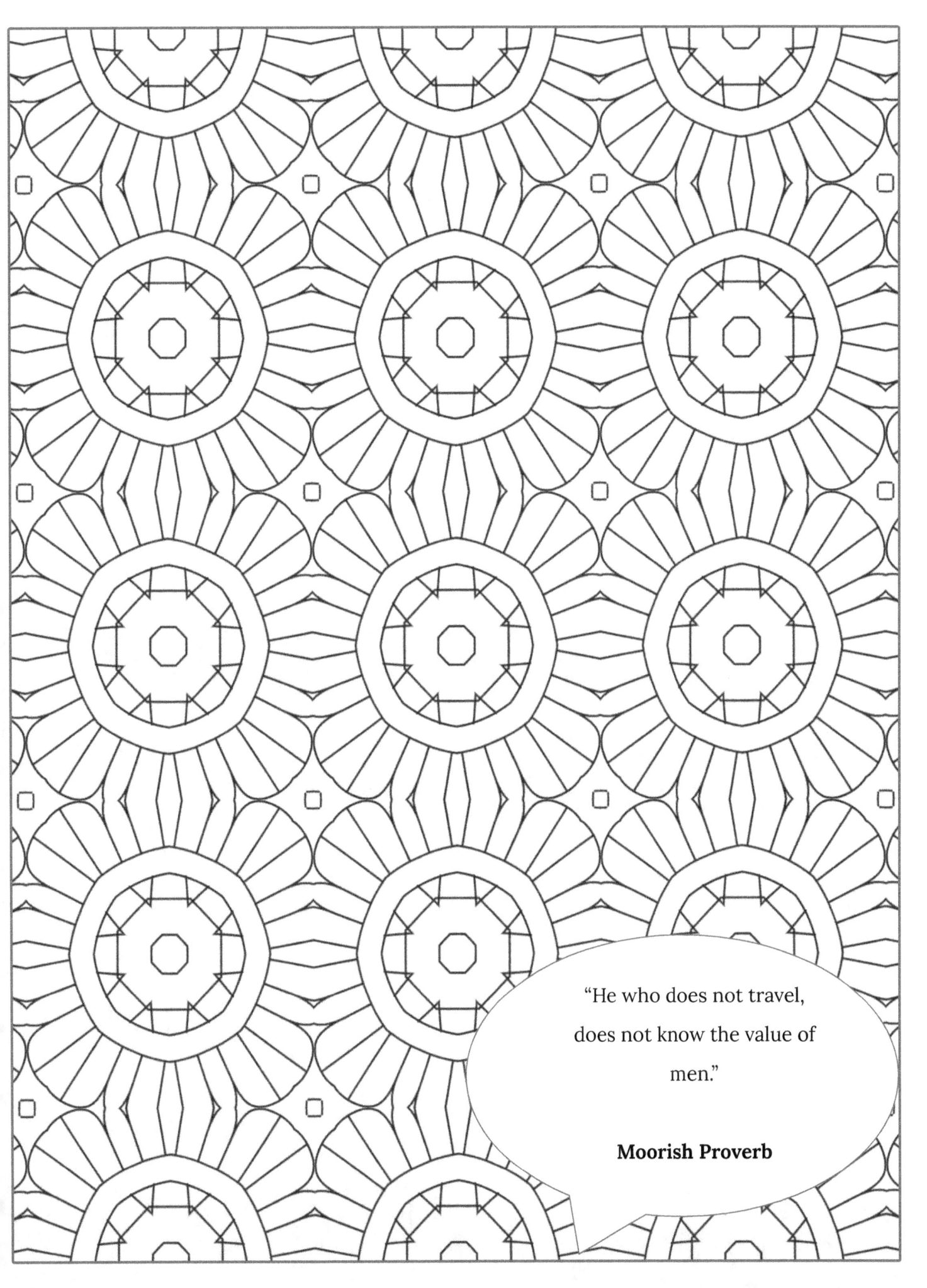

"He who does not travel, does not know the value of men."

Moorish Proverb

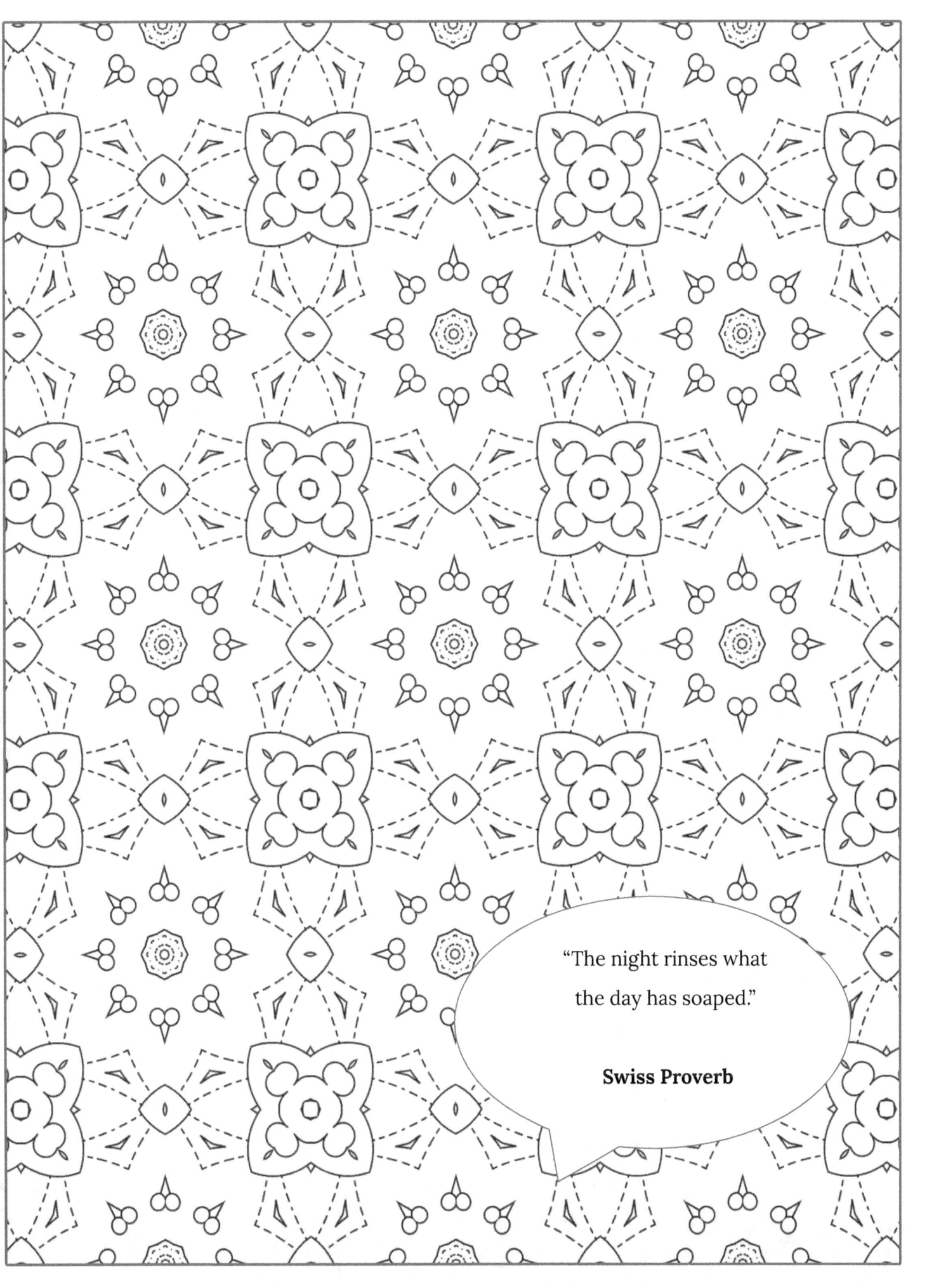

"The night rinses what the day has soaped."

Swiss Proverb

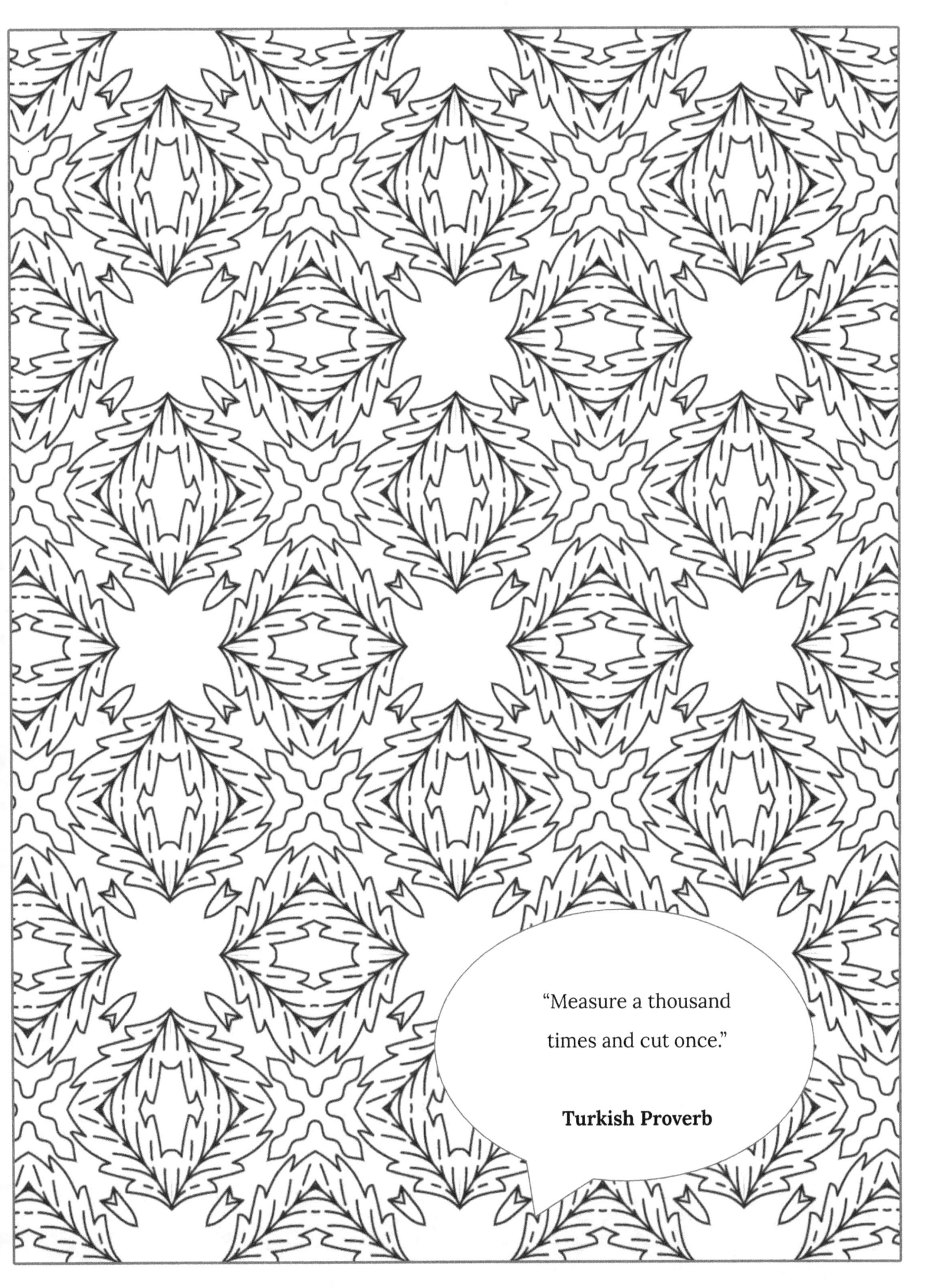

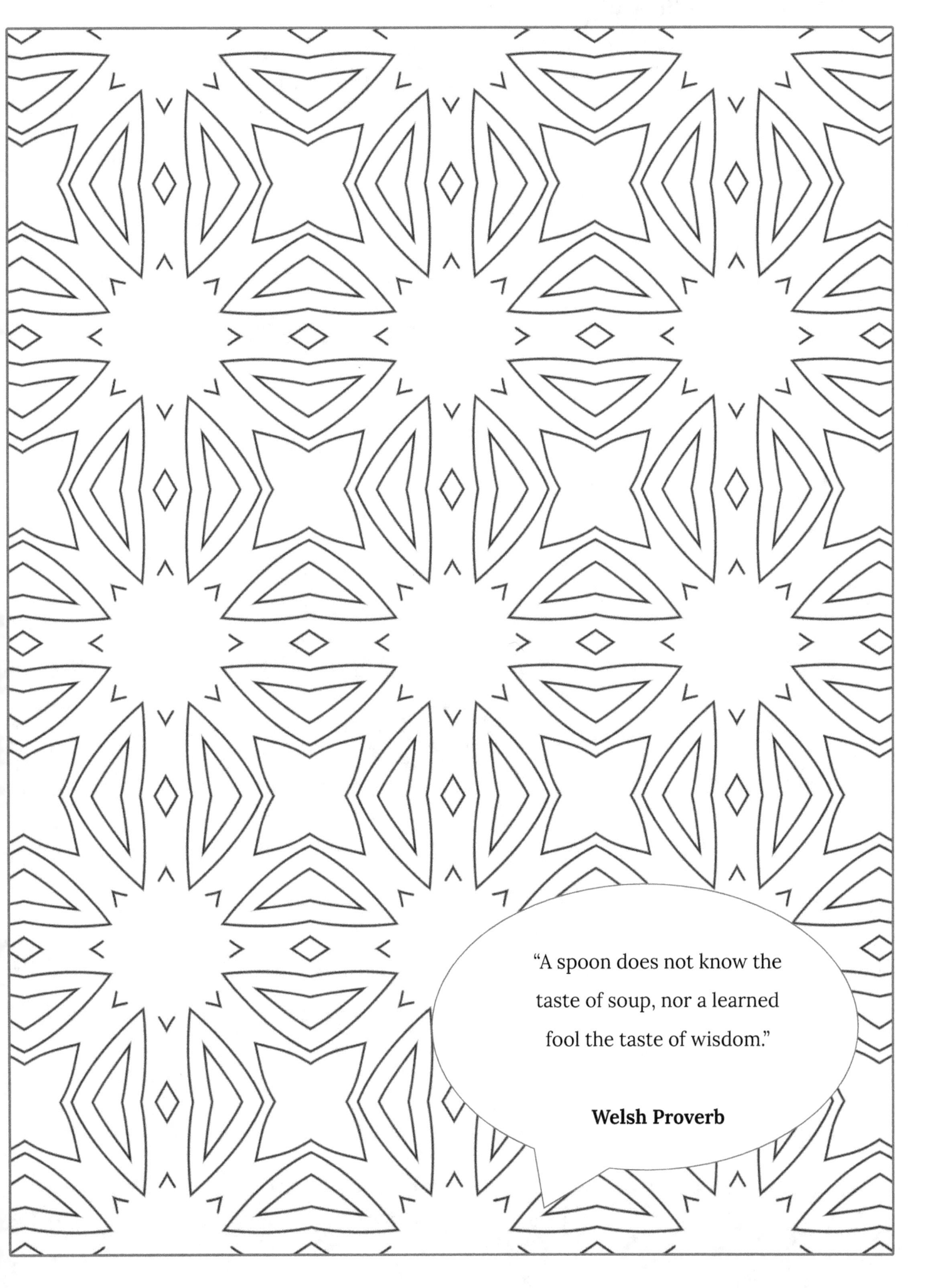

"A spoon does not know the taste of soup, nor a learned fool the taste of wisdom."

Welsh Proverb

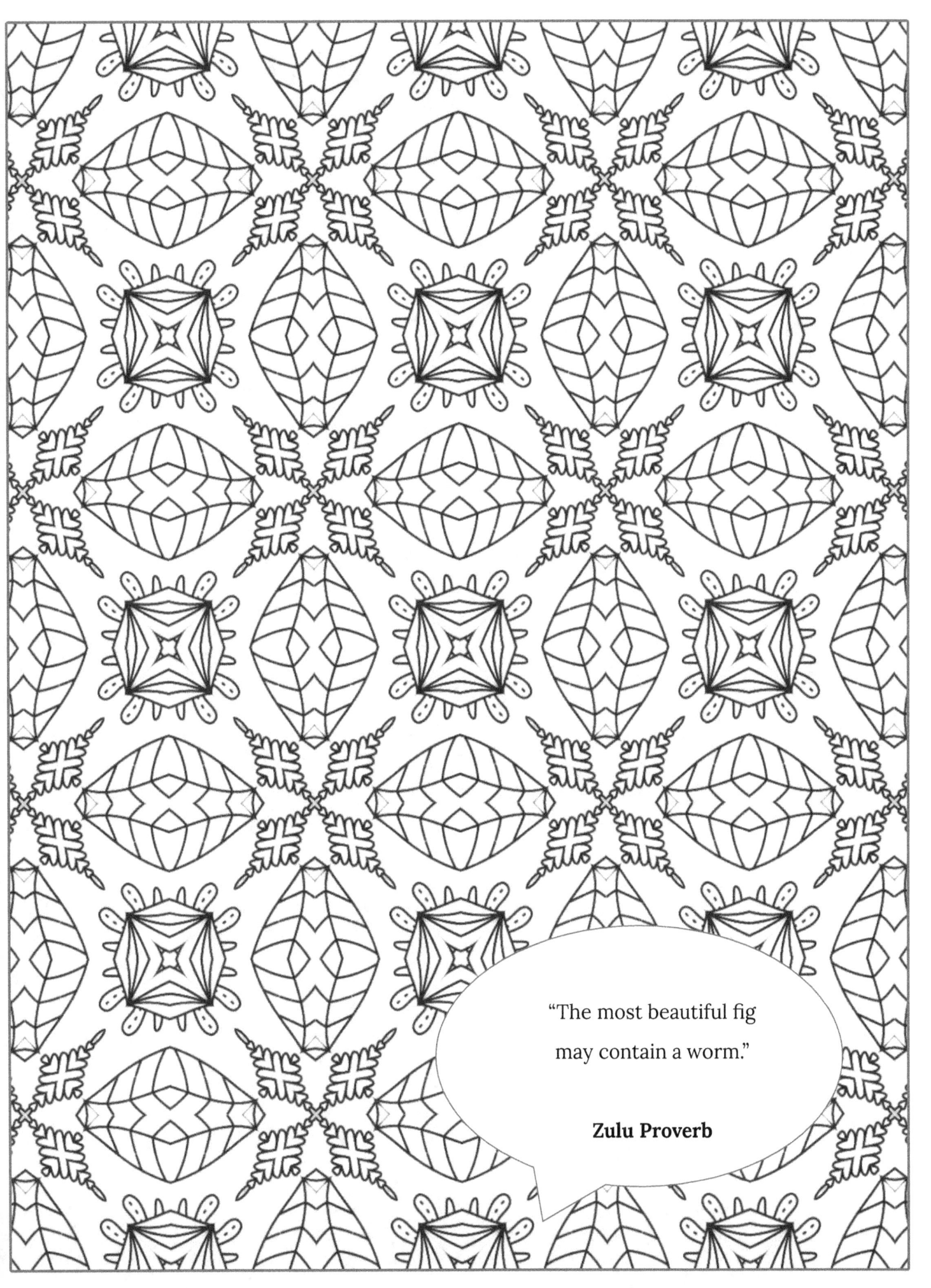

"The most beautiful fig may contain a worm."

Zulu Proverb

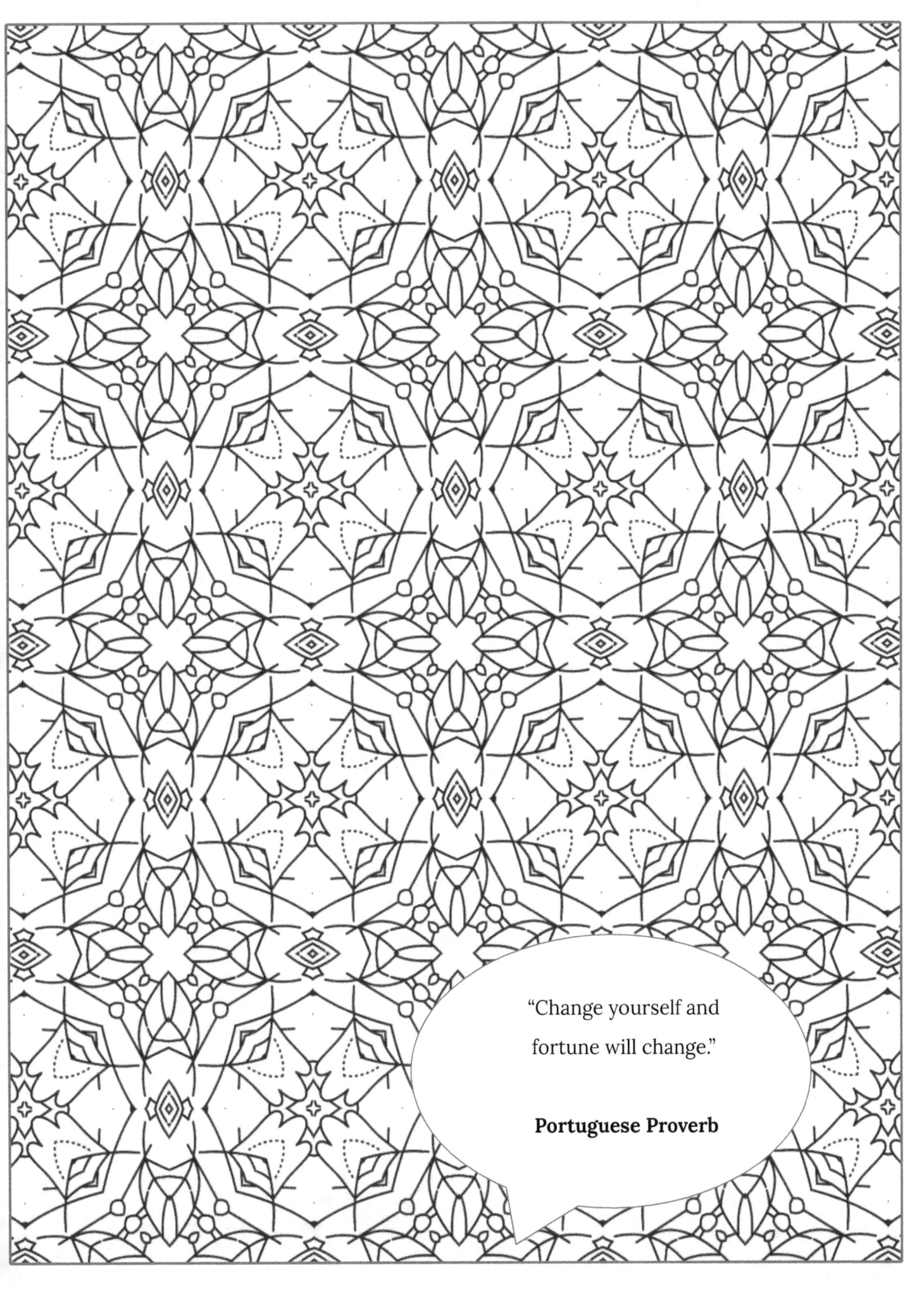

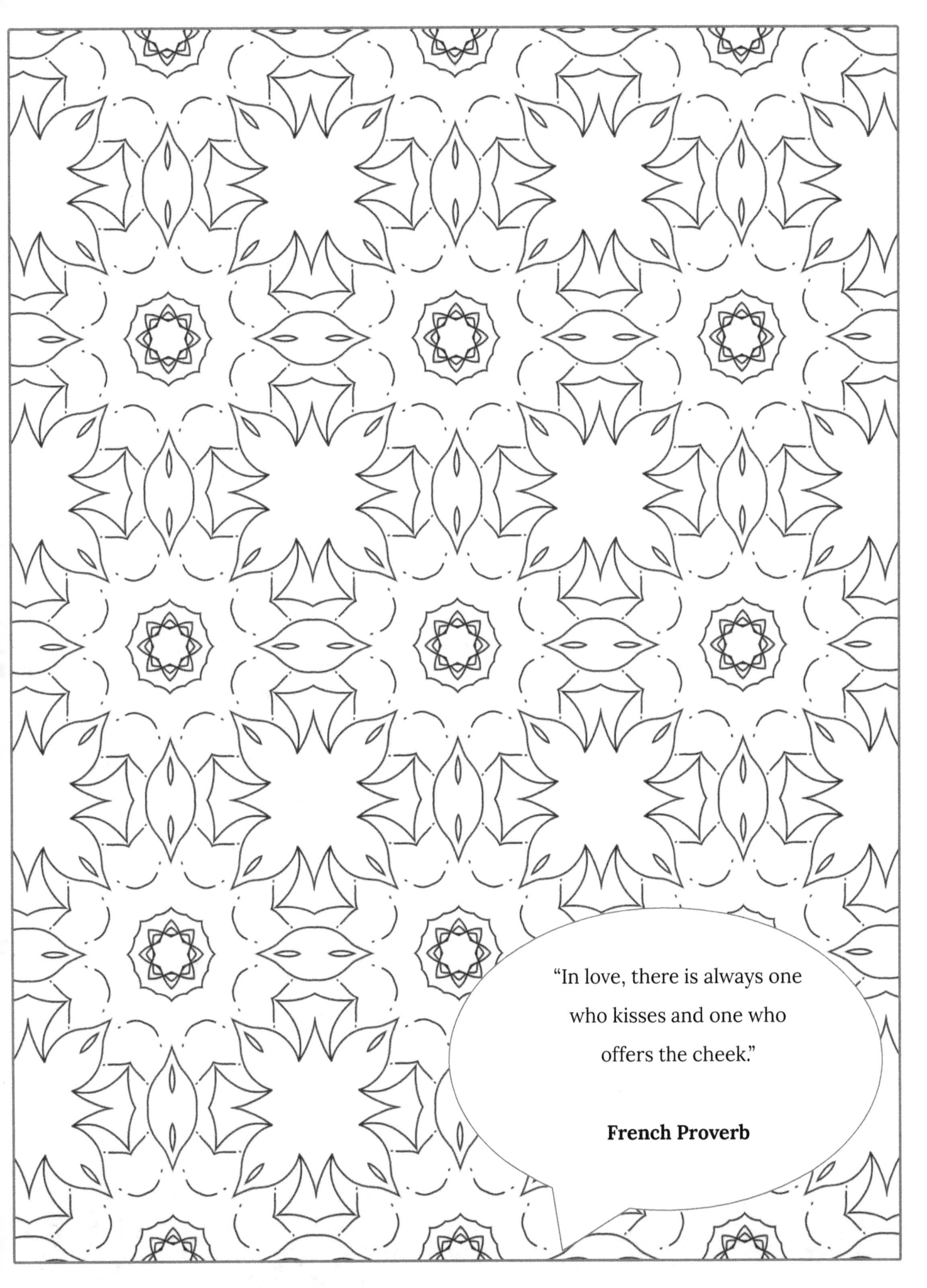

"In love, there is always one who kisses and one who offers the cheek."

French Proverb

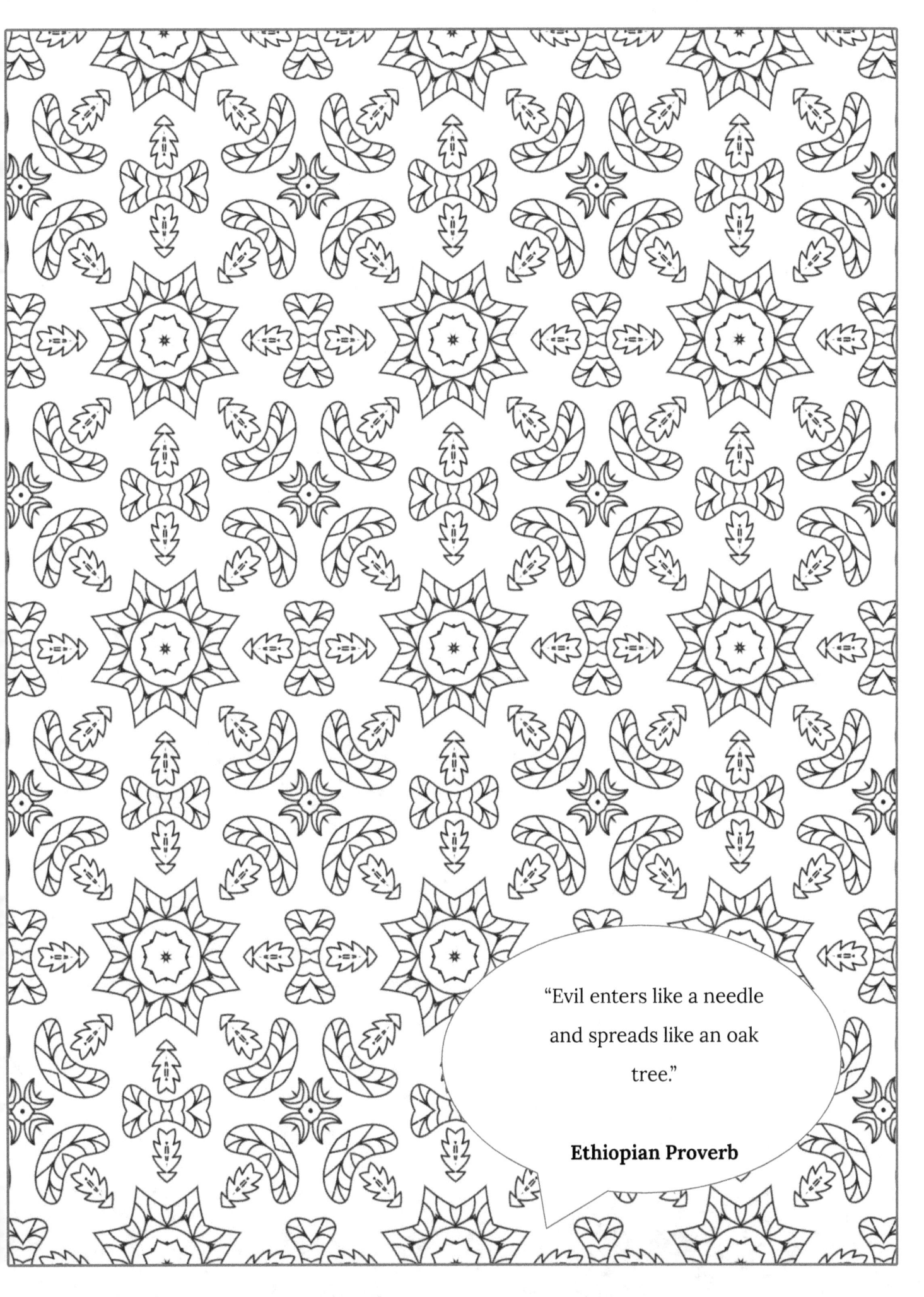

"Evil enters like a needle and spreads like an oak tree."

Ethiopian Proverb

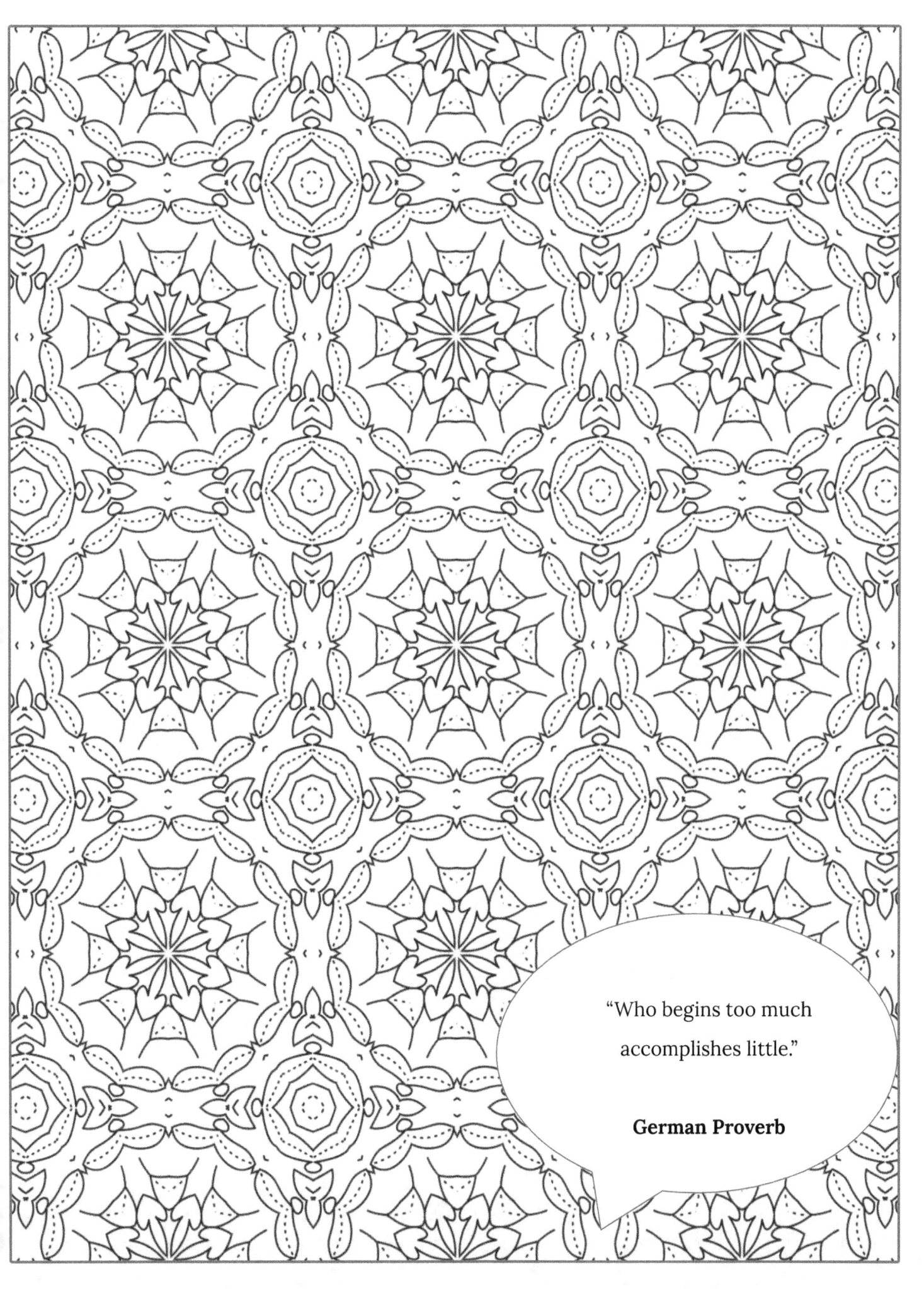

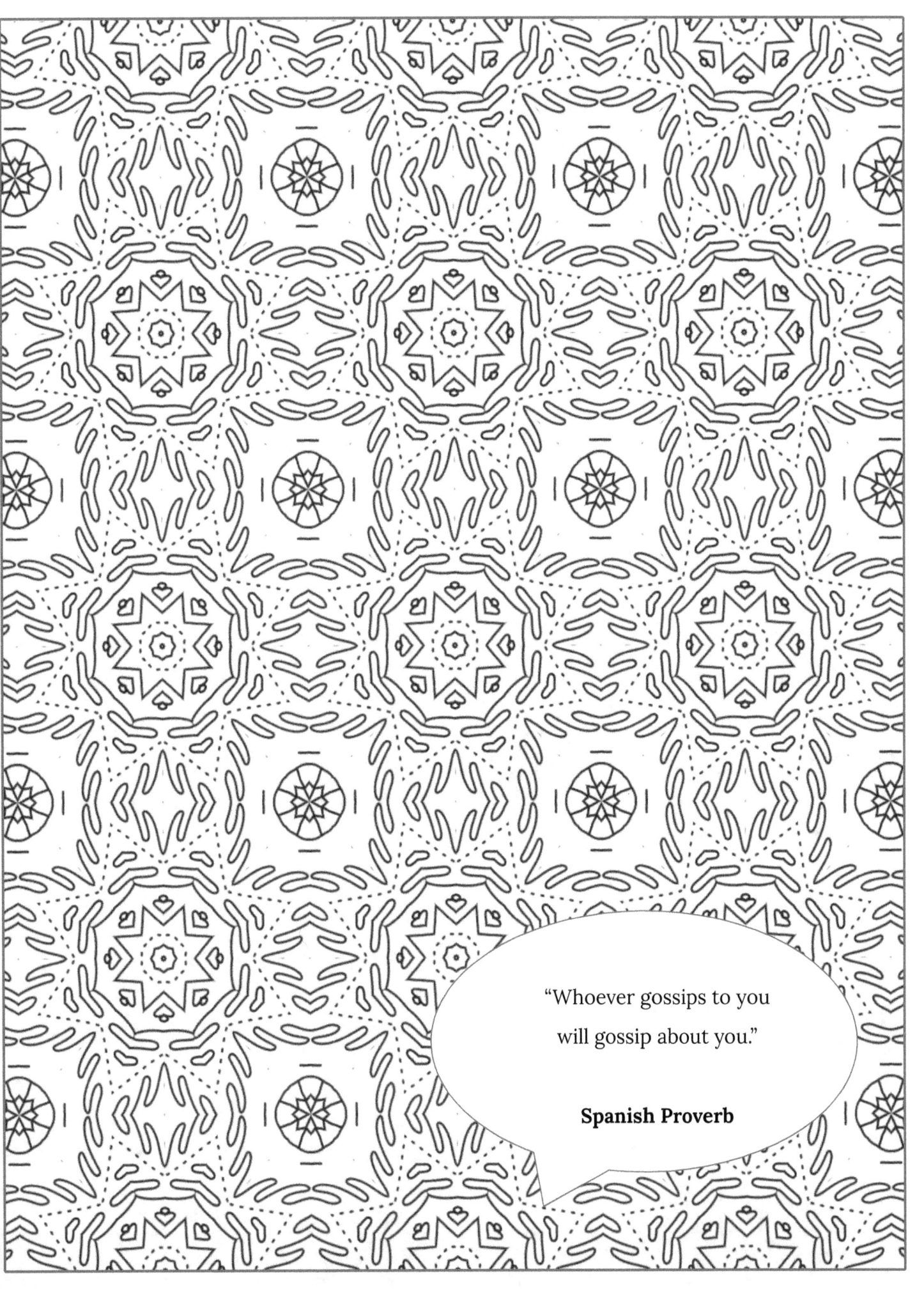

"Whoever gossips to you will gossip about you."

Spanish Proverb

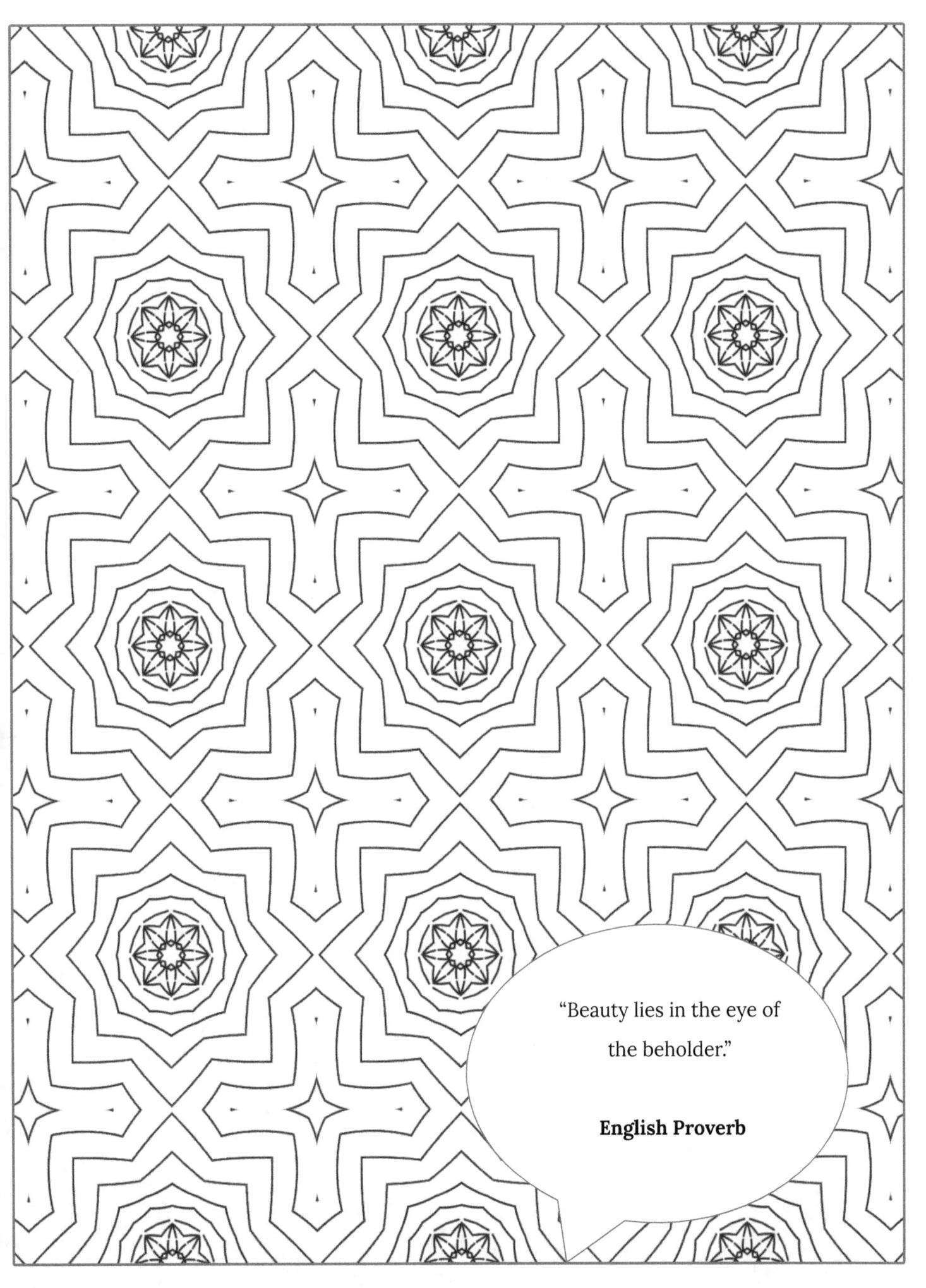

"Beauty lies in the eye of the beholder."

English Proverb

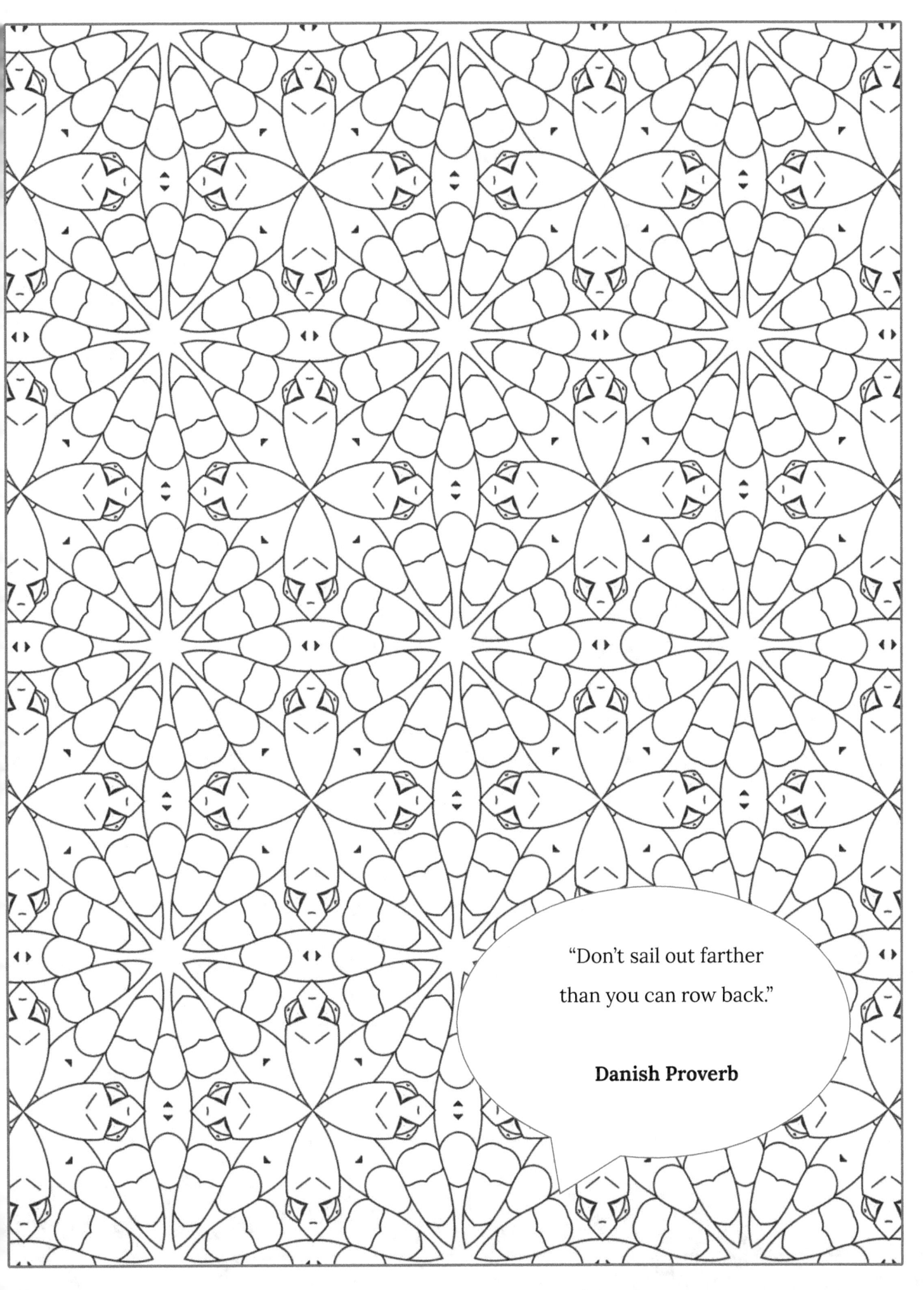

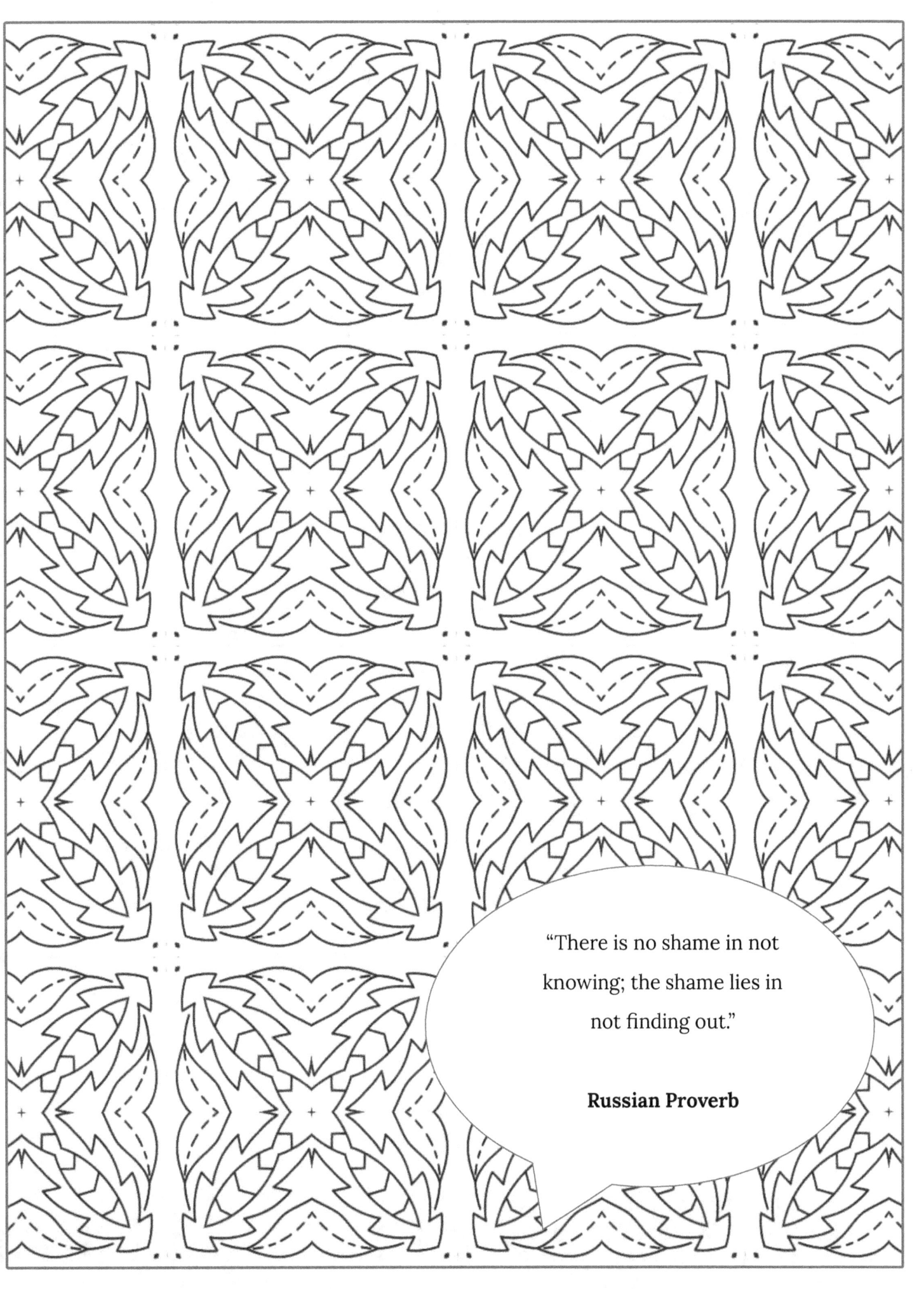

"There is no shame in not knowing; the shame lies in not finding out."

Russian Proverb

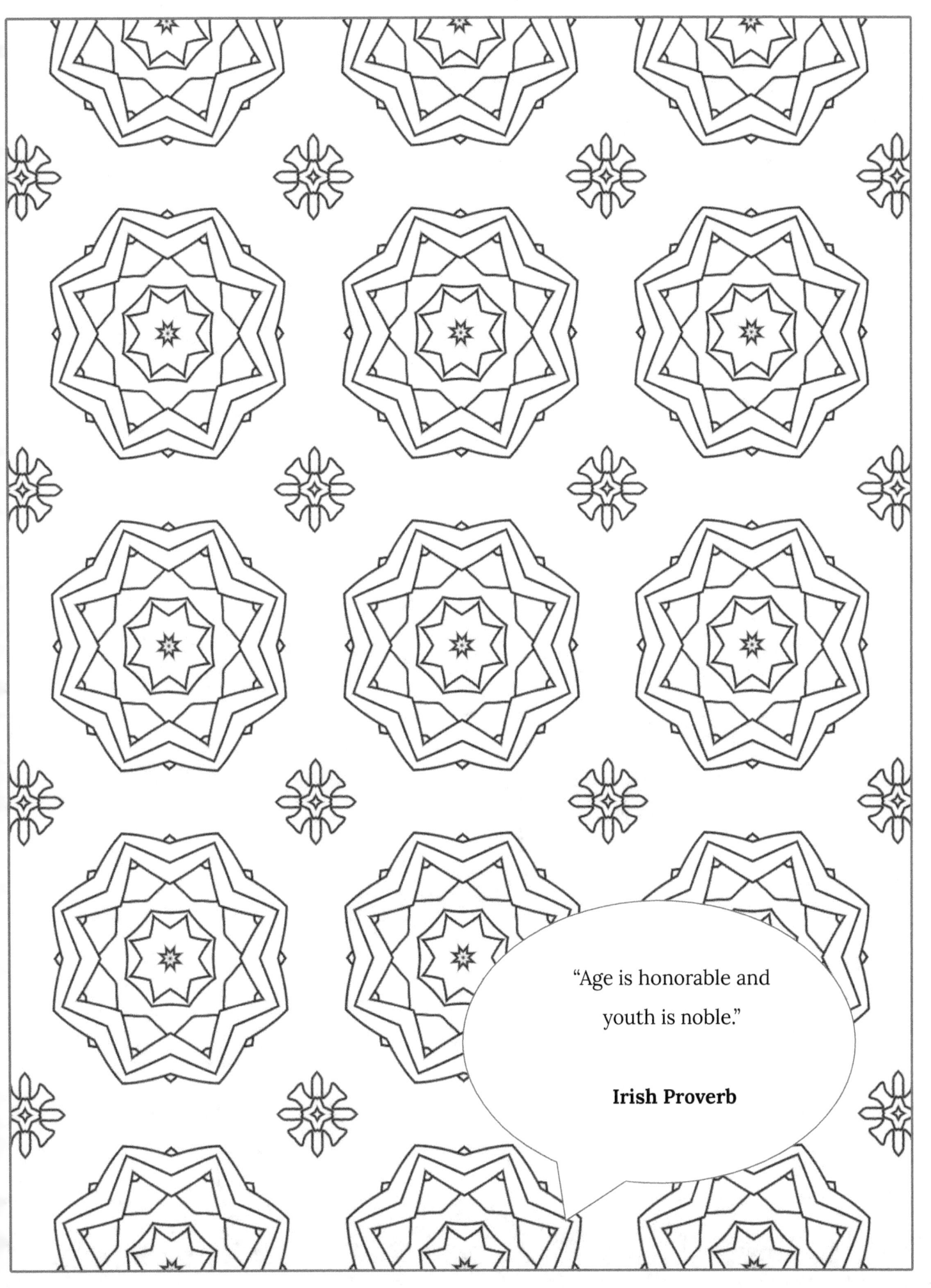

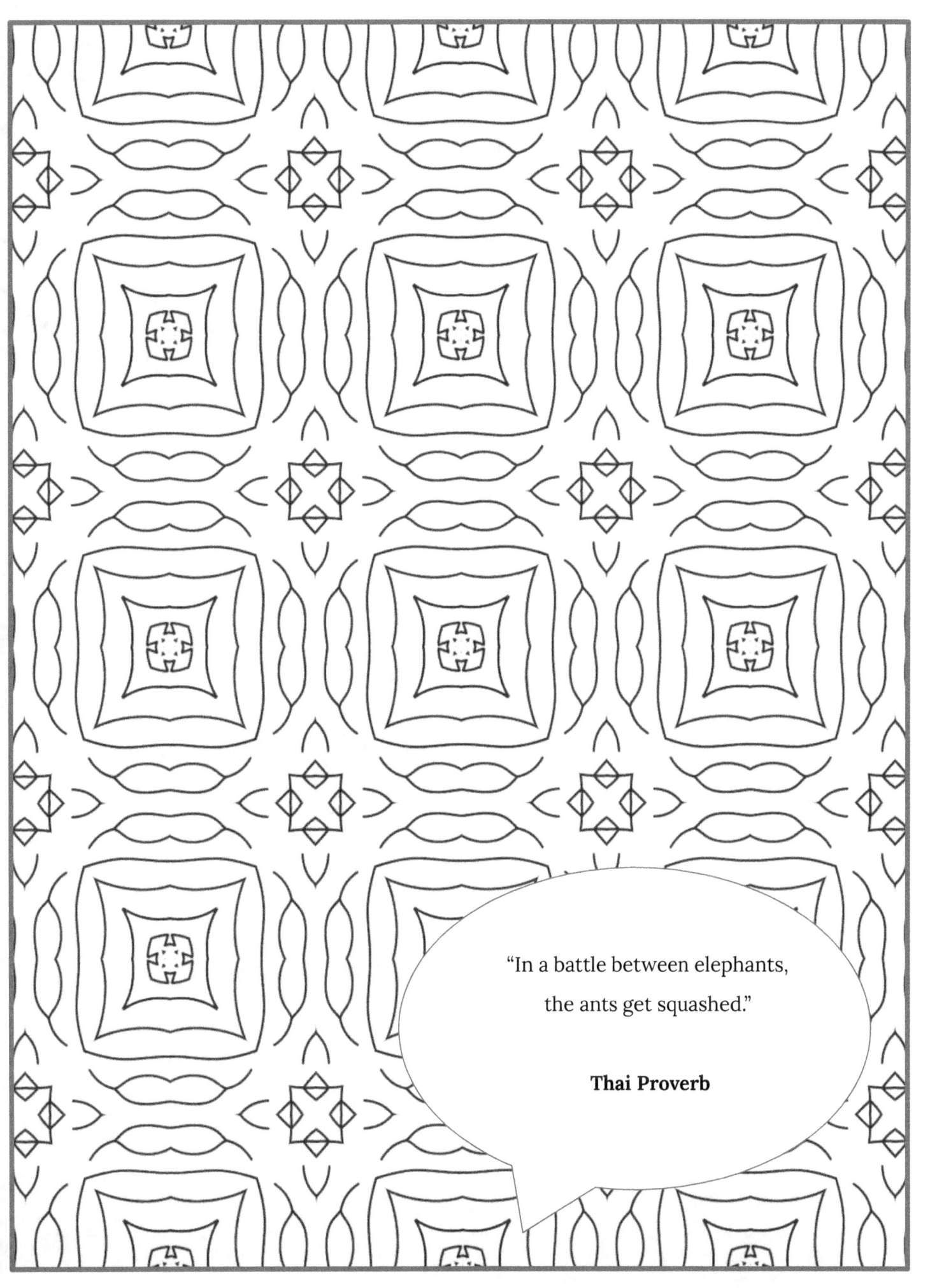

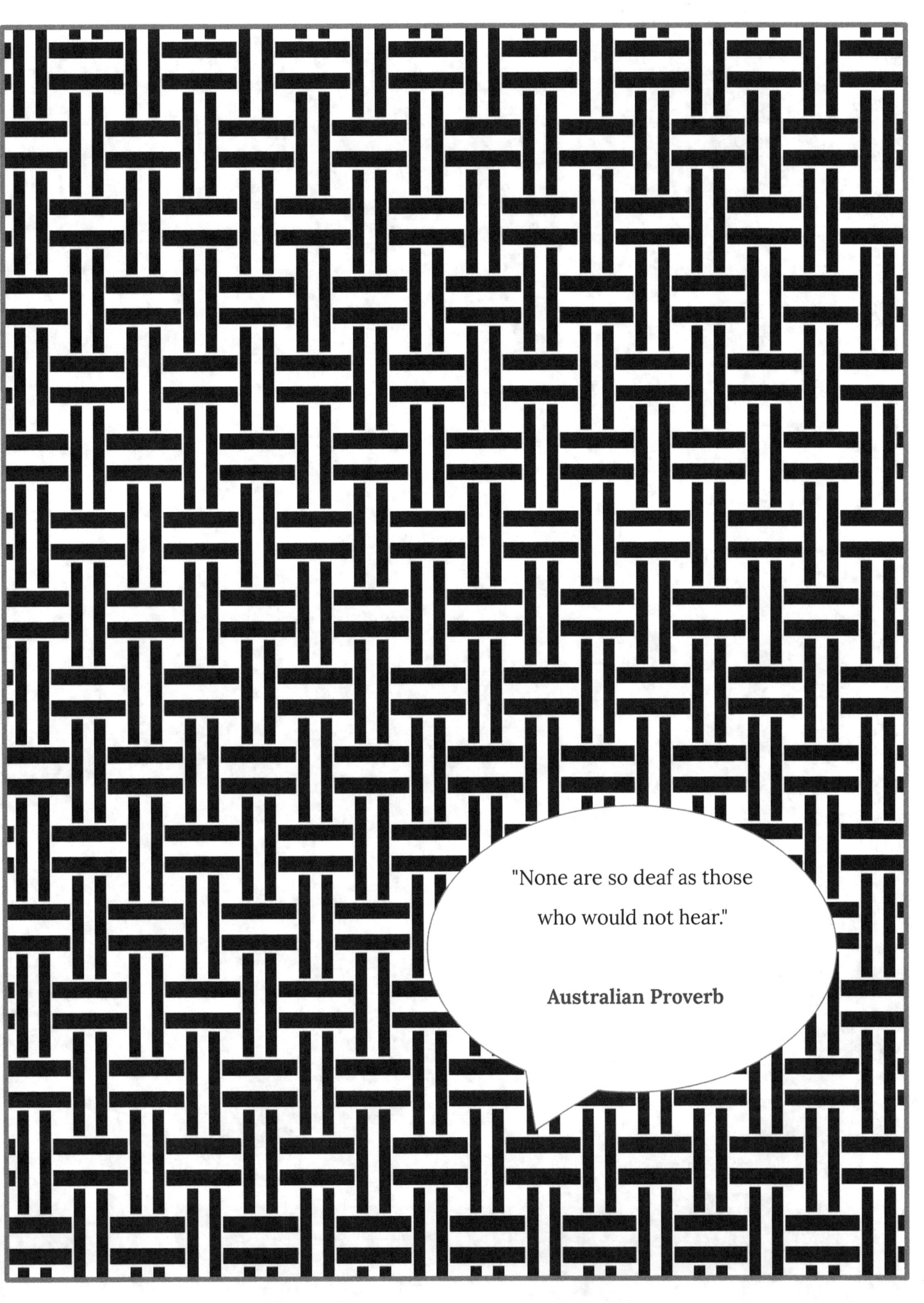

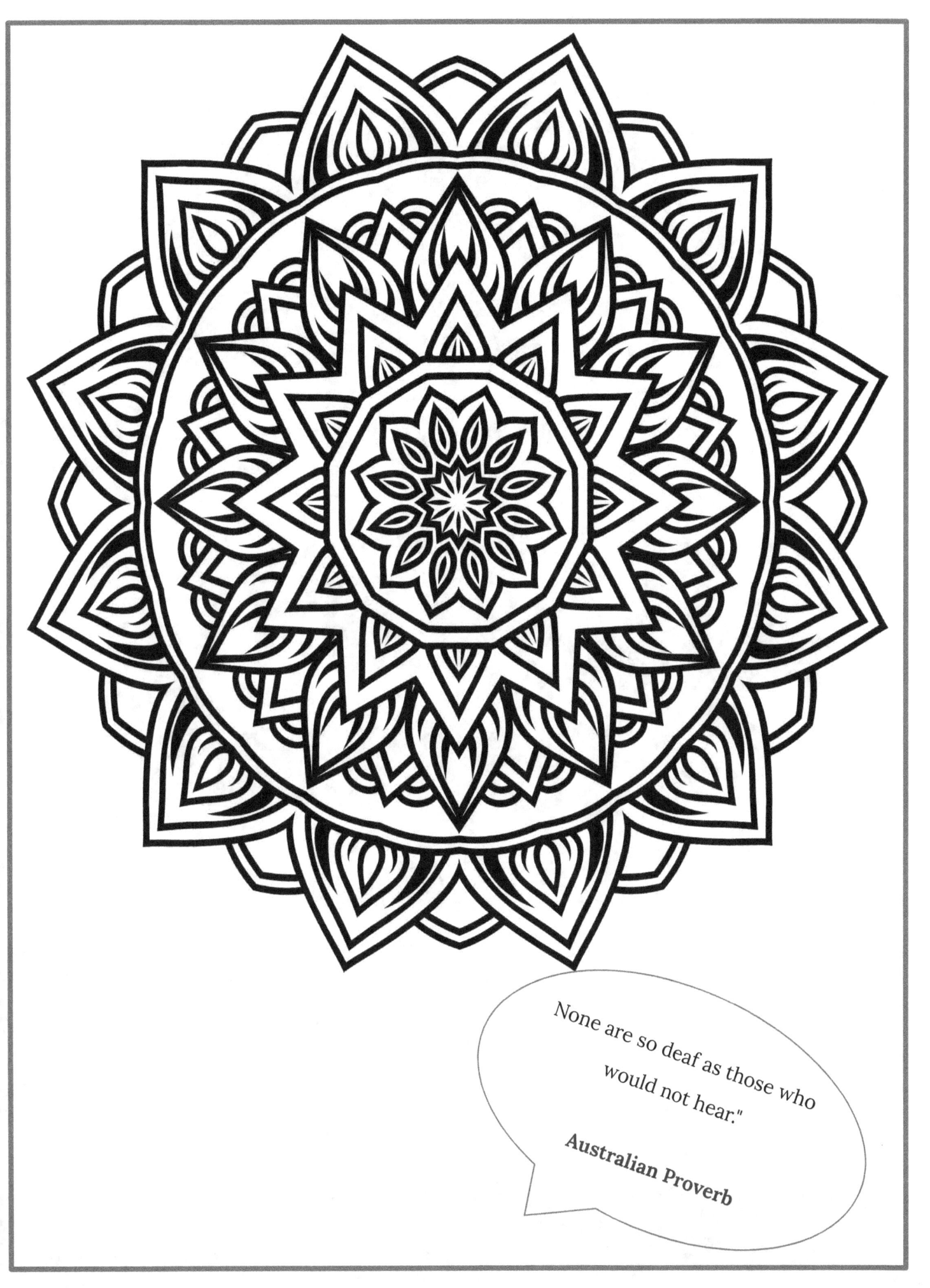

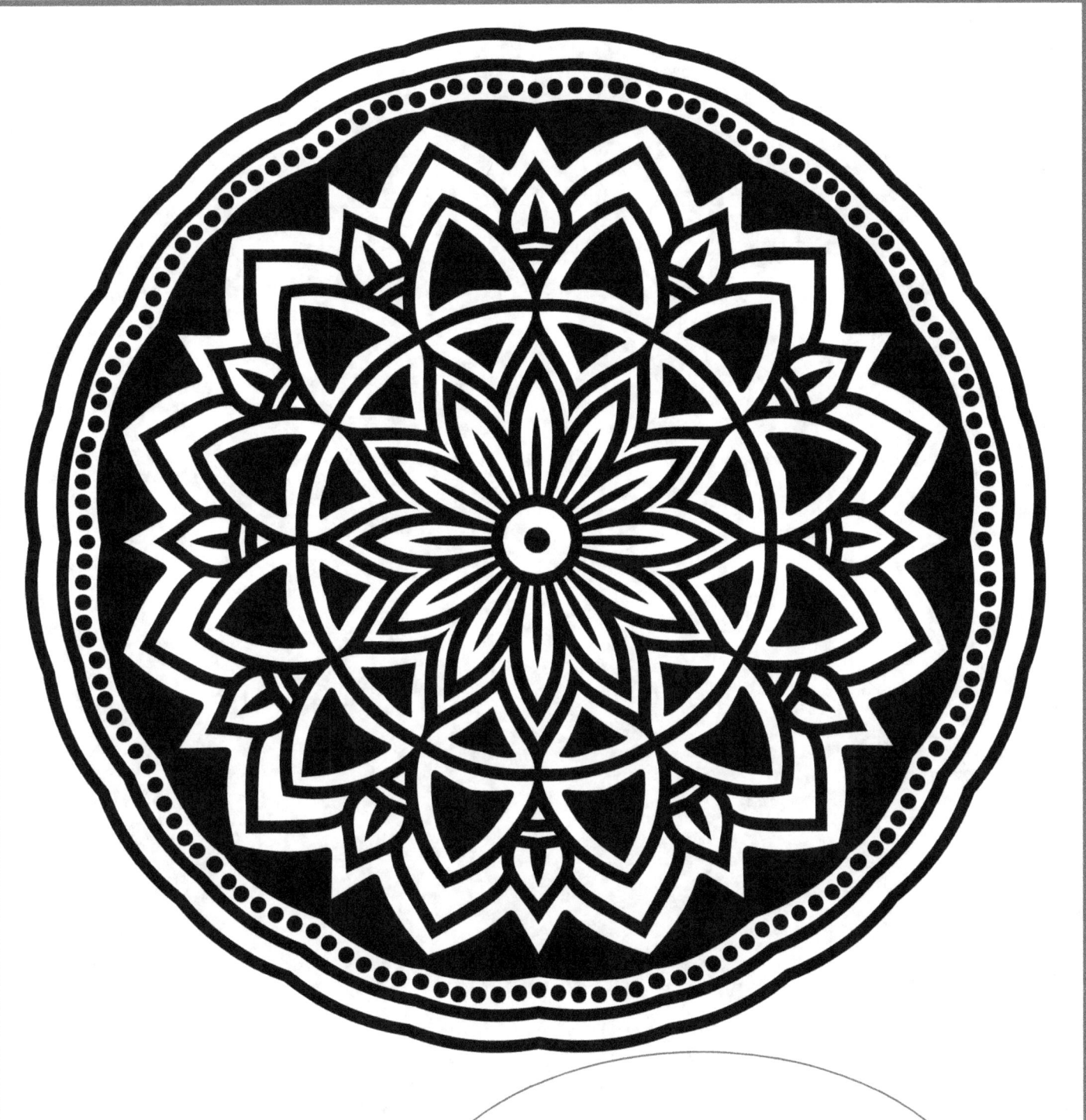

"When building a house, don't measure the timbers in the forest."

Liberian proverb

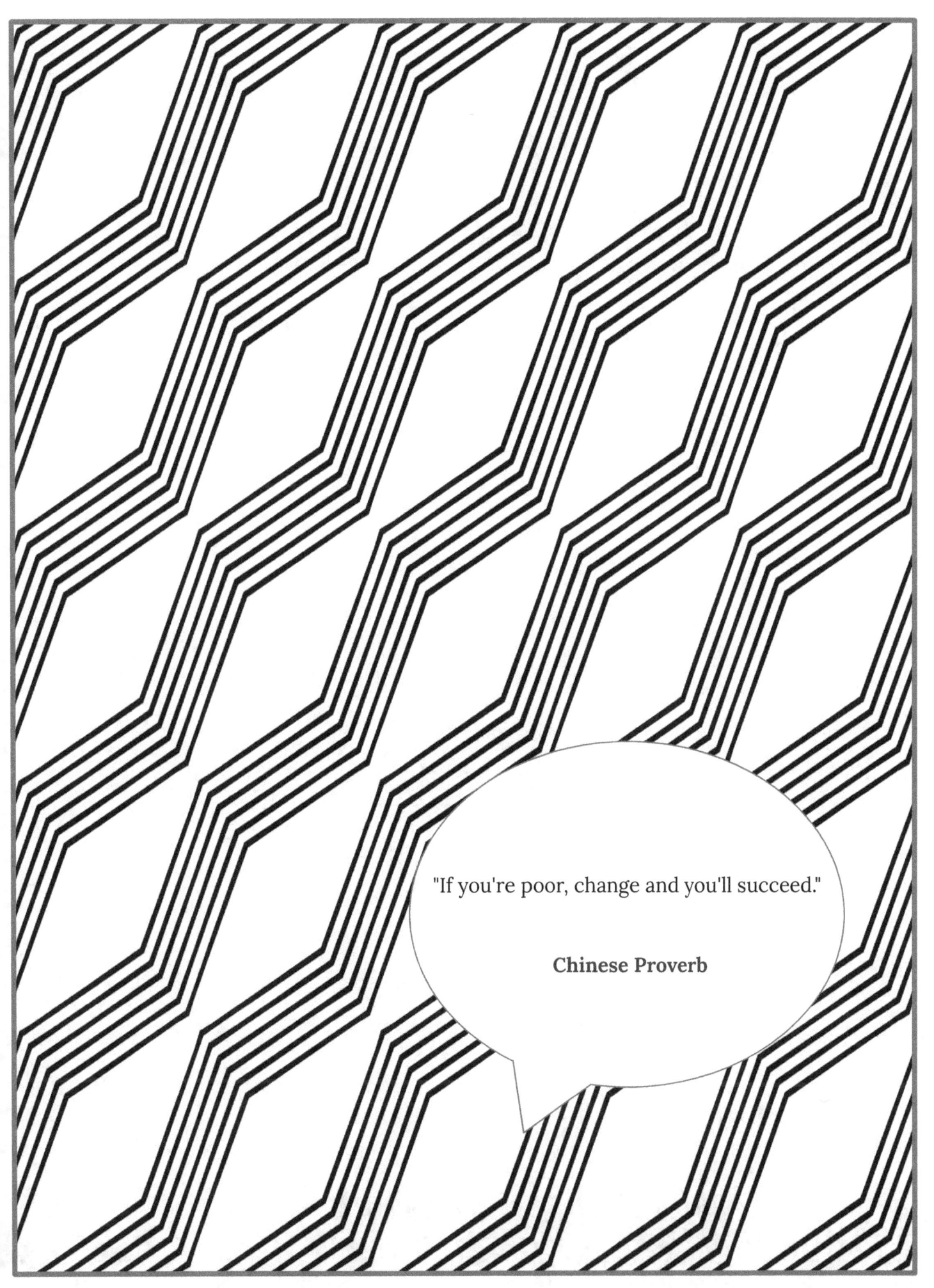

"The wolf has a thick neck because he does his job on his own."

Bulgarian Proverb

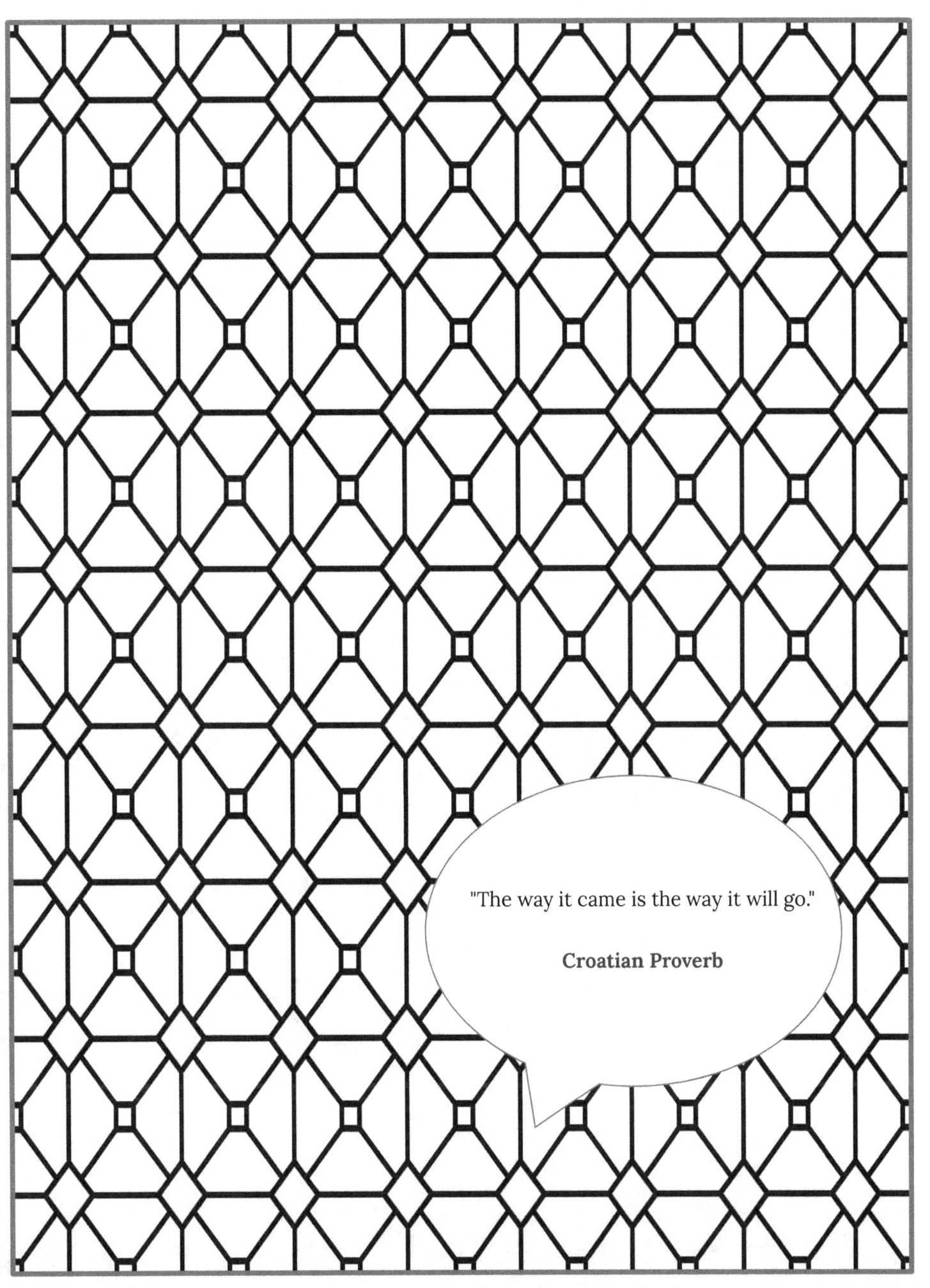

"The way it came is the way it will go."

Croatian Proverb

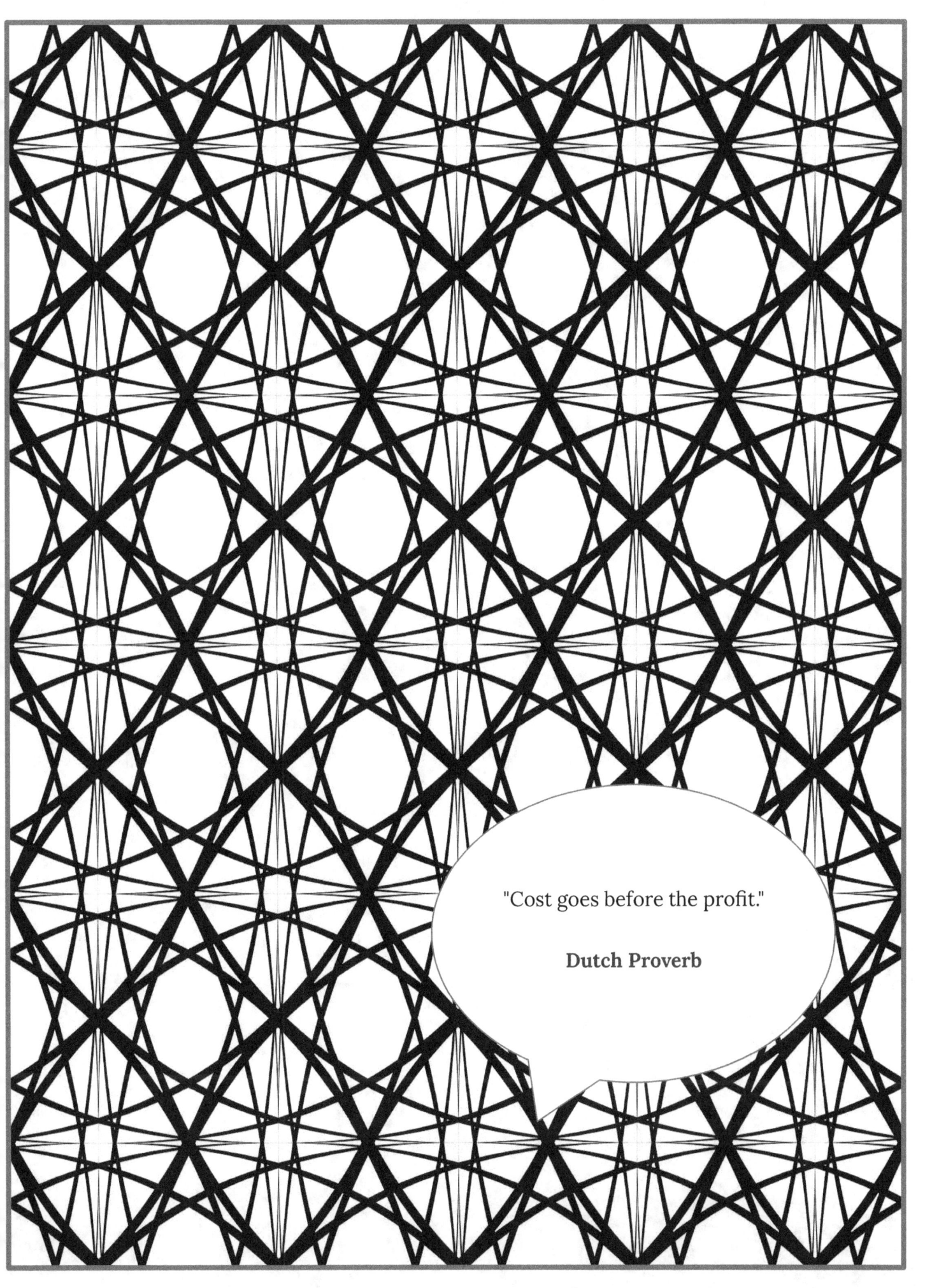

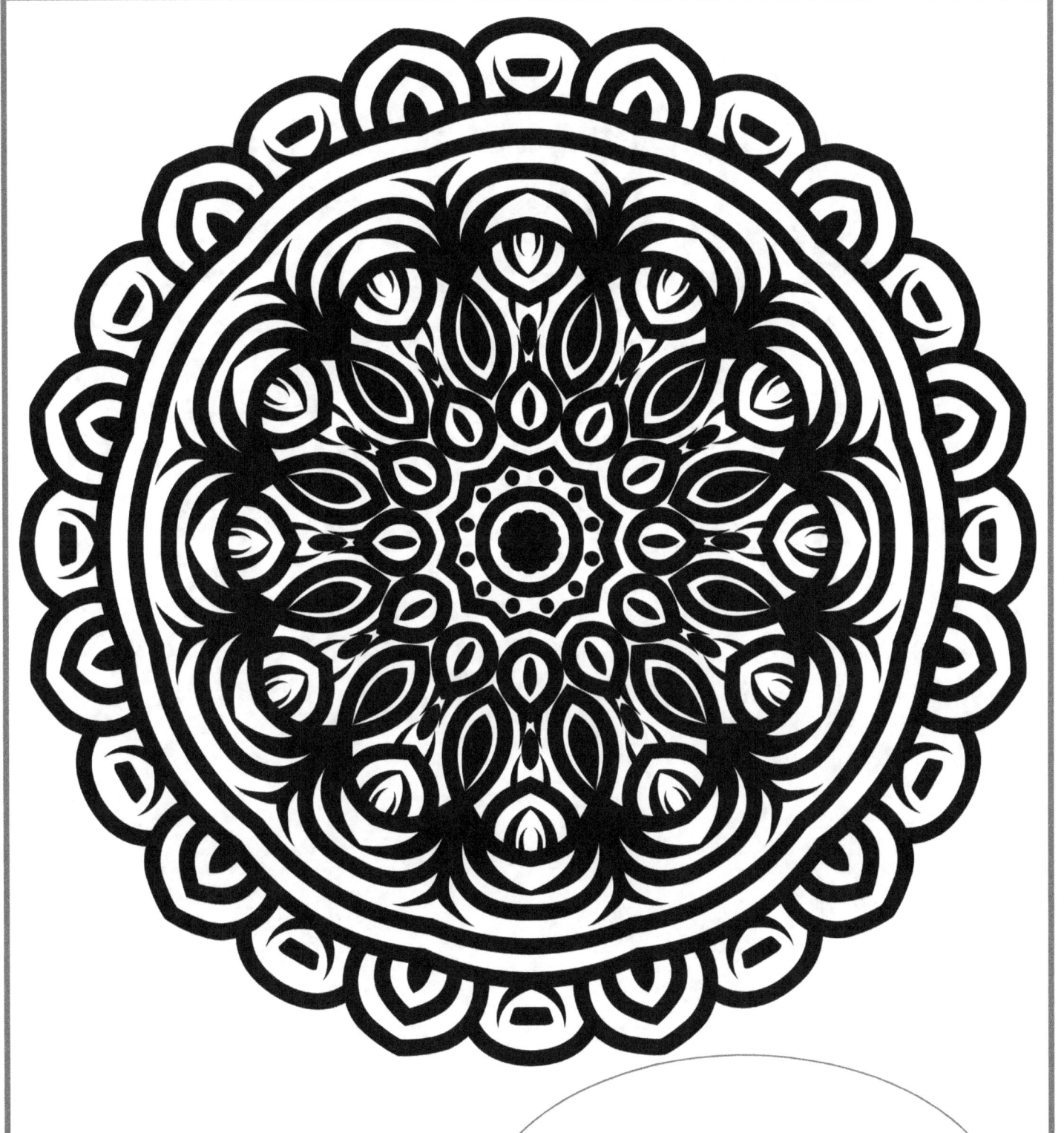

"The pen is mightier than the sword."

English Proverb

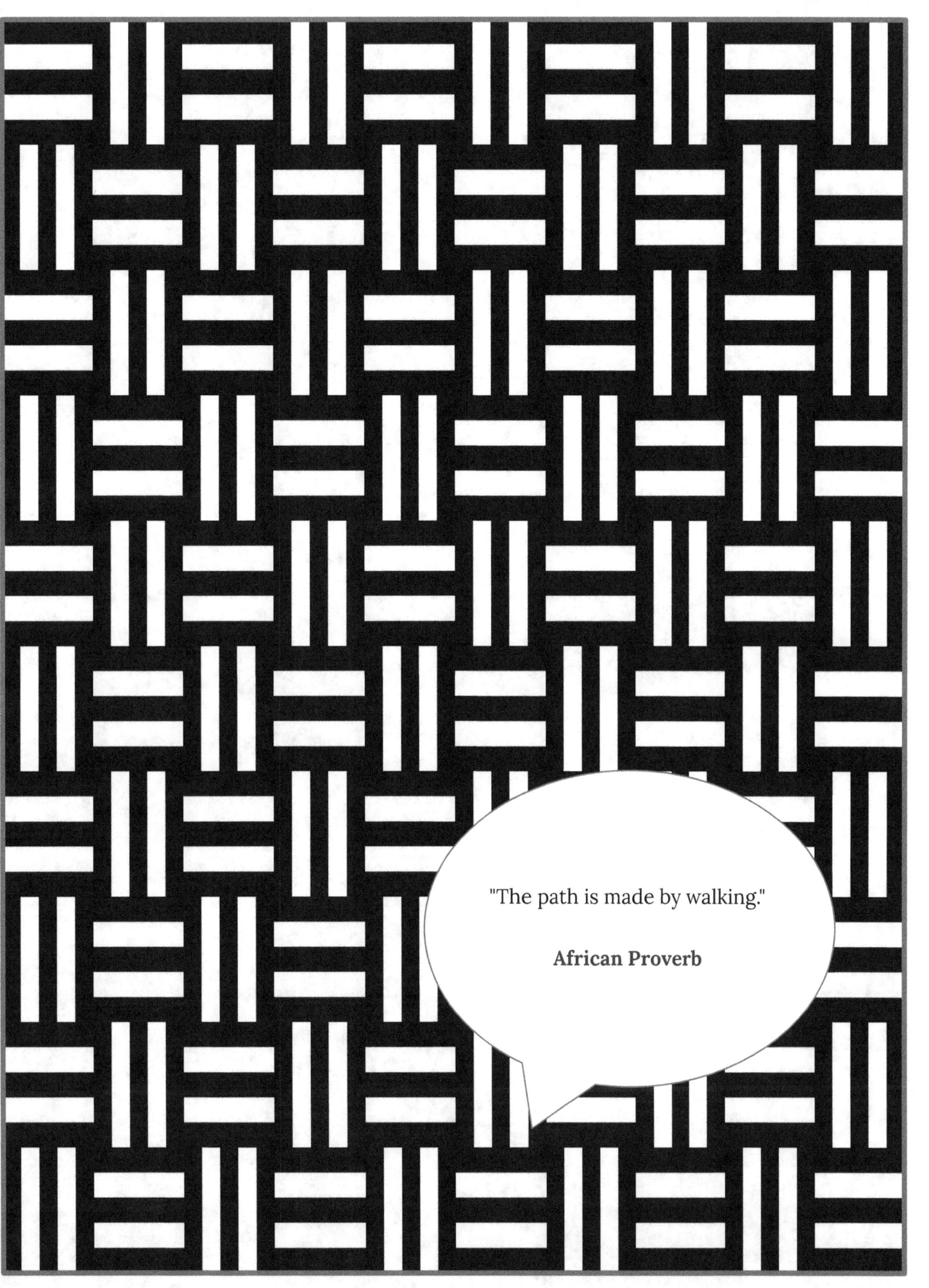

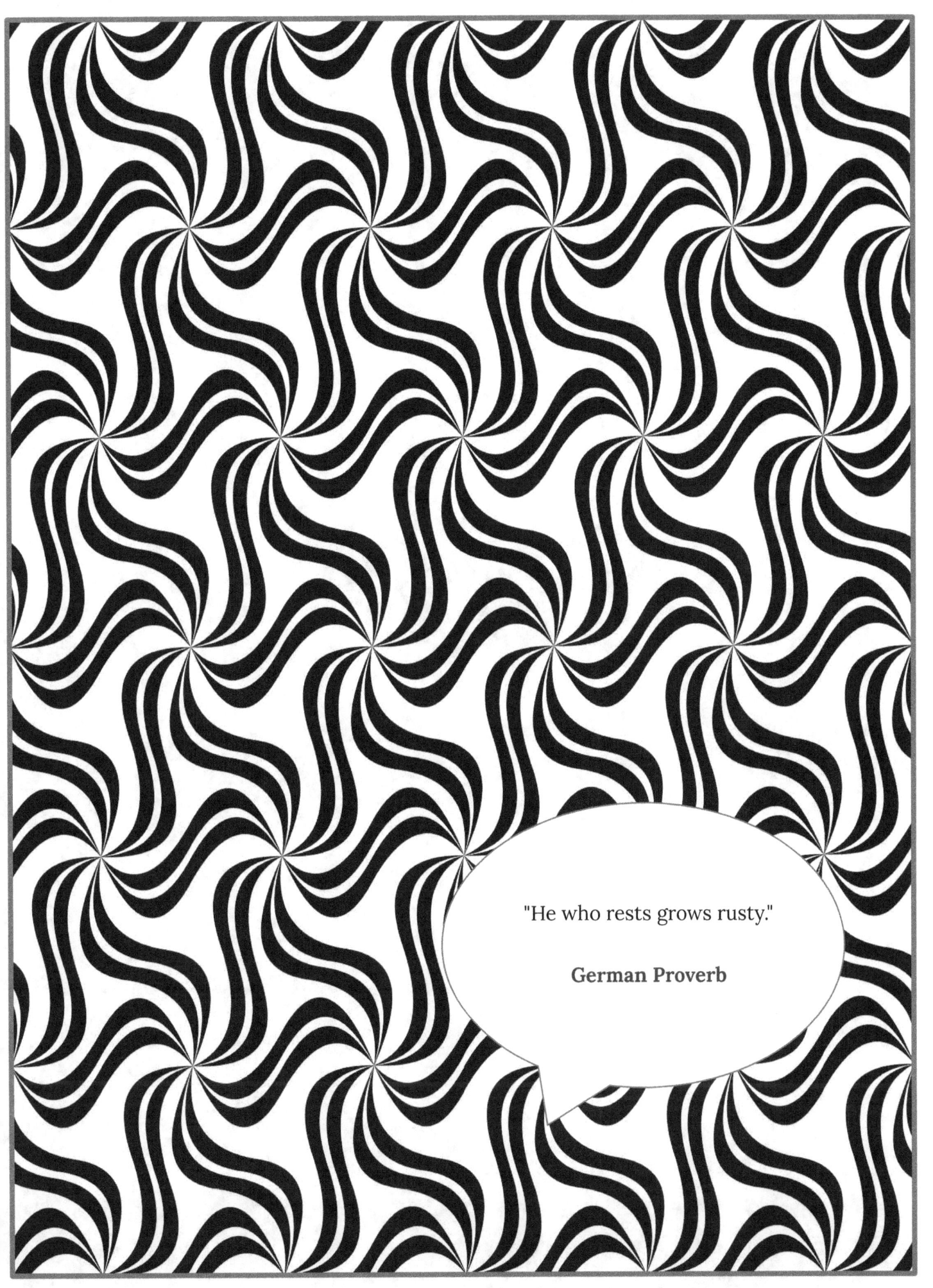

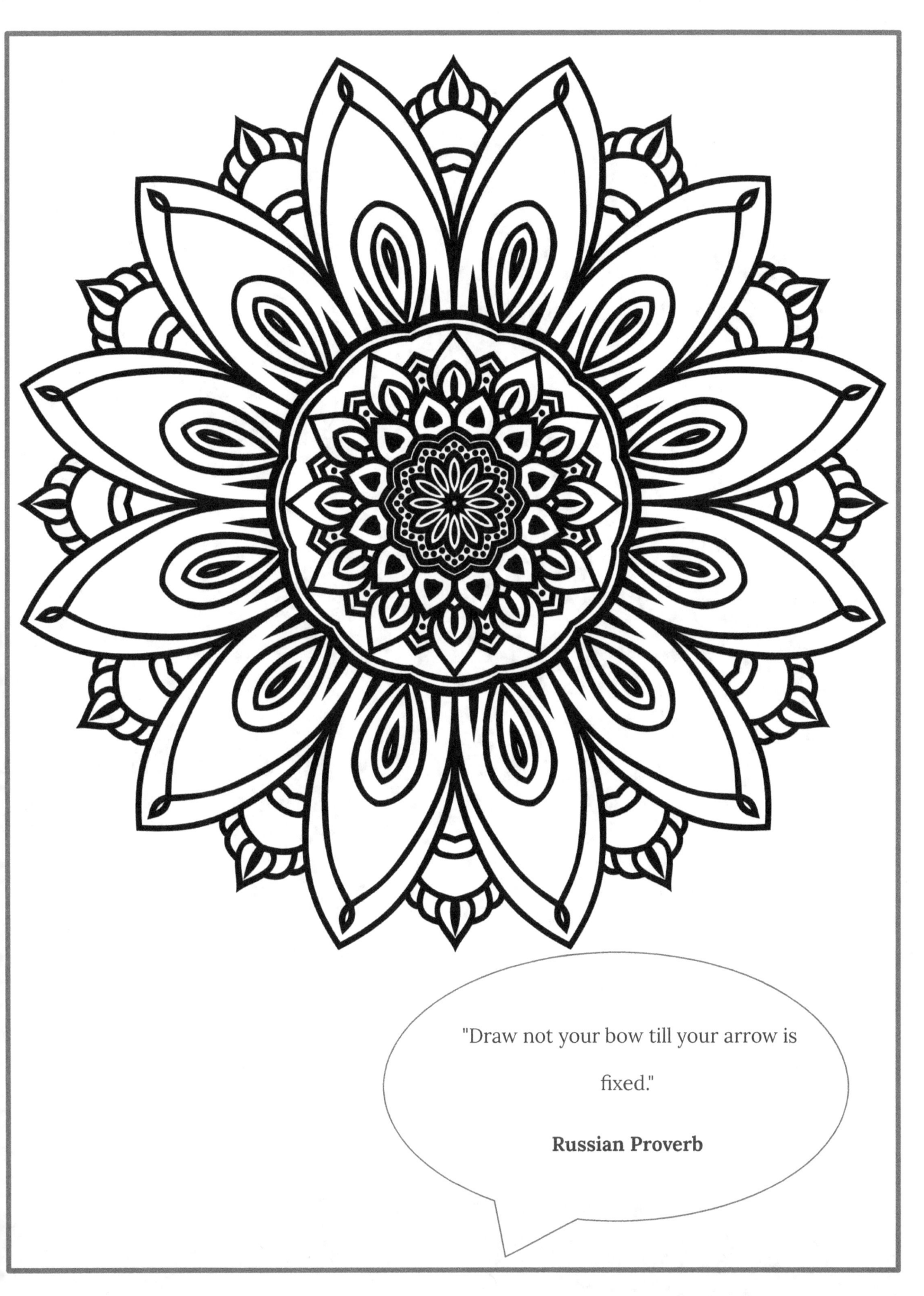

"Draw not your bow till your arrow is fixed."

Russian Proverb

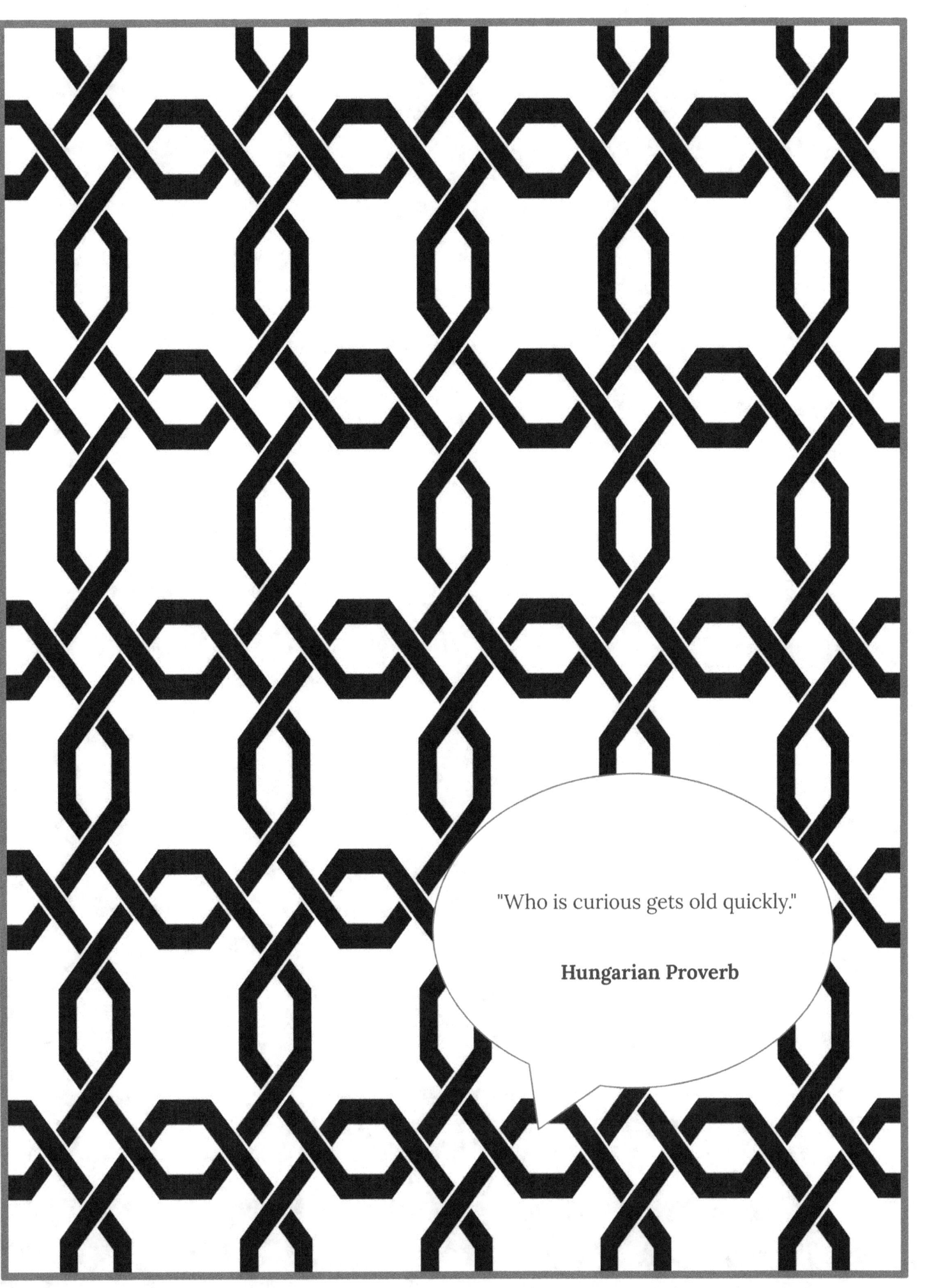

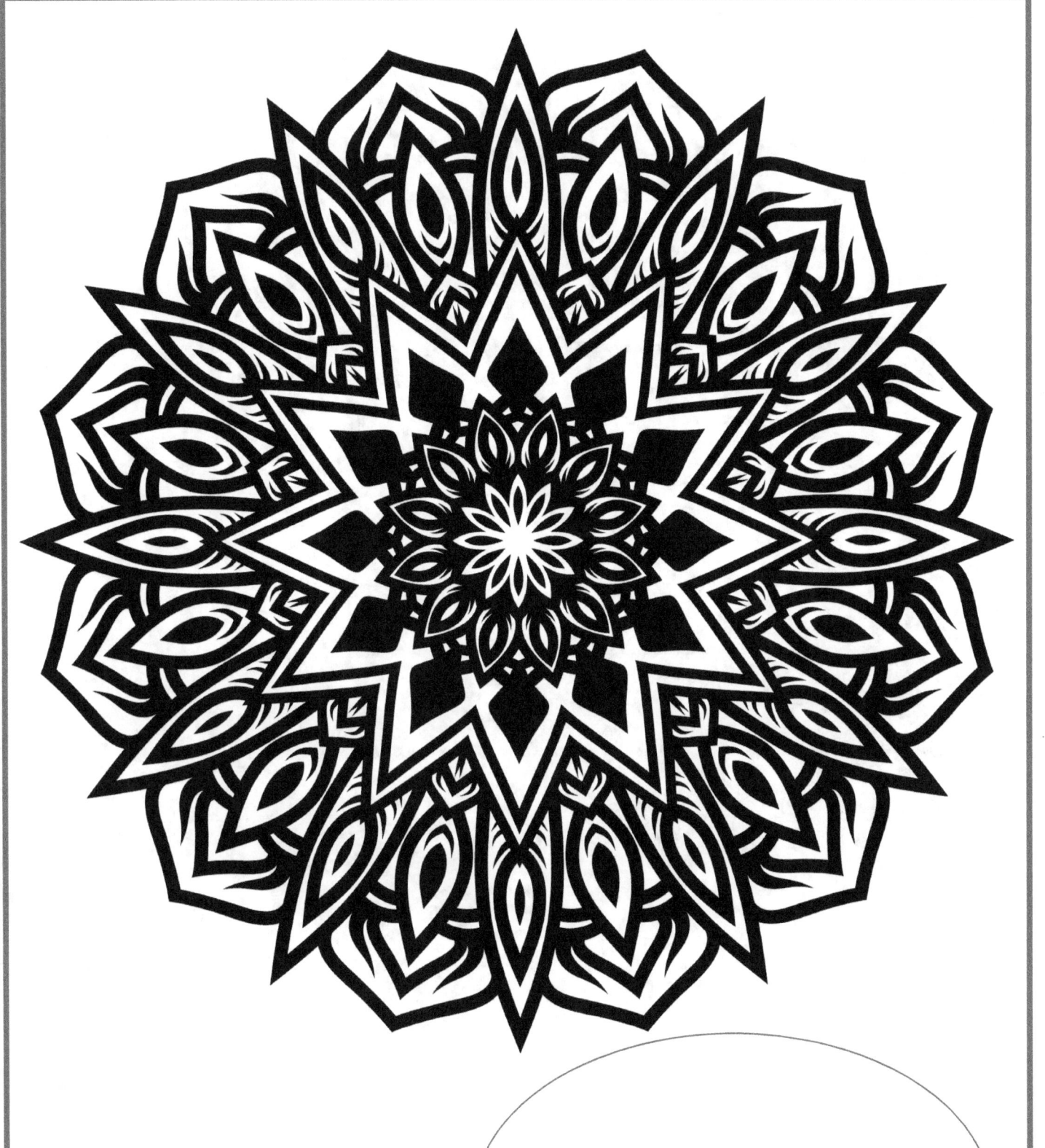

"A king's child is a slave elsewhere."

African Proverb

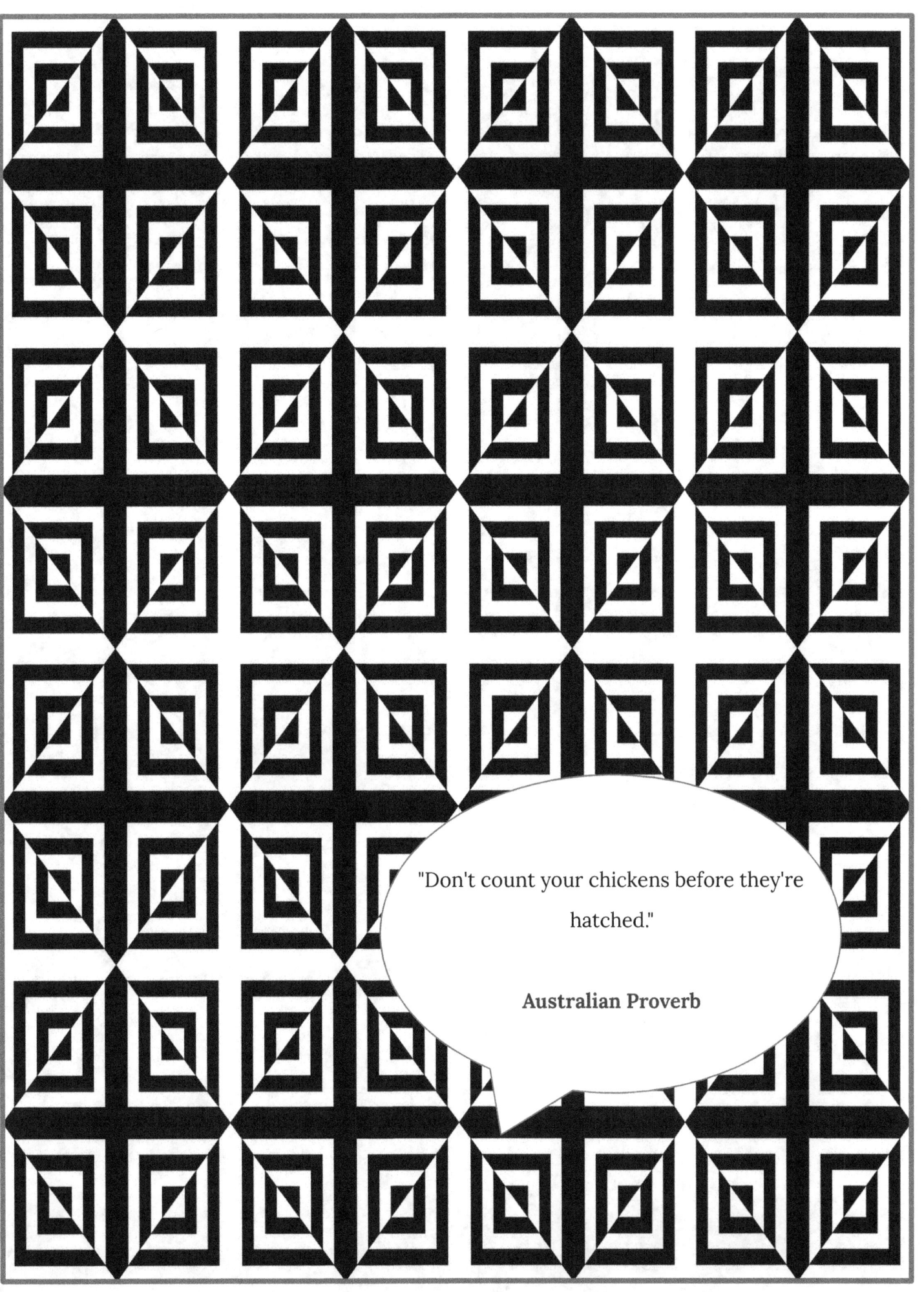

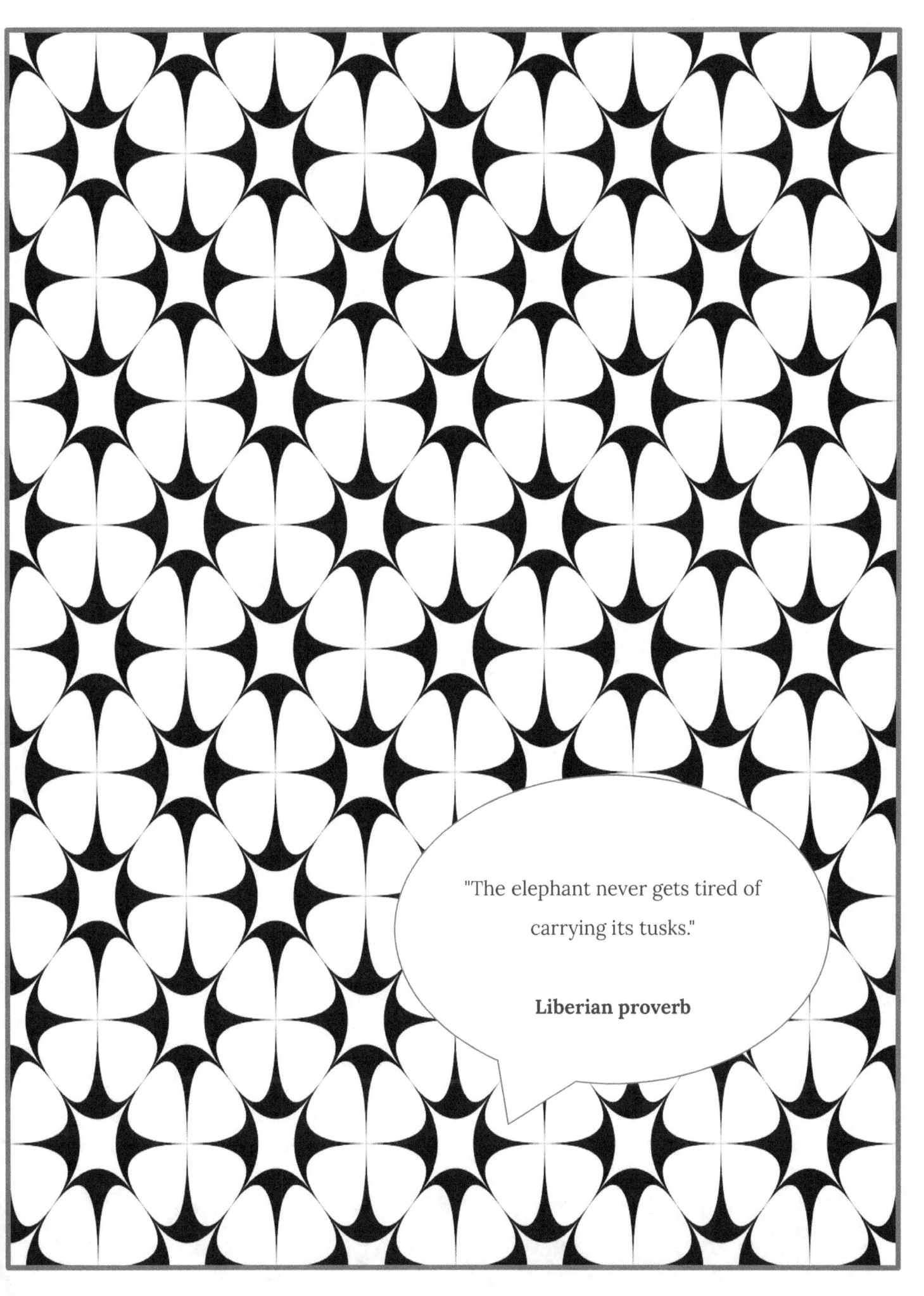

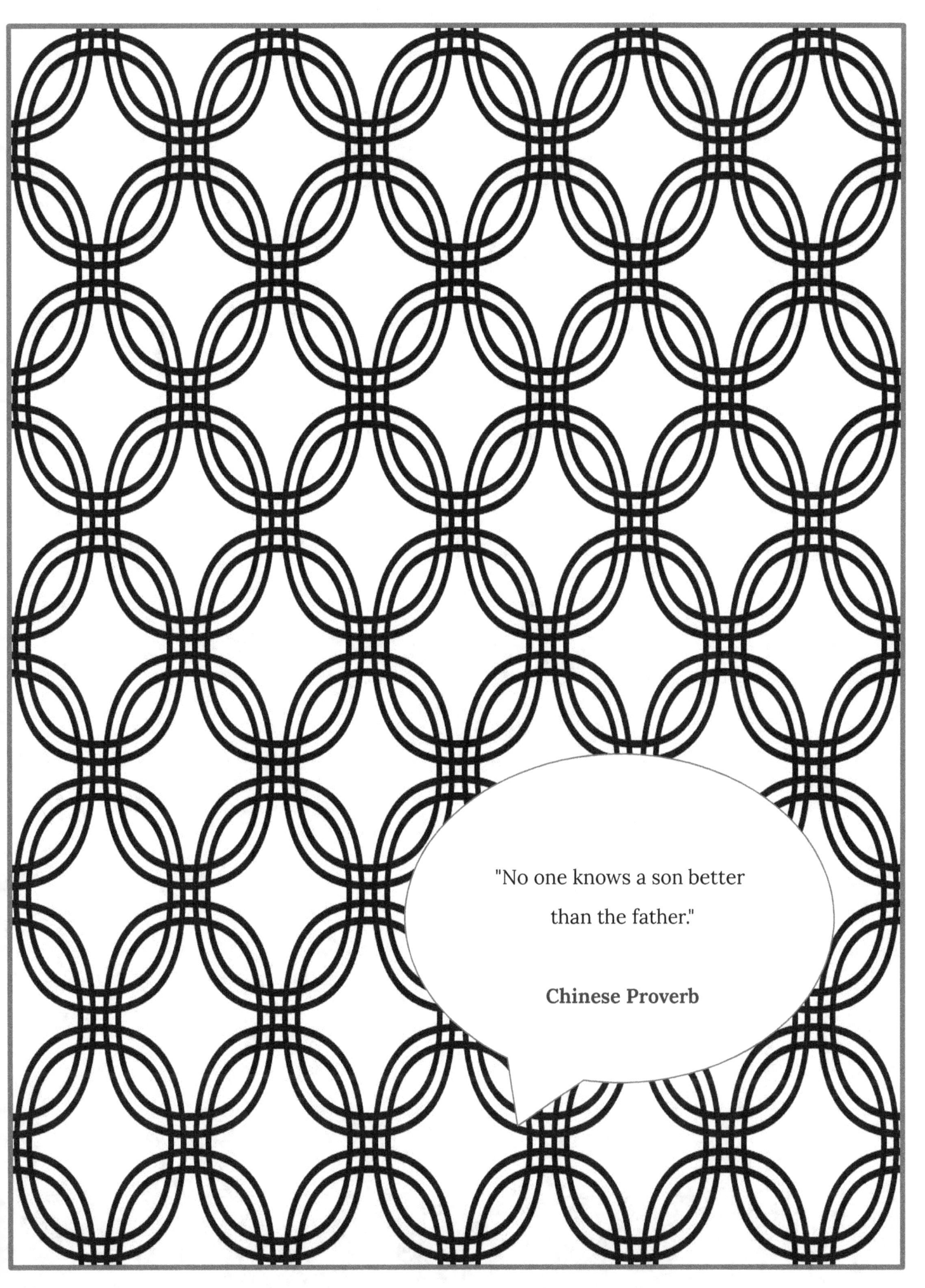

"No one knows a son better than the father."

Chinese Proverb

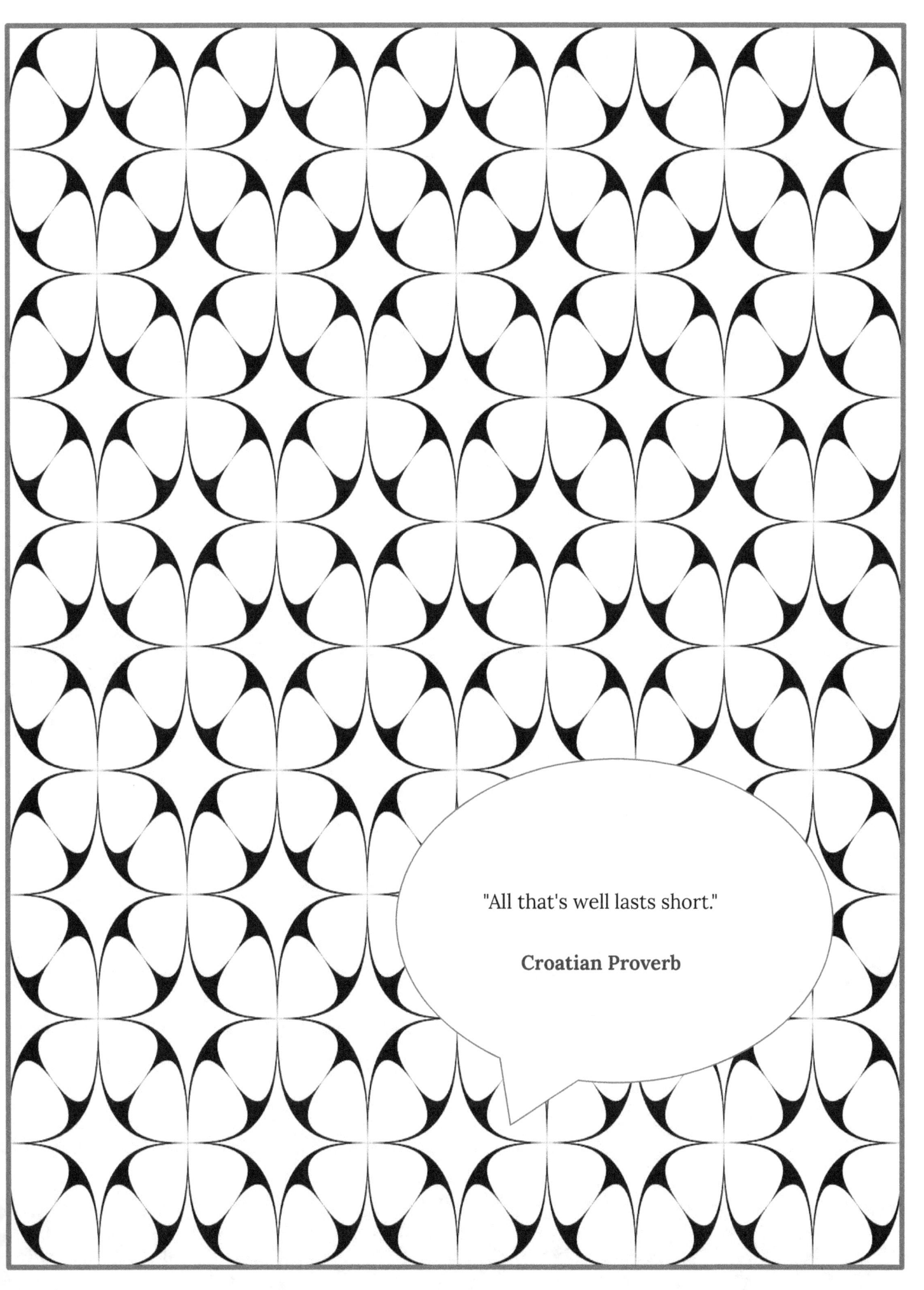

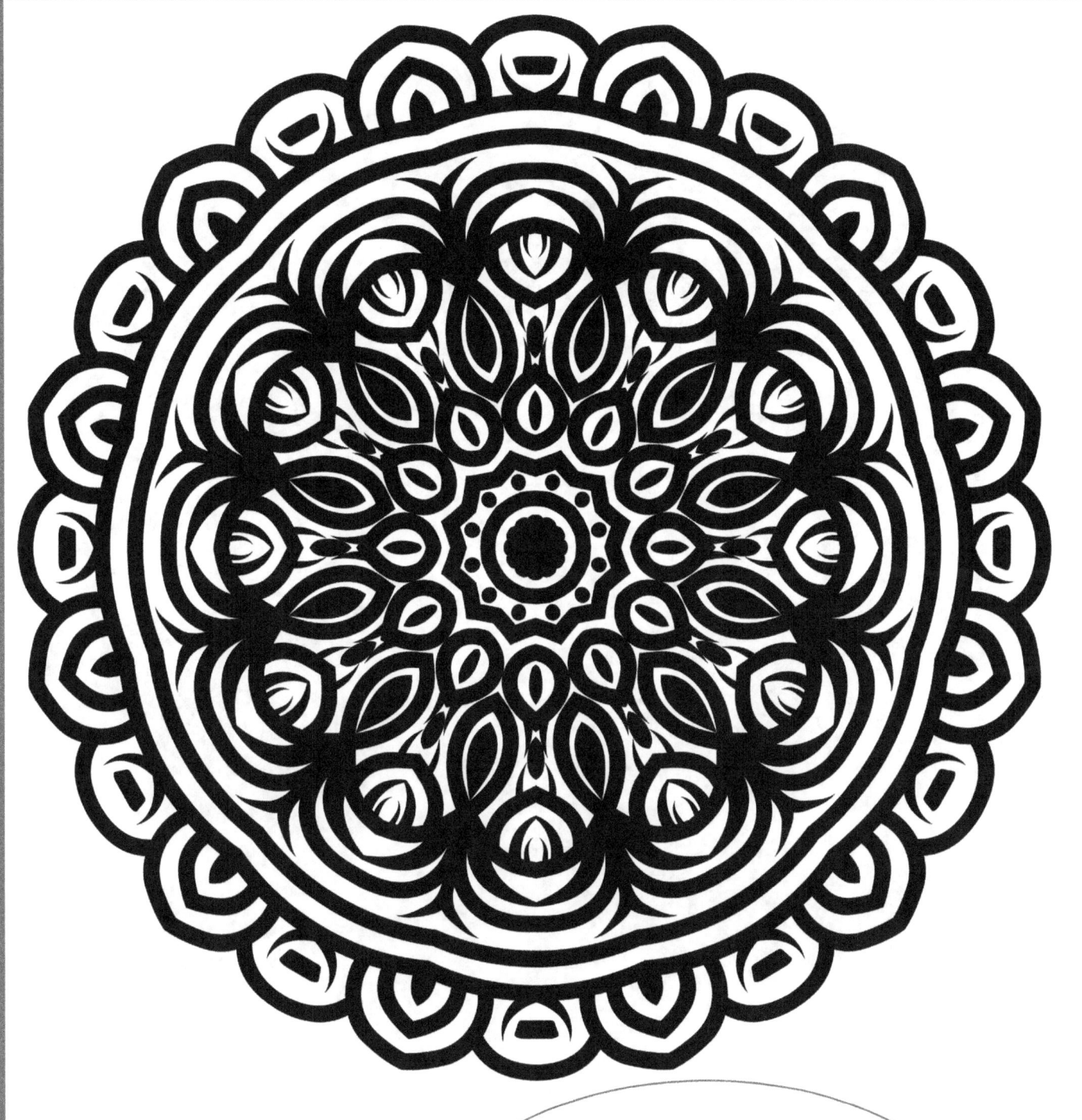

"When the rich make war, it's the poor that die."

Russian Proverb

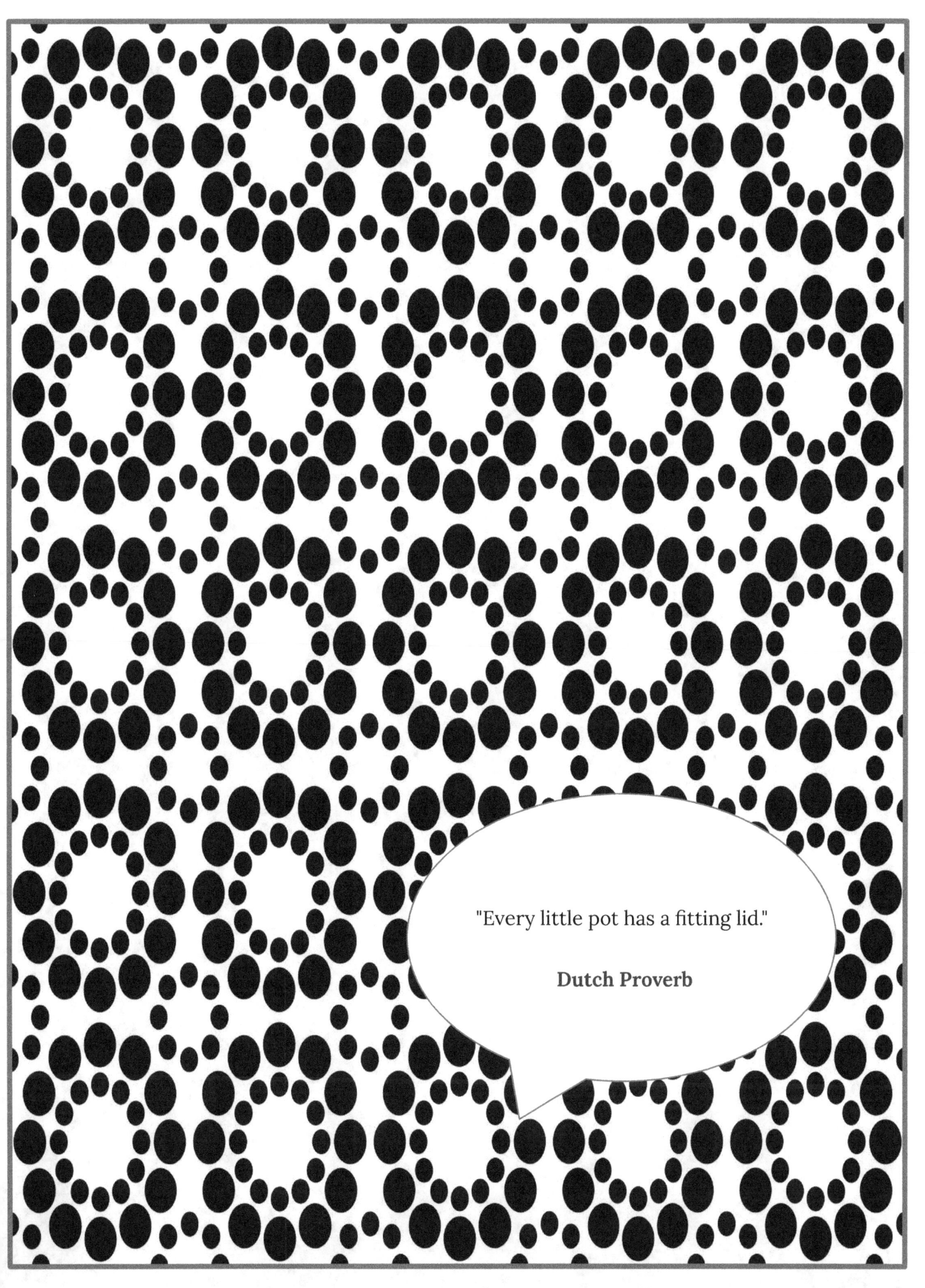

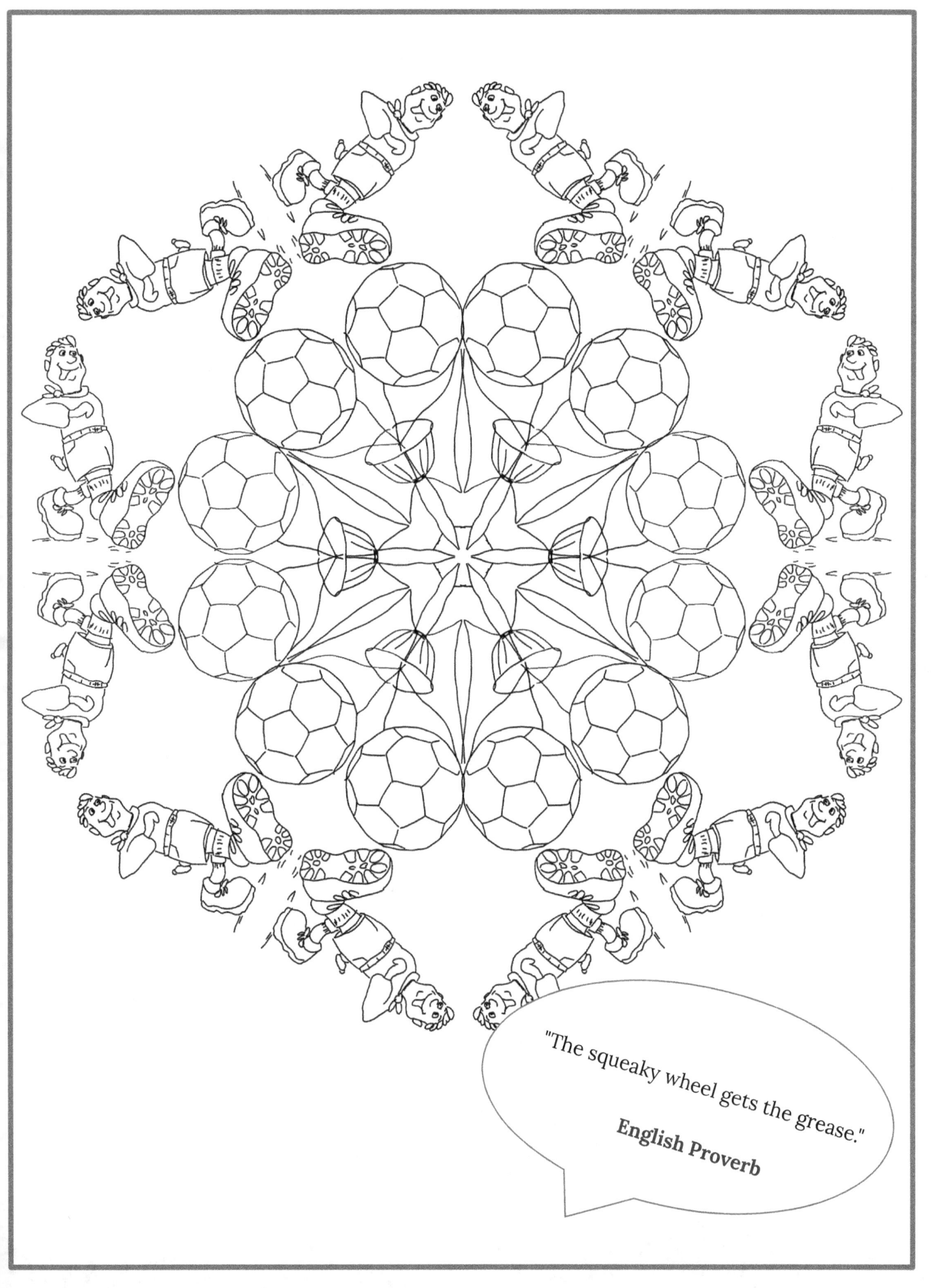

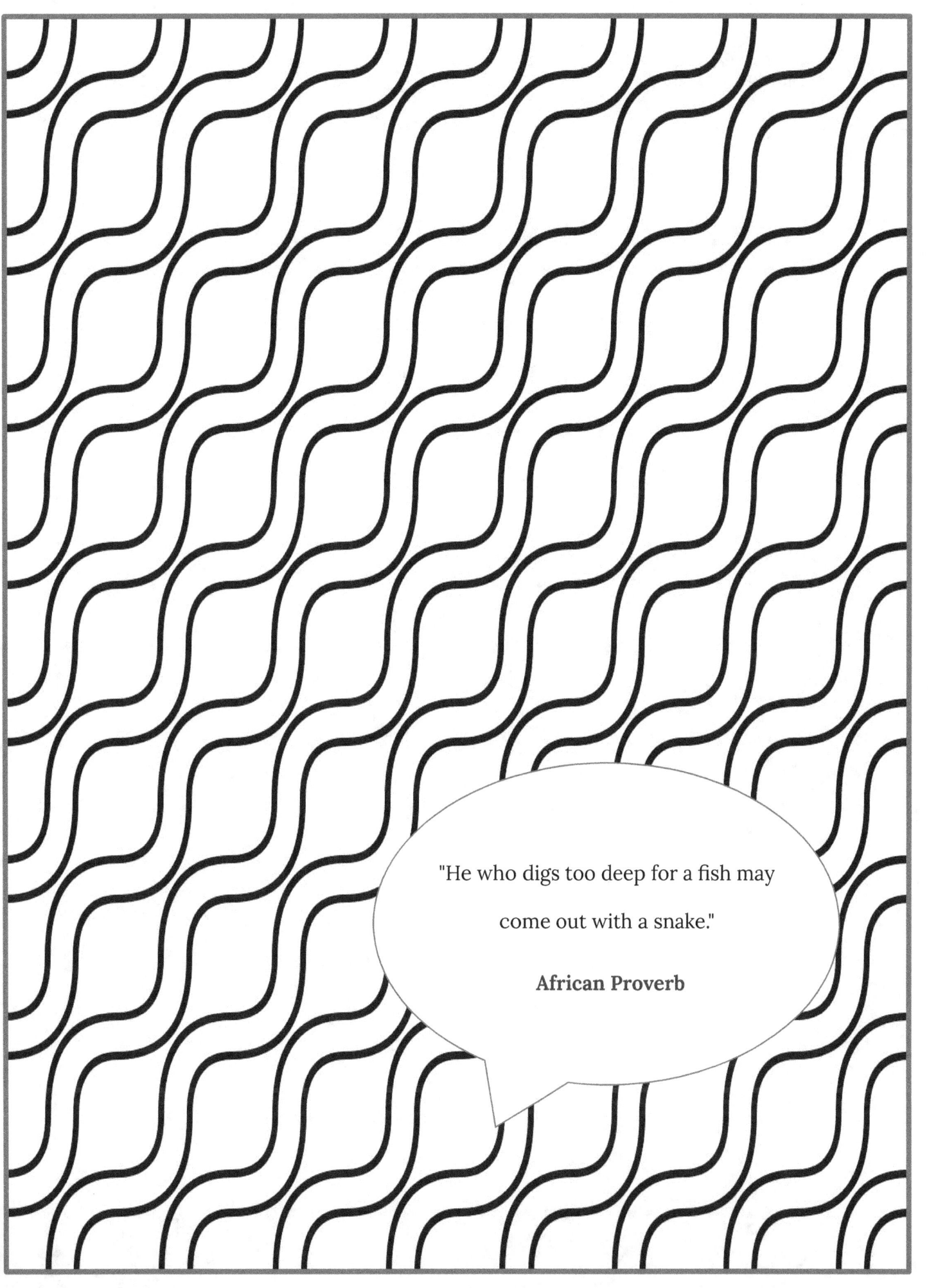

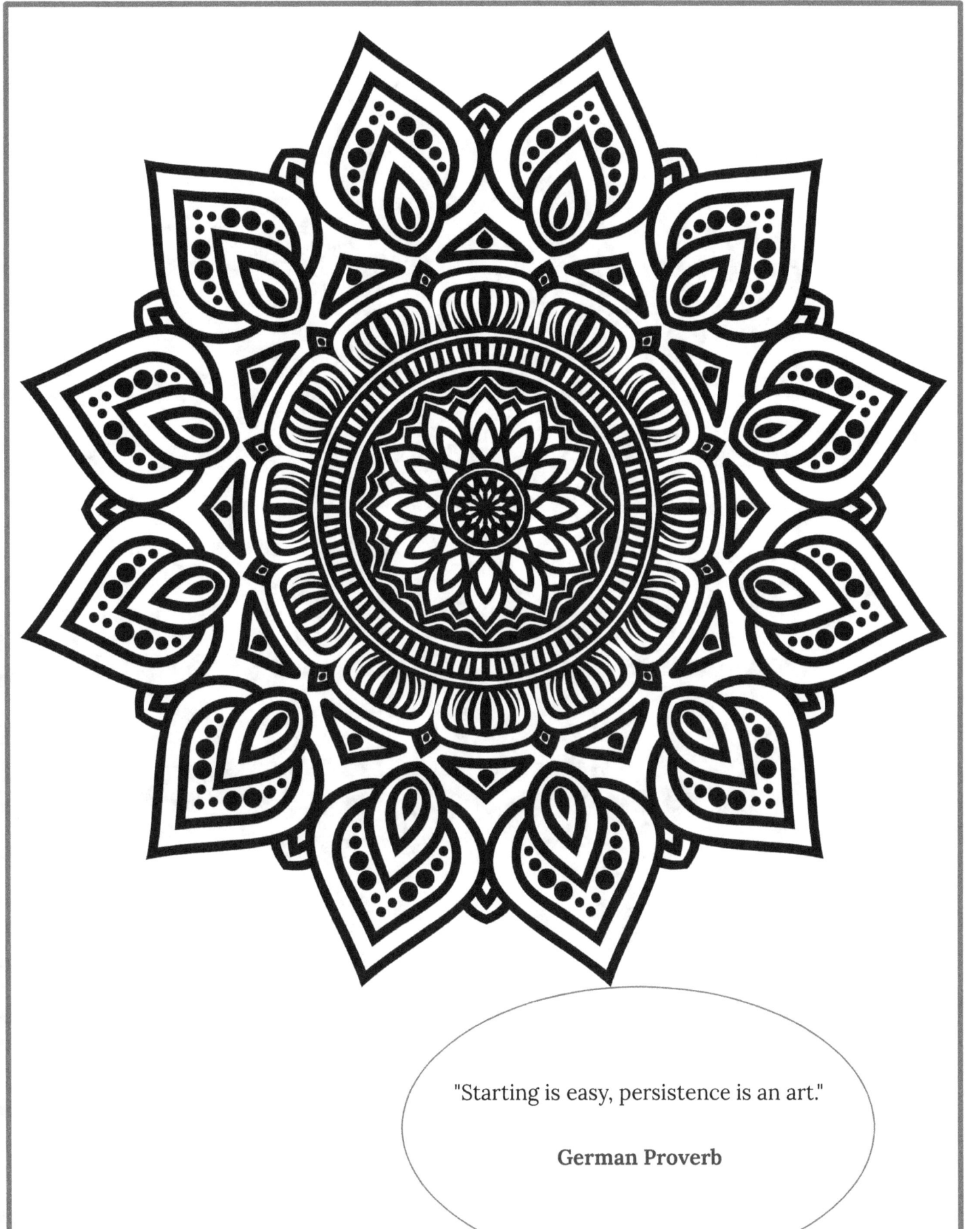

"Starting is easy, persistence is an art."

German Proverb

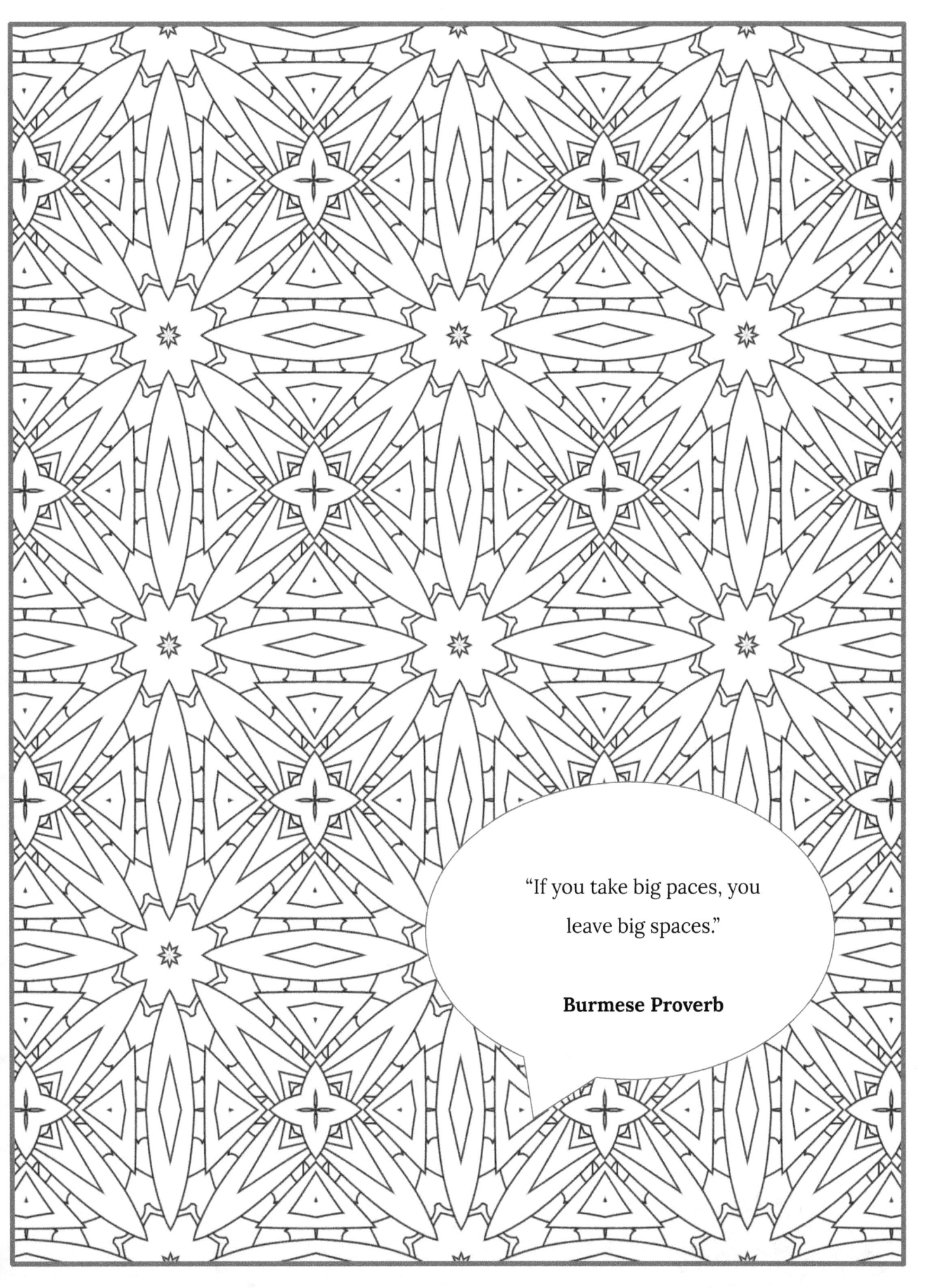

"If you take big paces, you leave big spaces."

Burmese Proverb

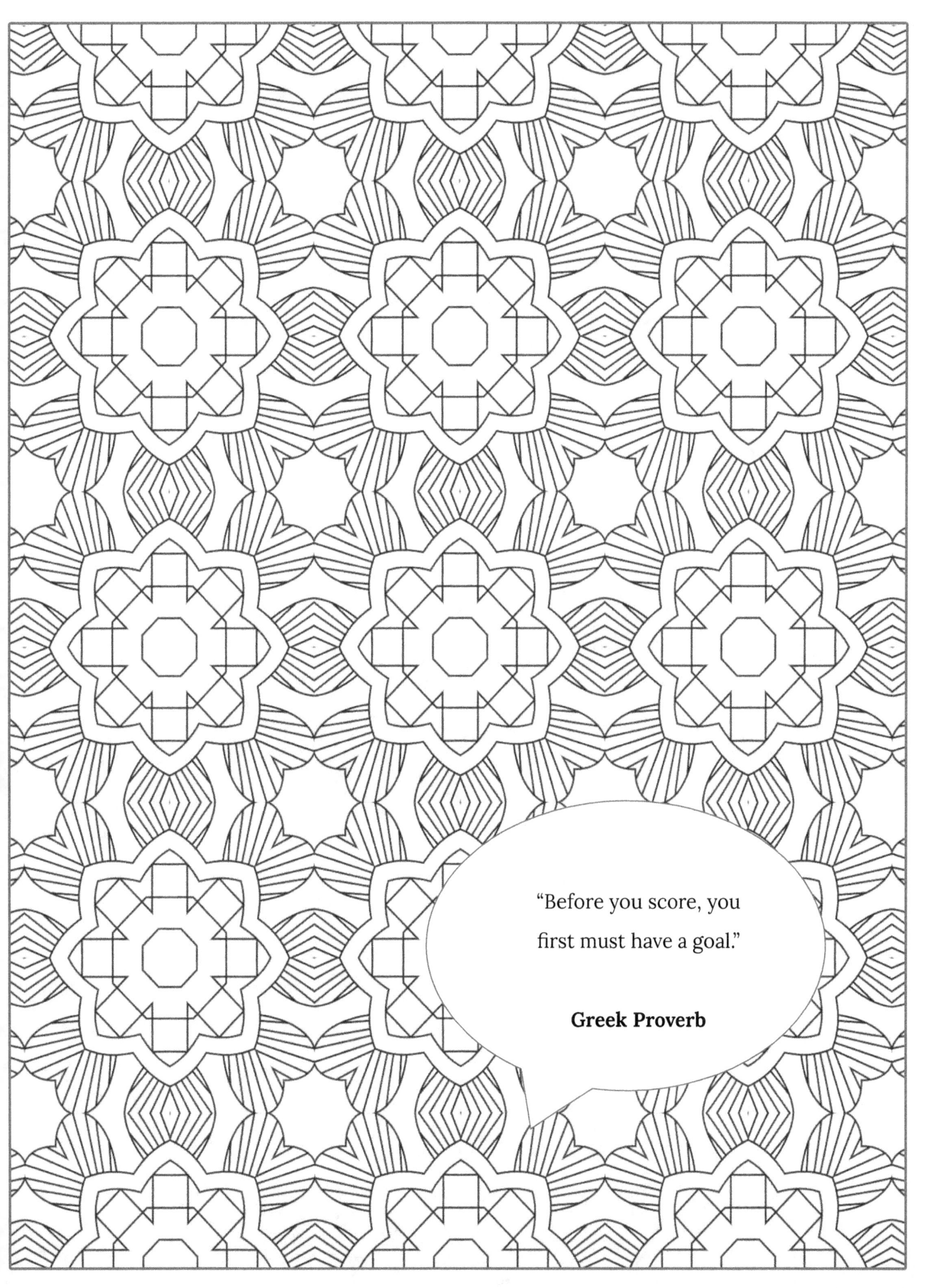

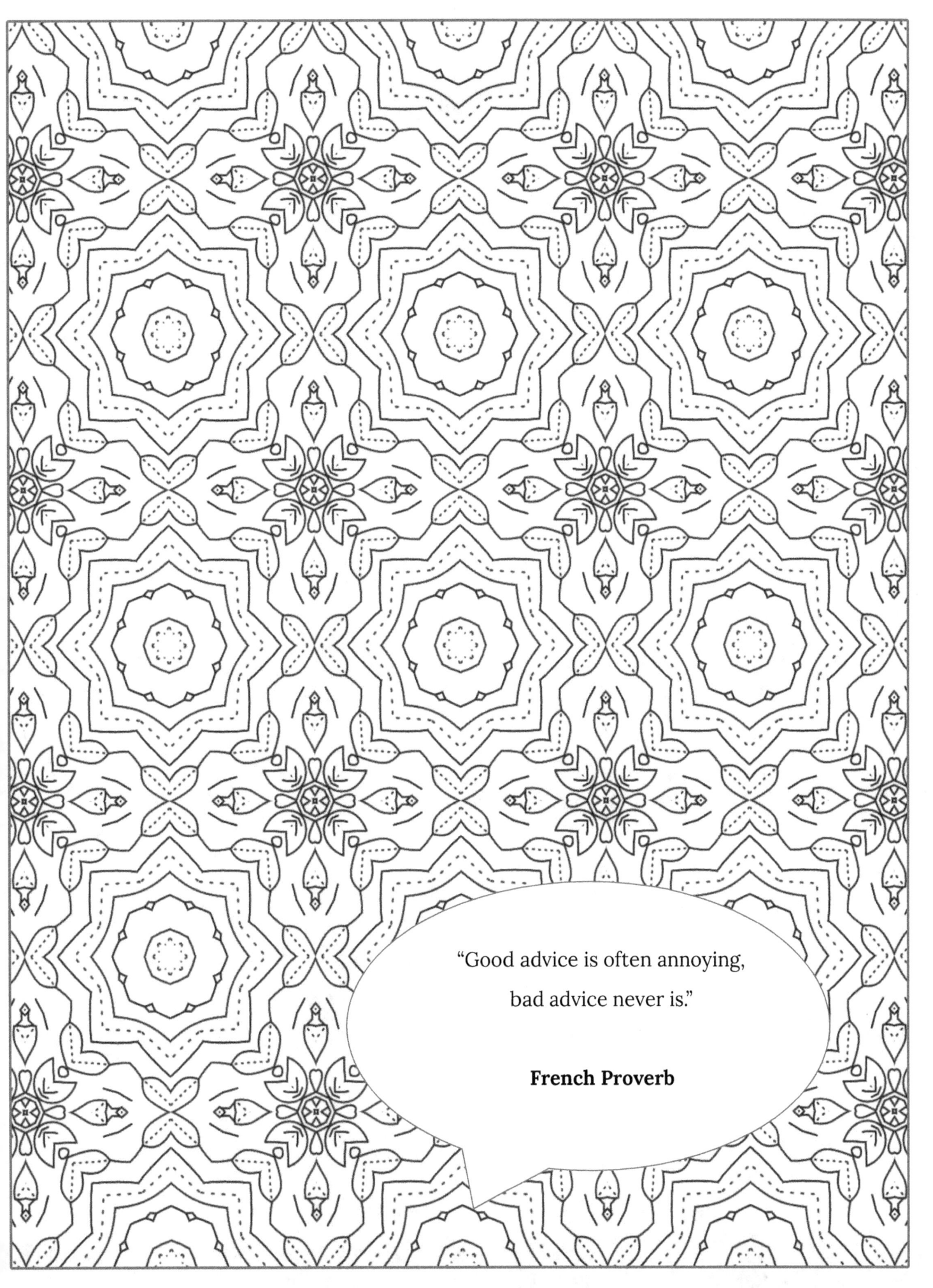

"Good advice is often annoying, bad advice never is."

French Proverb

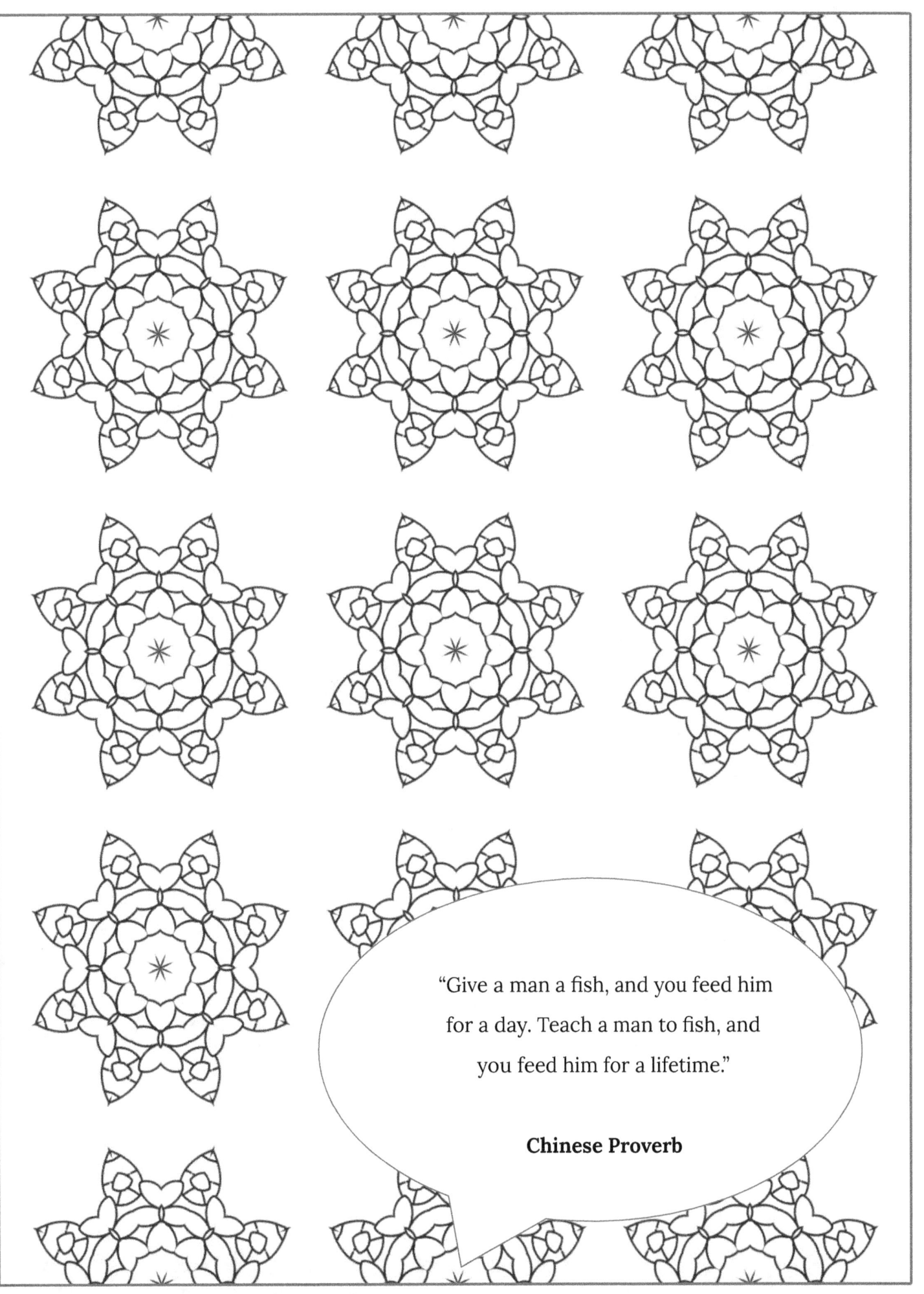

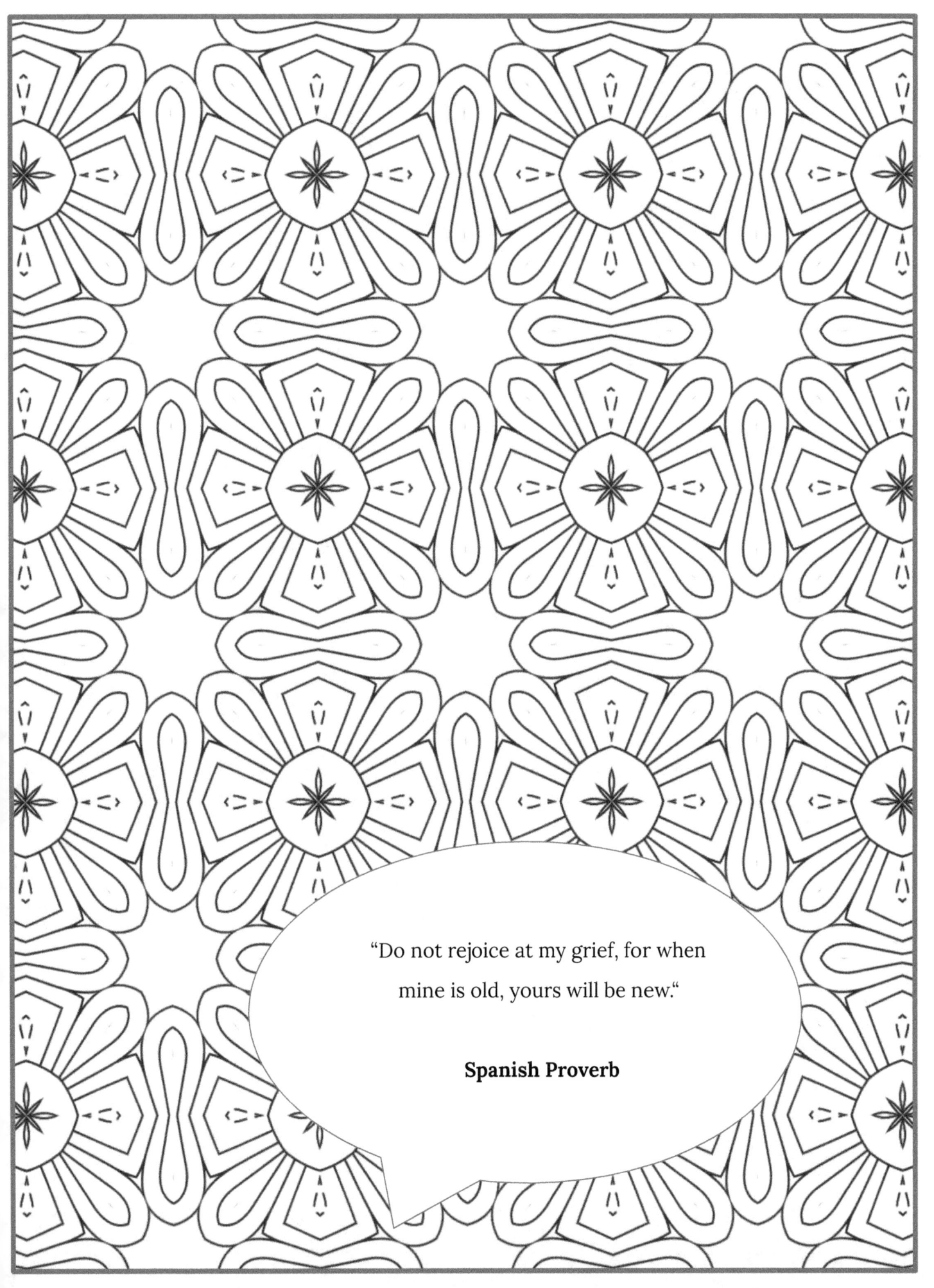

"Do not rejoice at my grief, for when mine is old, yours will be new."

Spanish Proverb

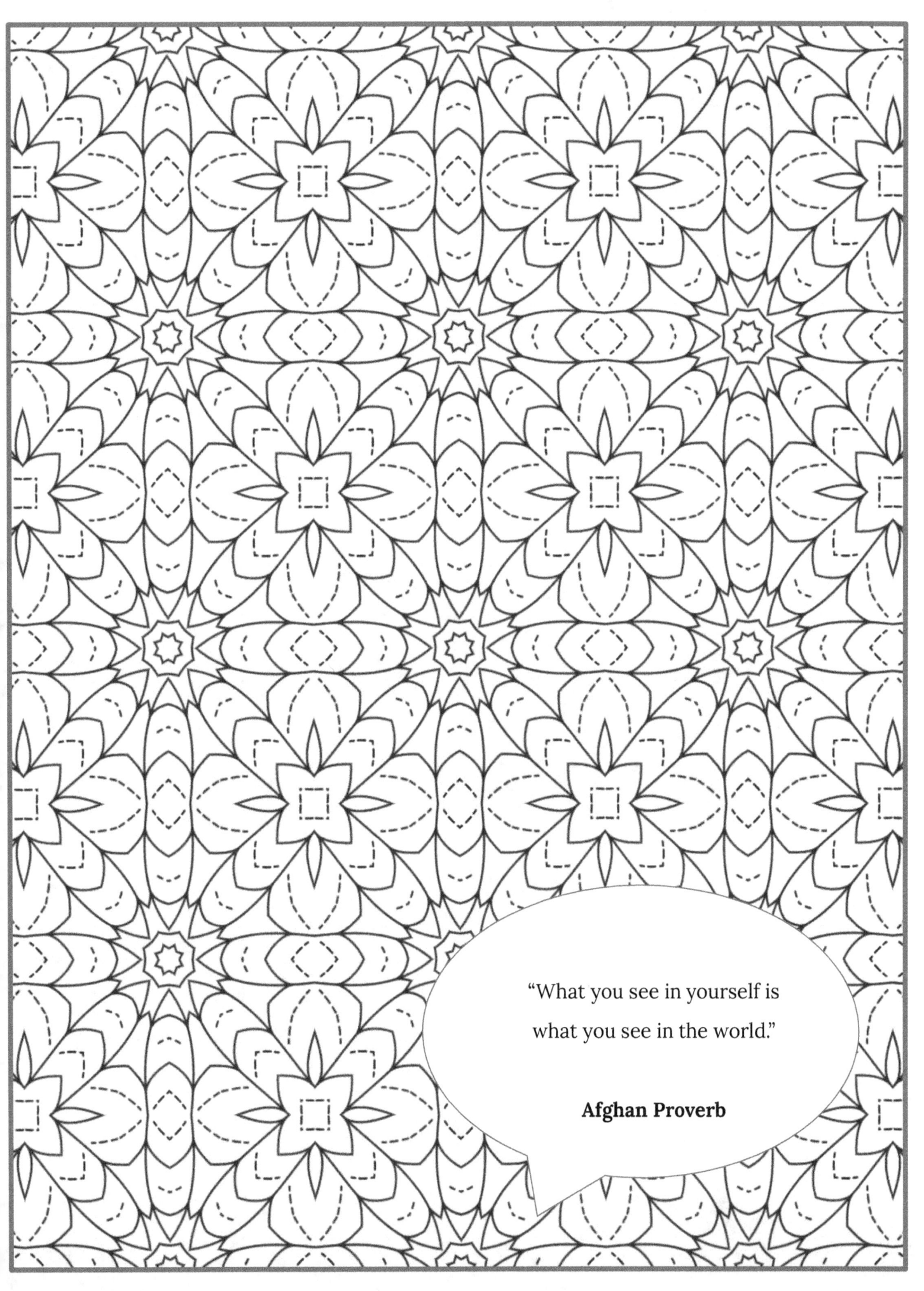

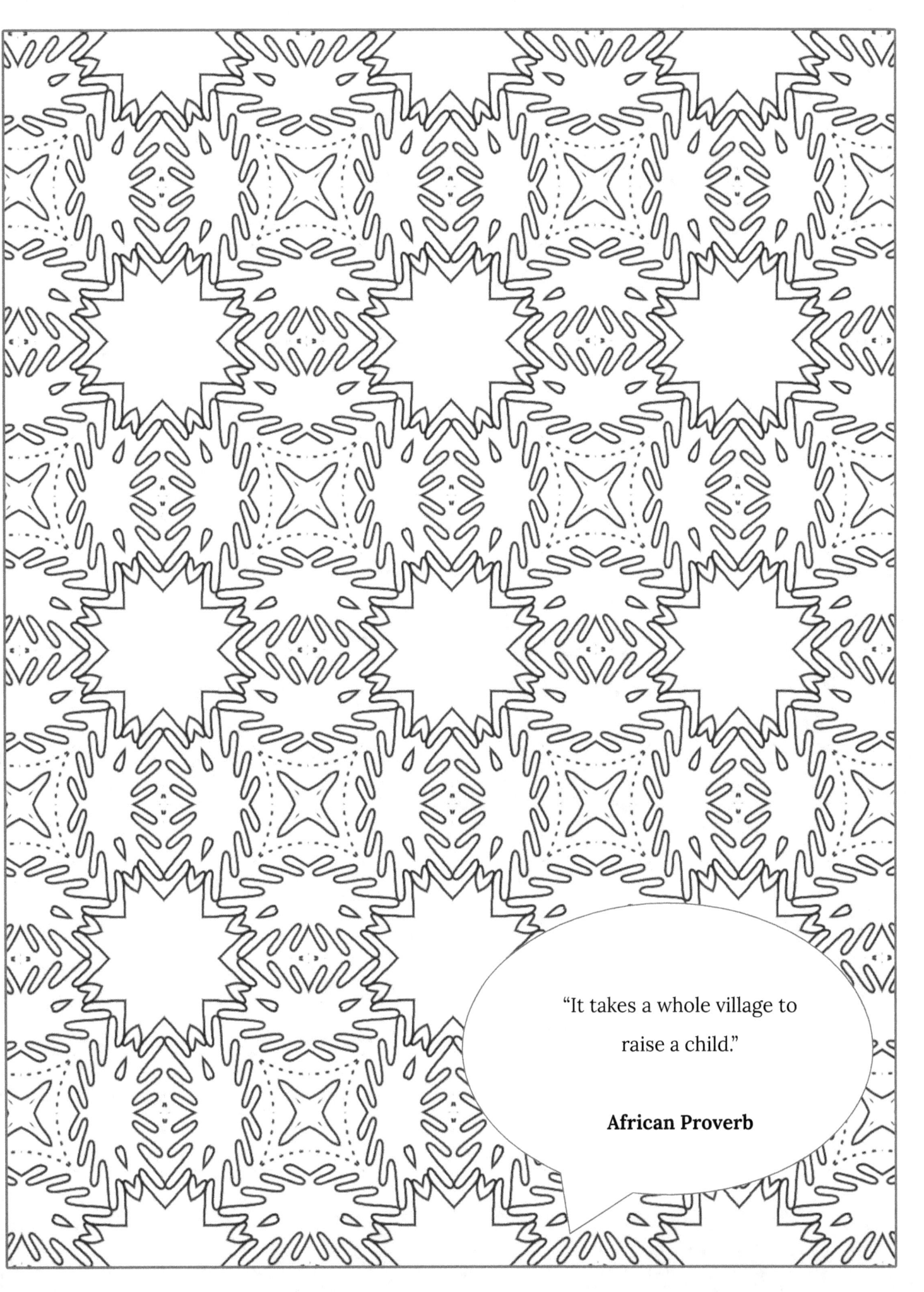

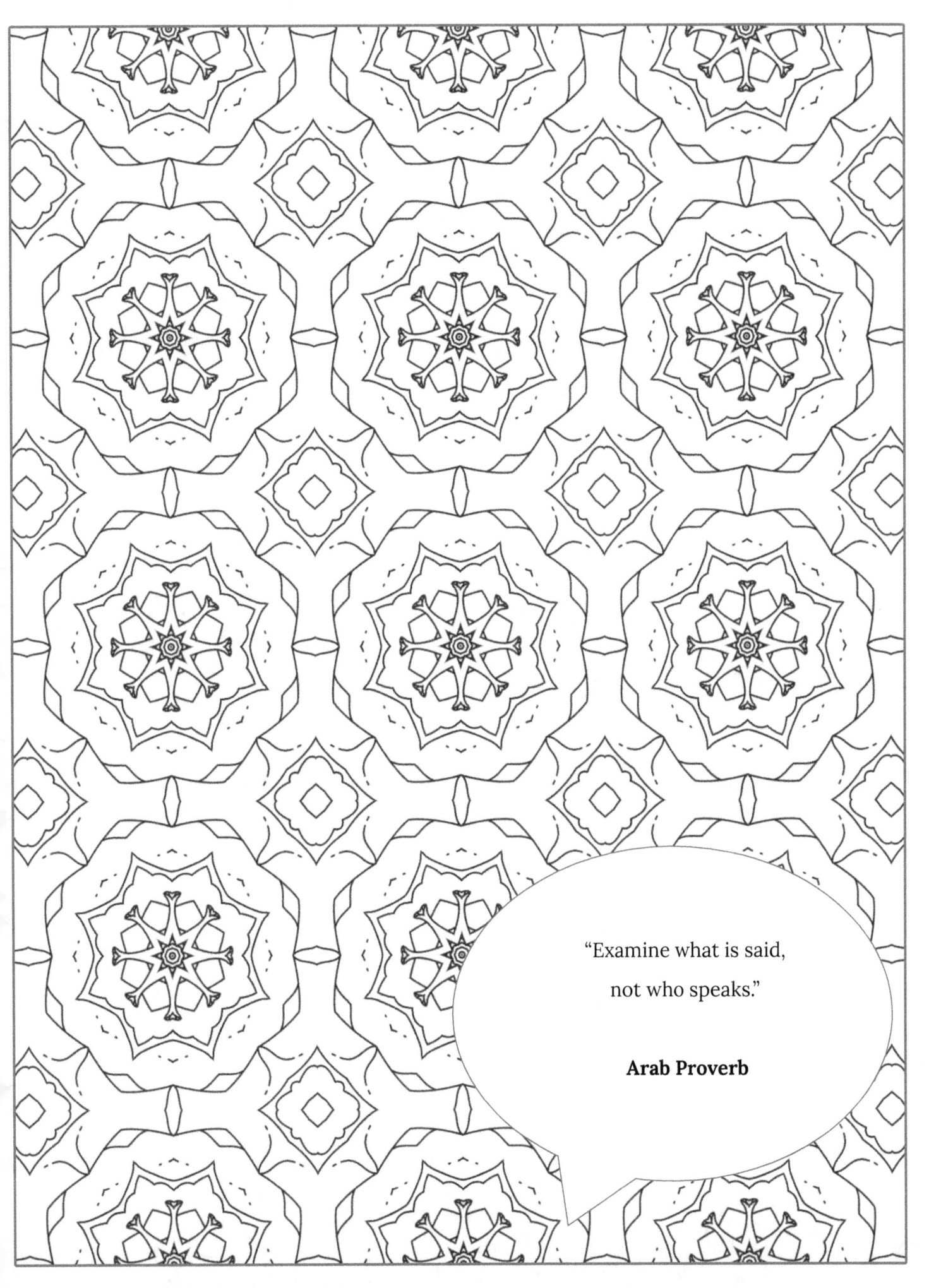

"Examine what is said, not who speaks."

Arab Proverb

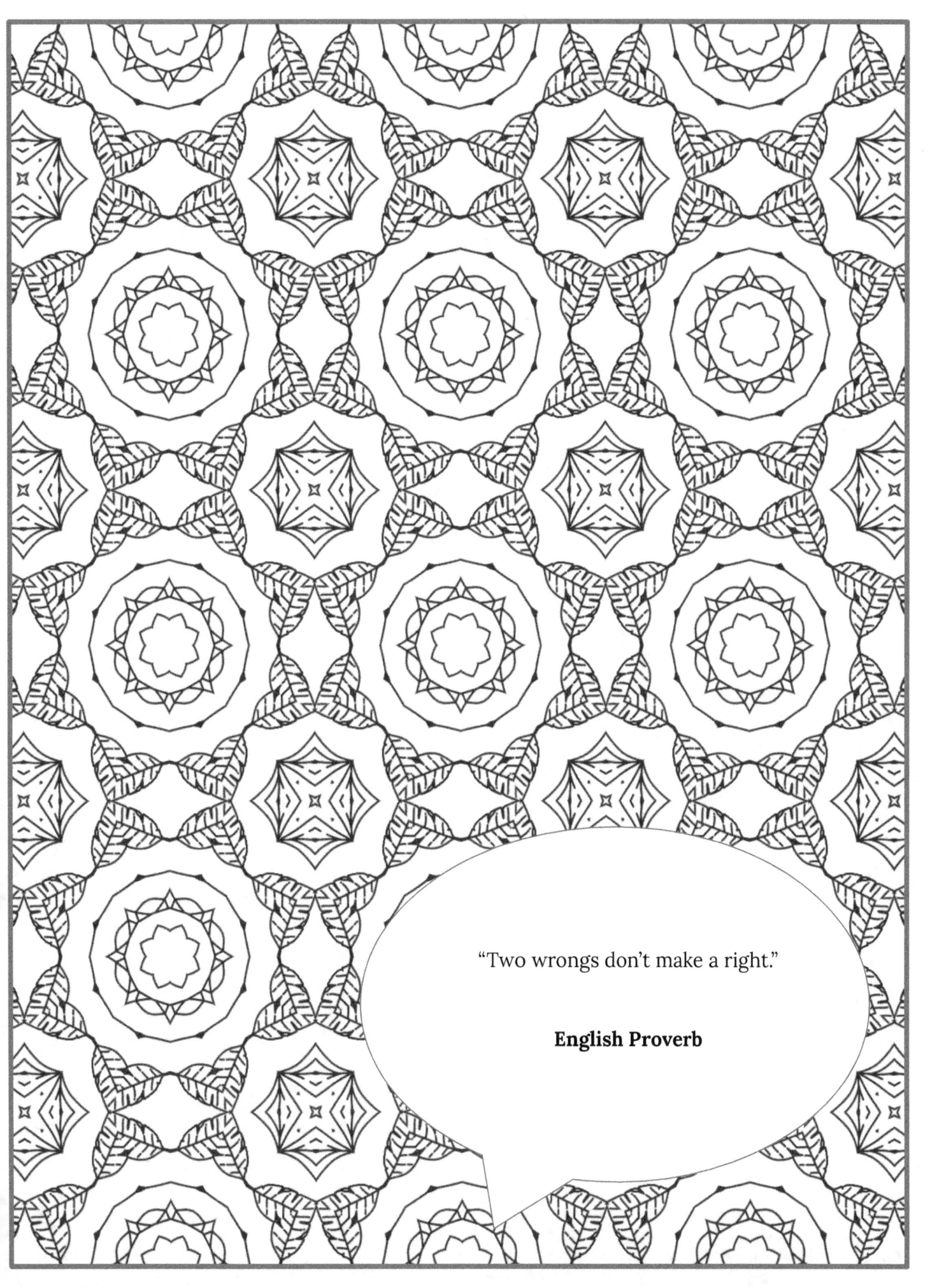

"Two wrongs don't make a right."

English Proverb

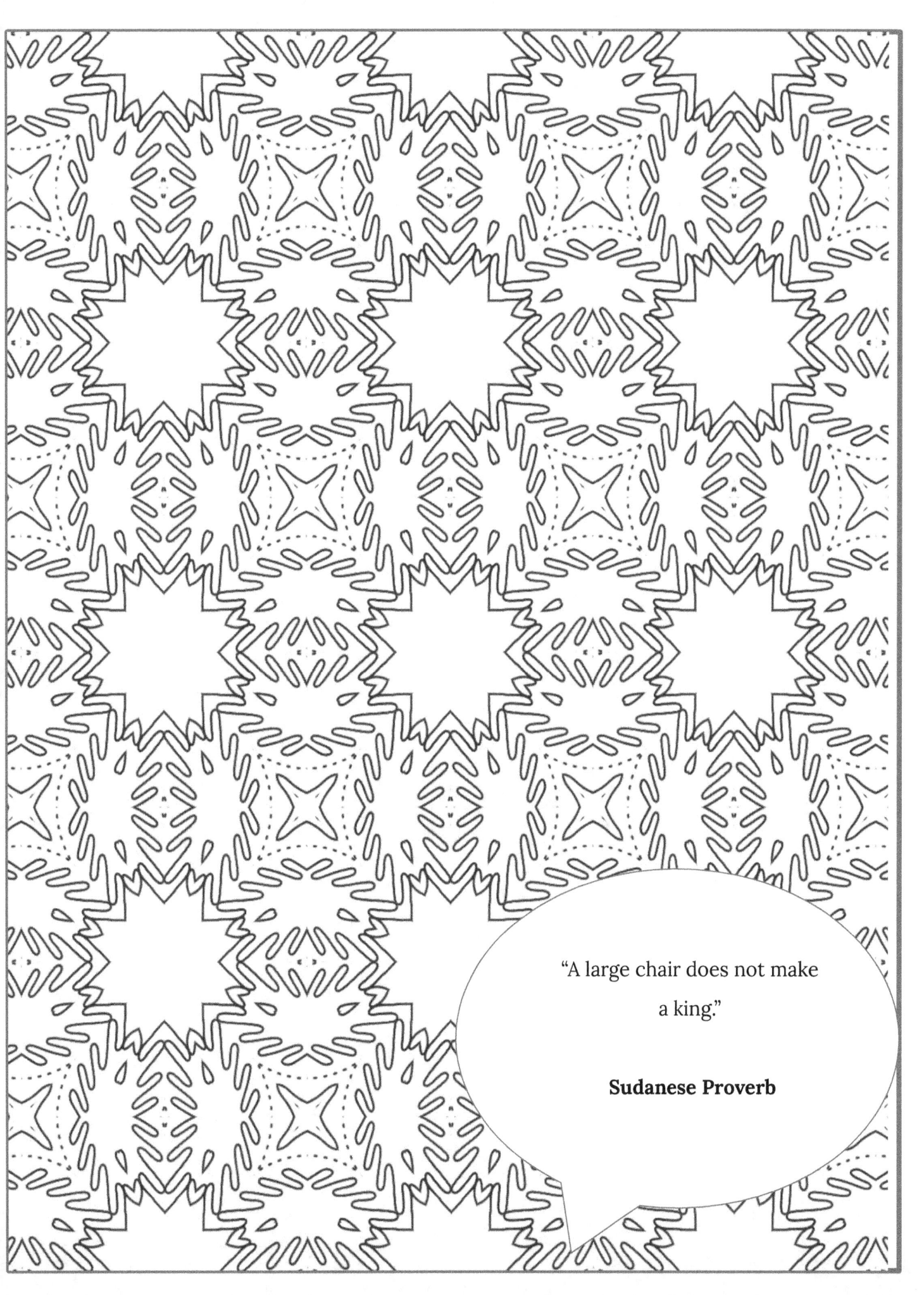

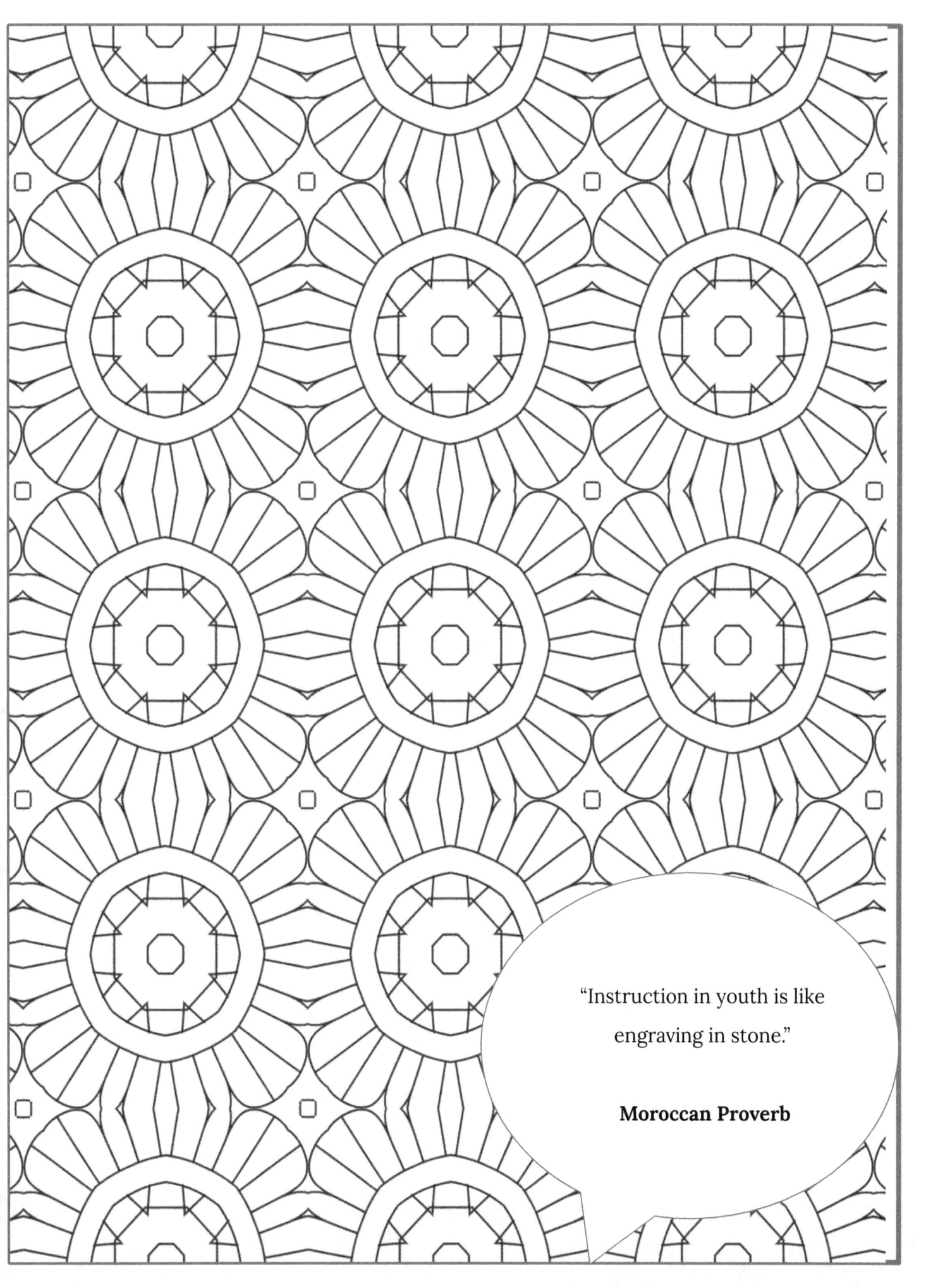

"Instruction in youth is like engraving in stone."

Moroccan Proverb

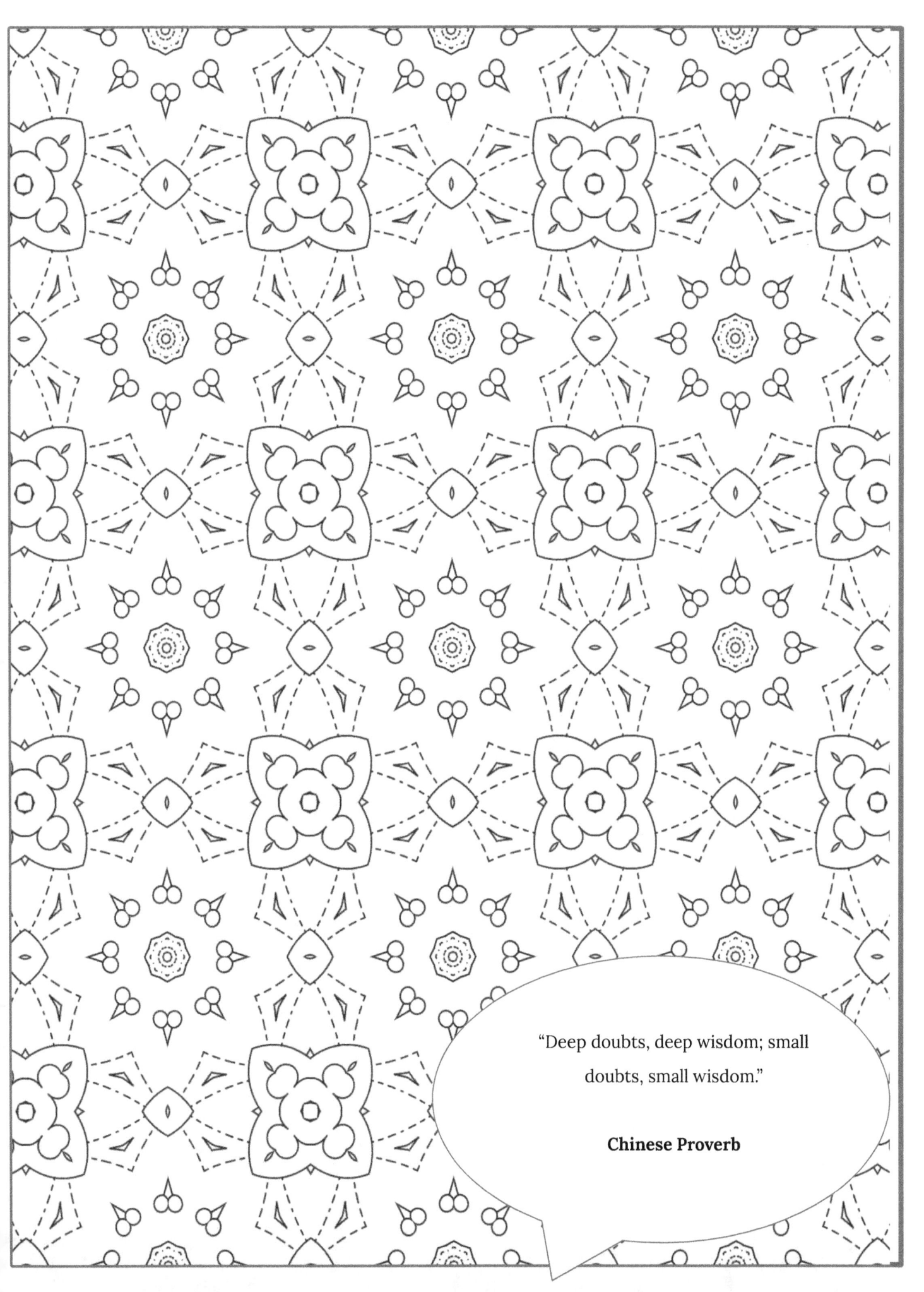

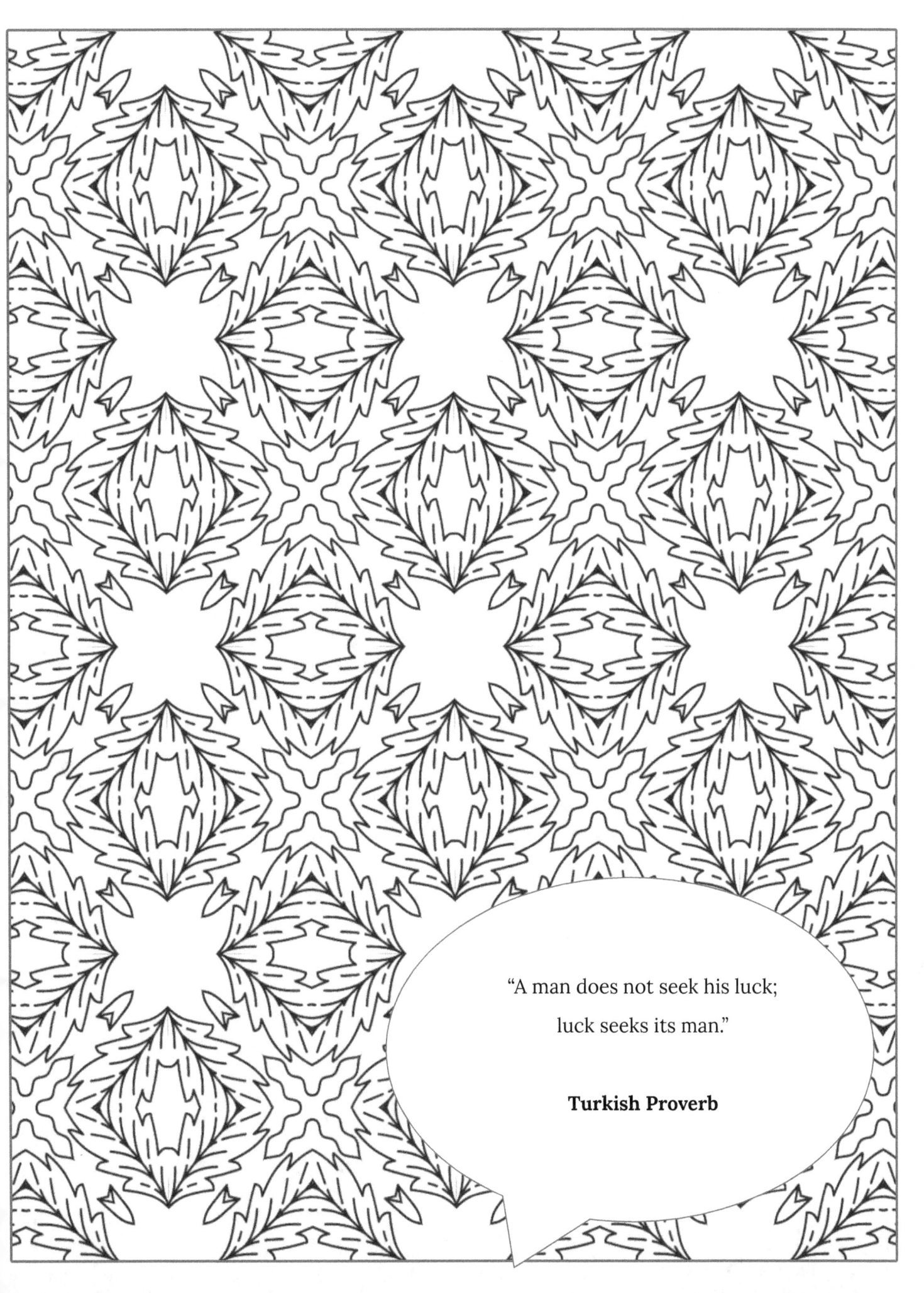

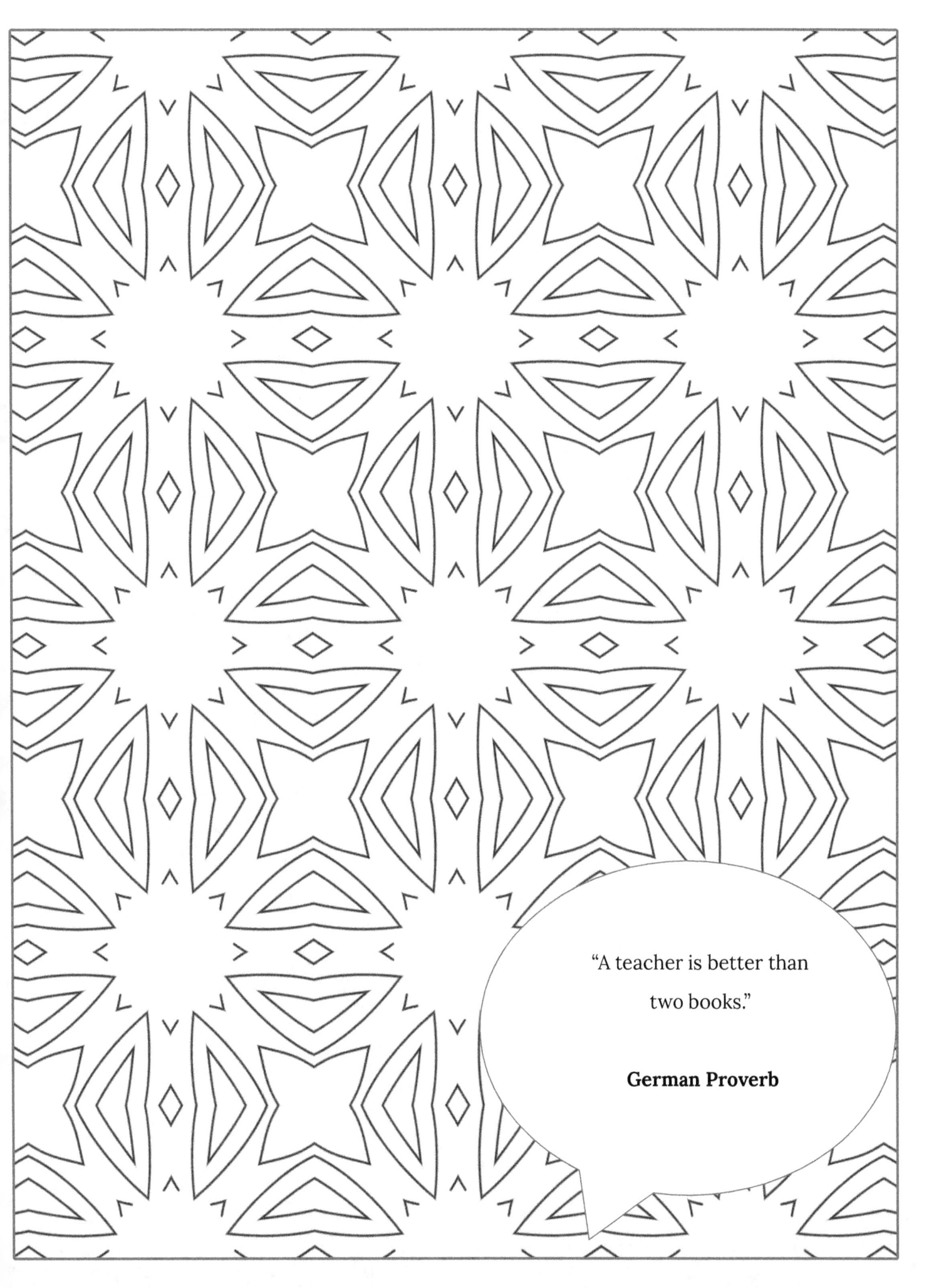

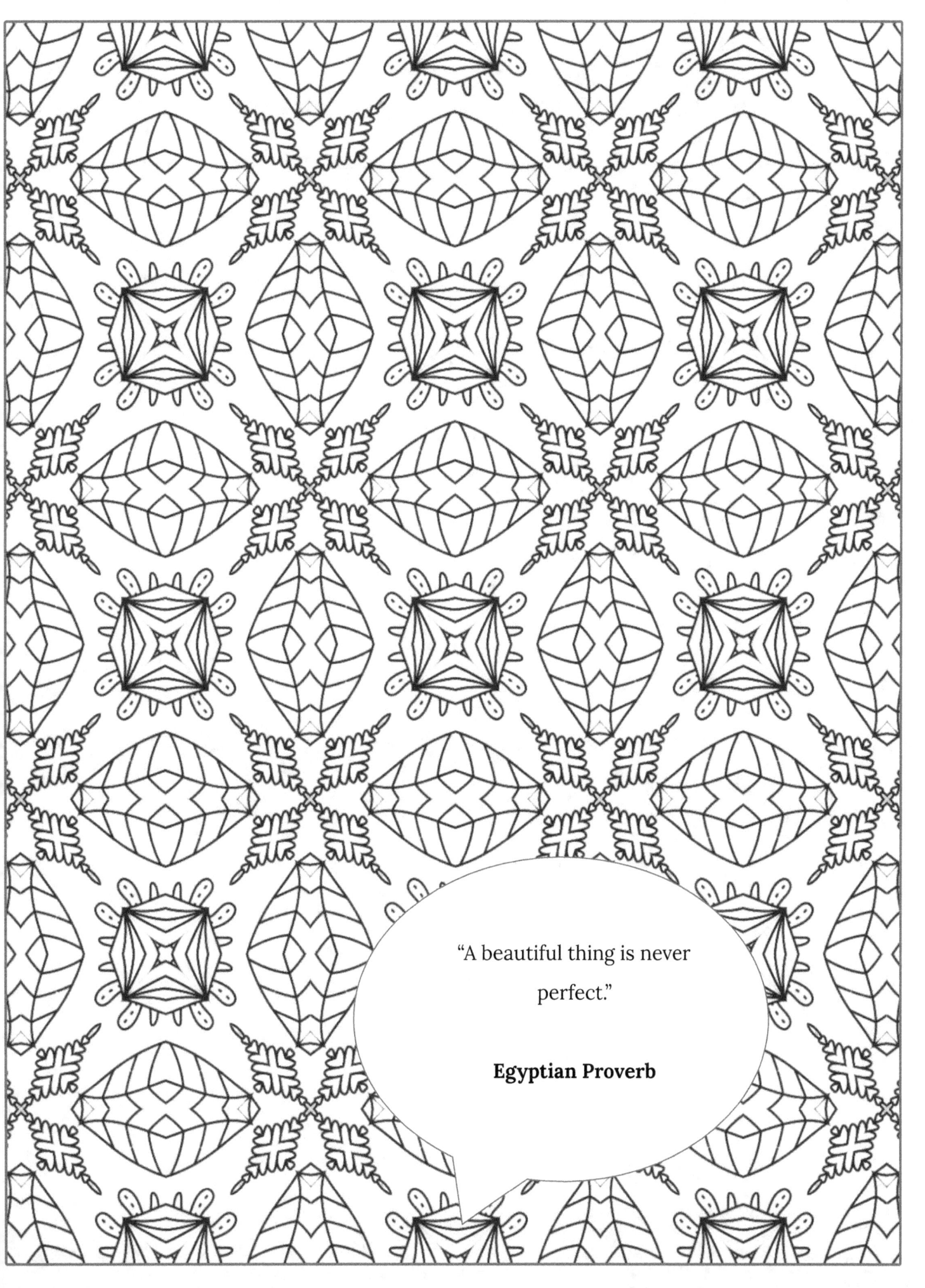

"A beautiful thing is never perfect."

Egyptian Proverb

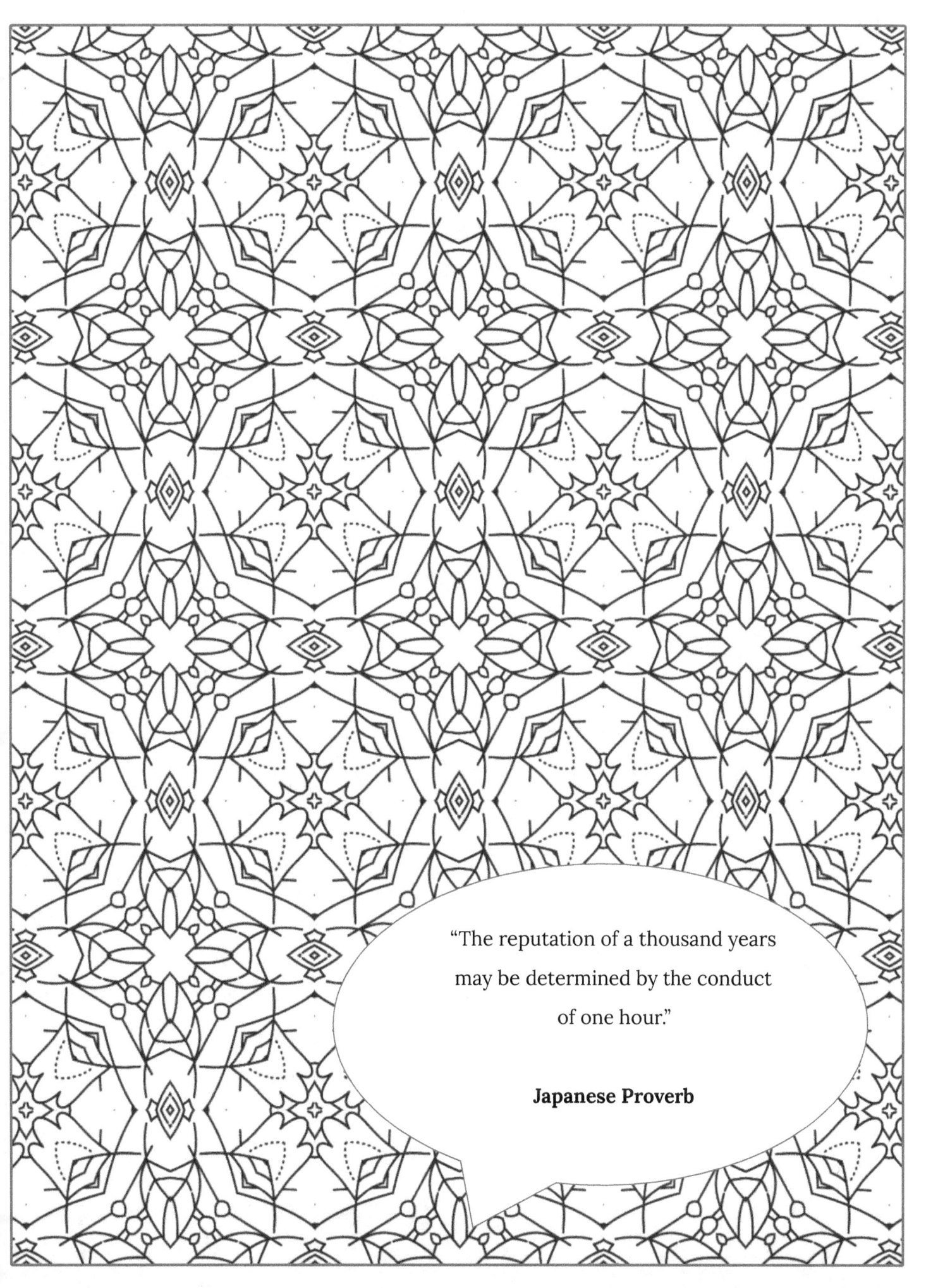

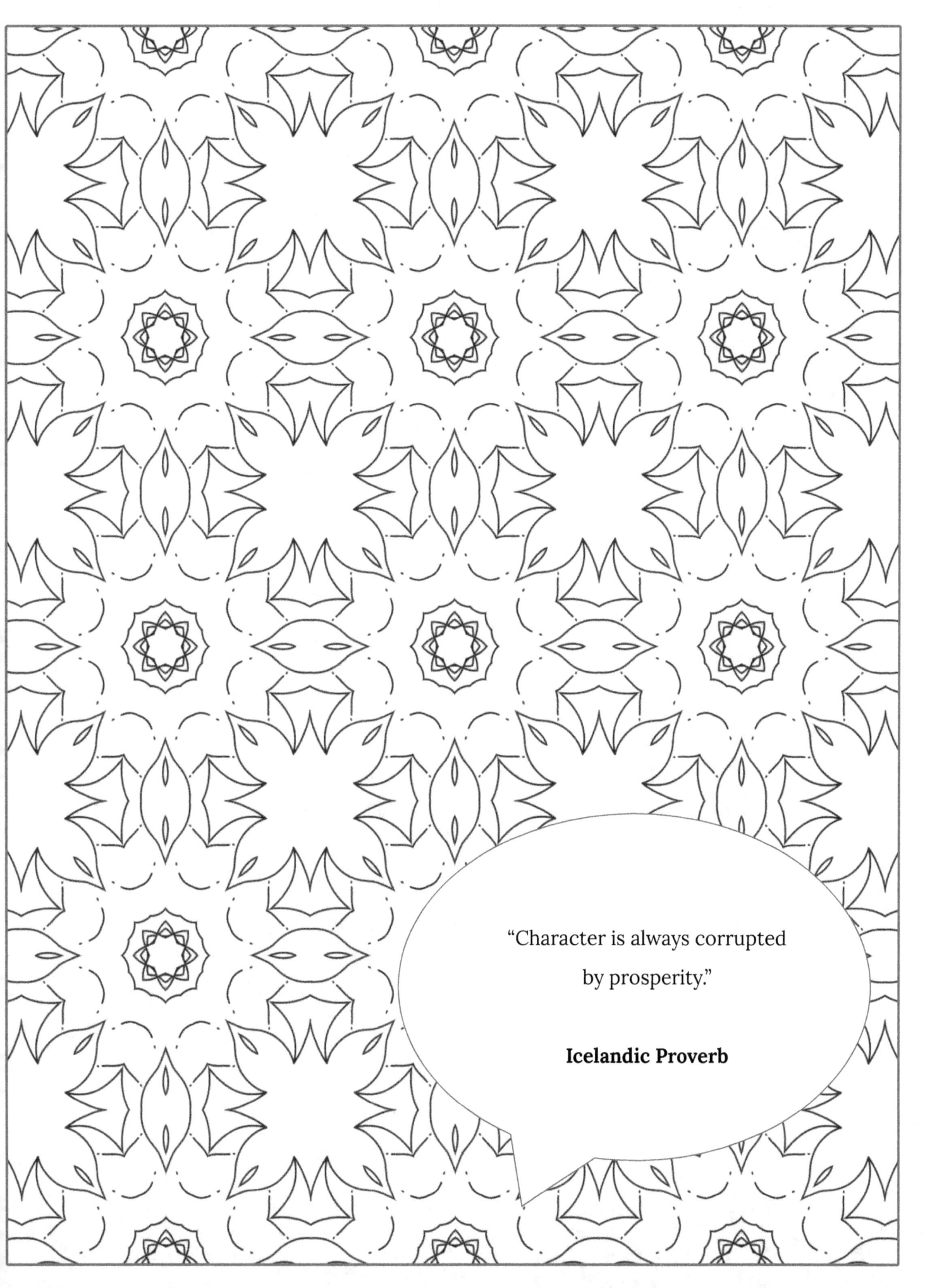

"Character is always corrupted by prosperity."

Icelandic Proverb

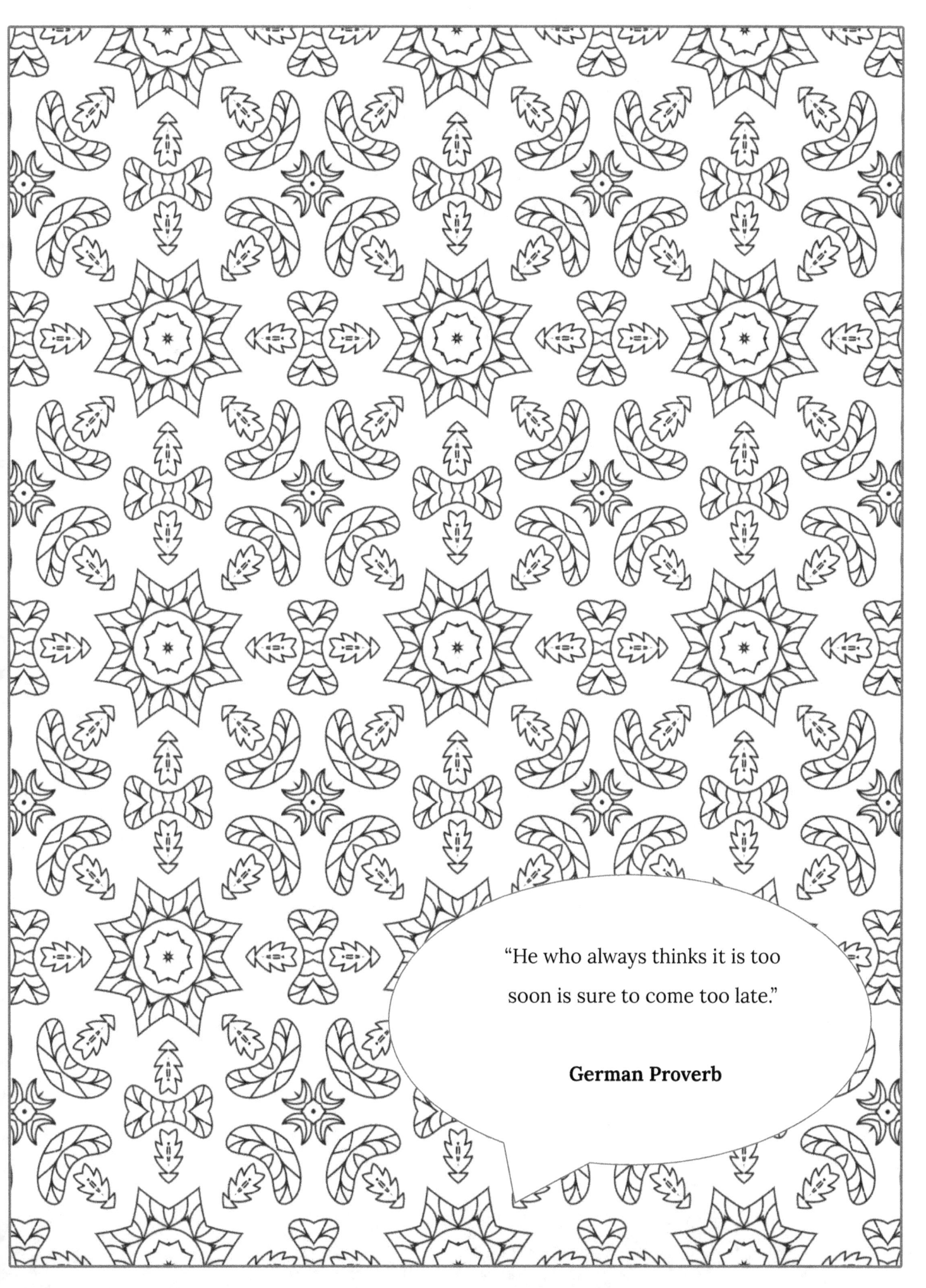

"He who always thinks it is too soon is sure to come too late."

German Proverb

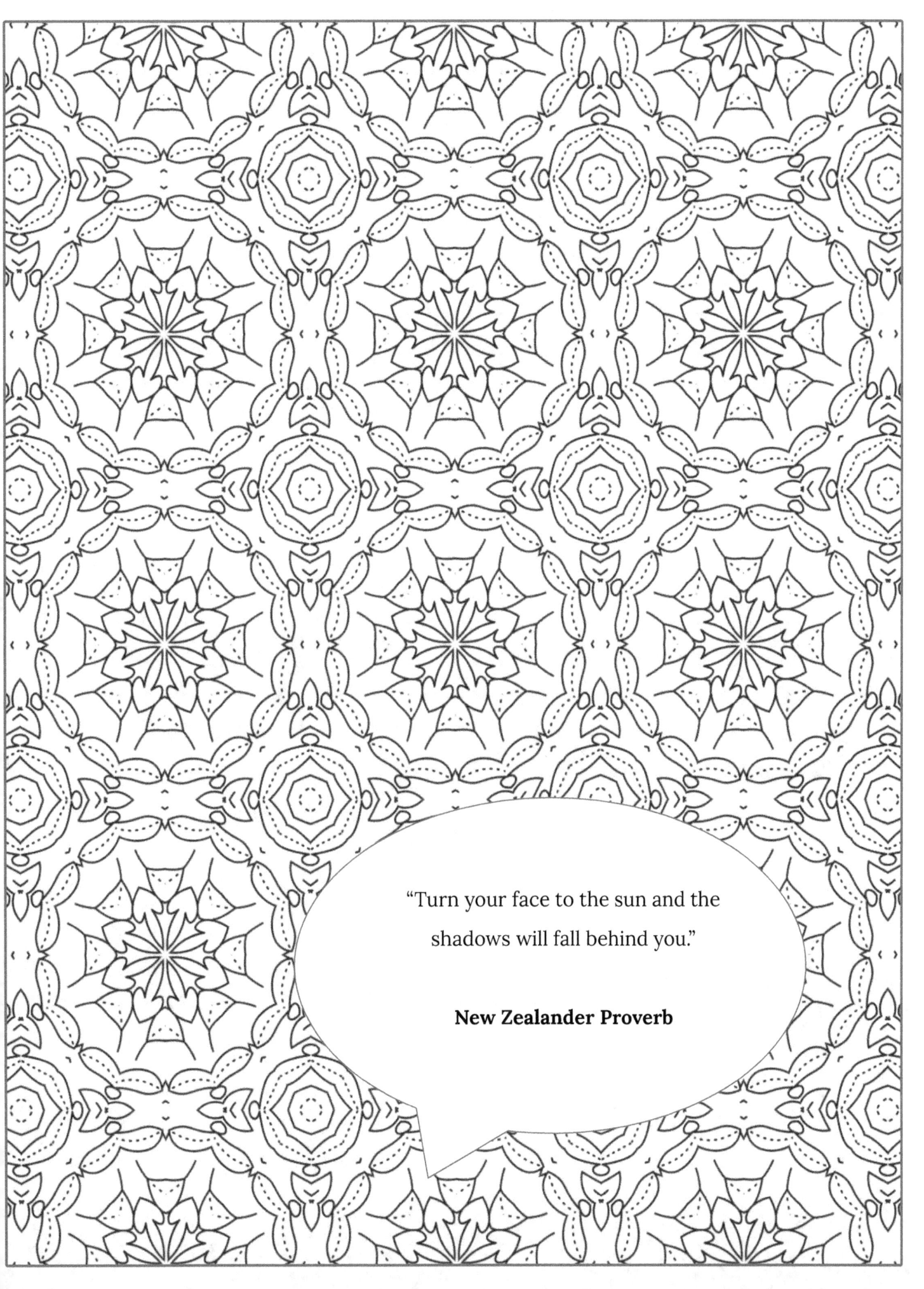

"Turn your face to the sun and the shadows will fall behind you."

New Zealander Proverb

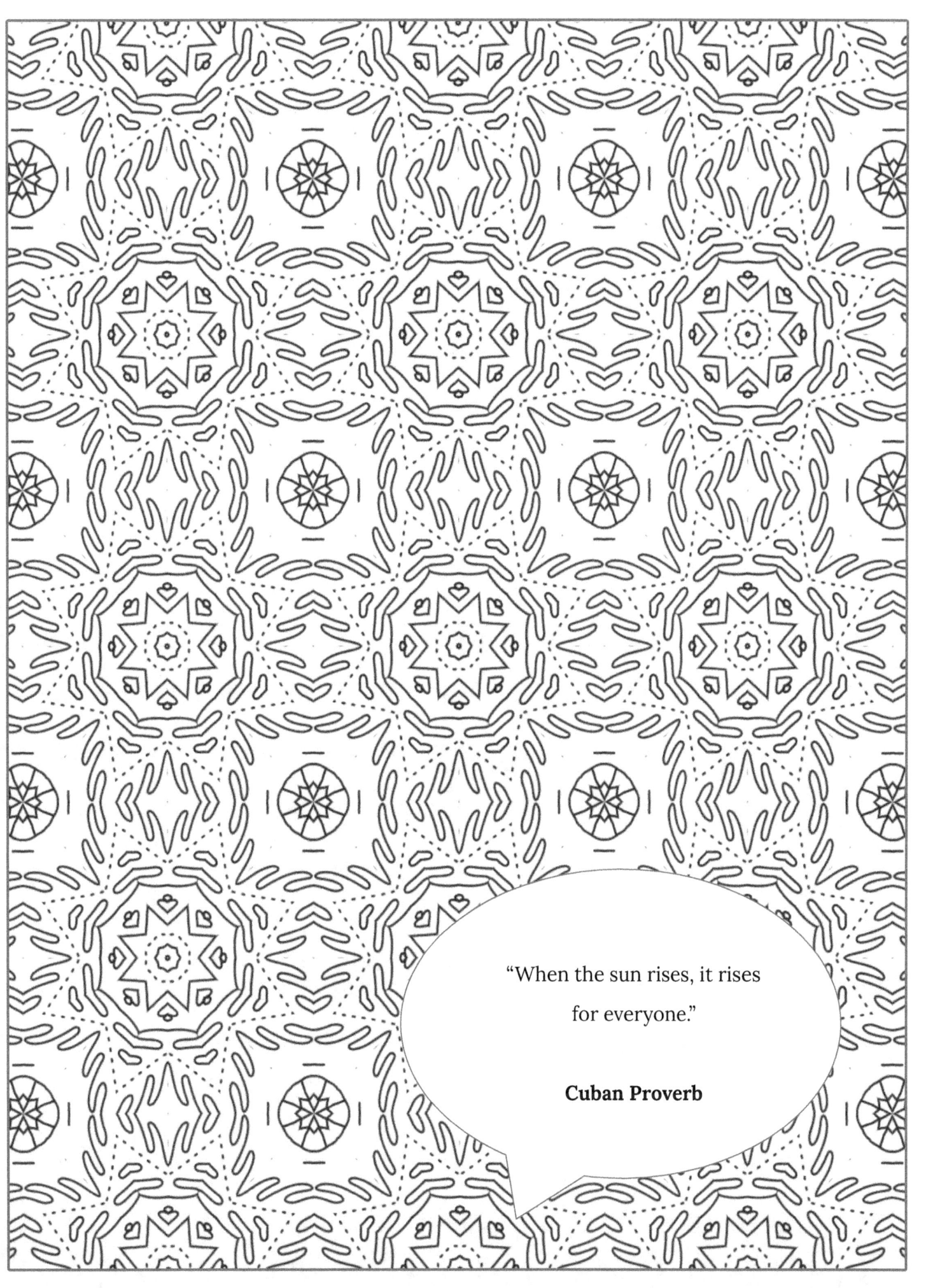

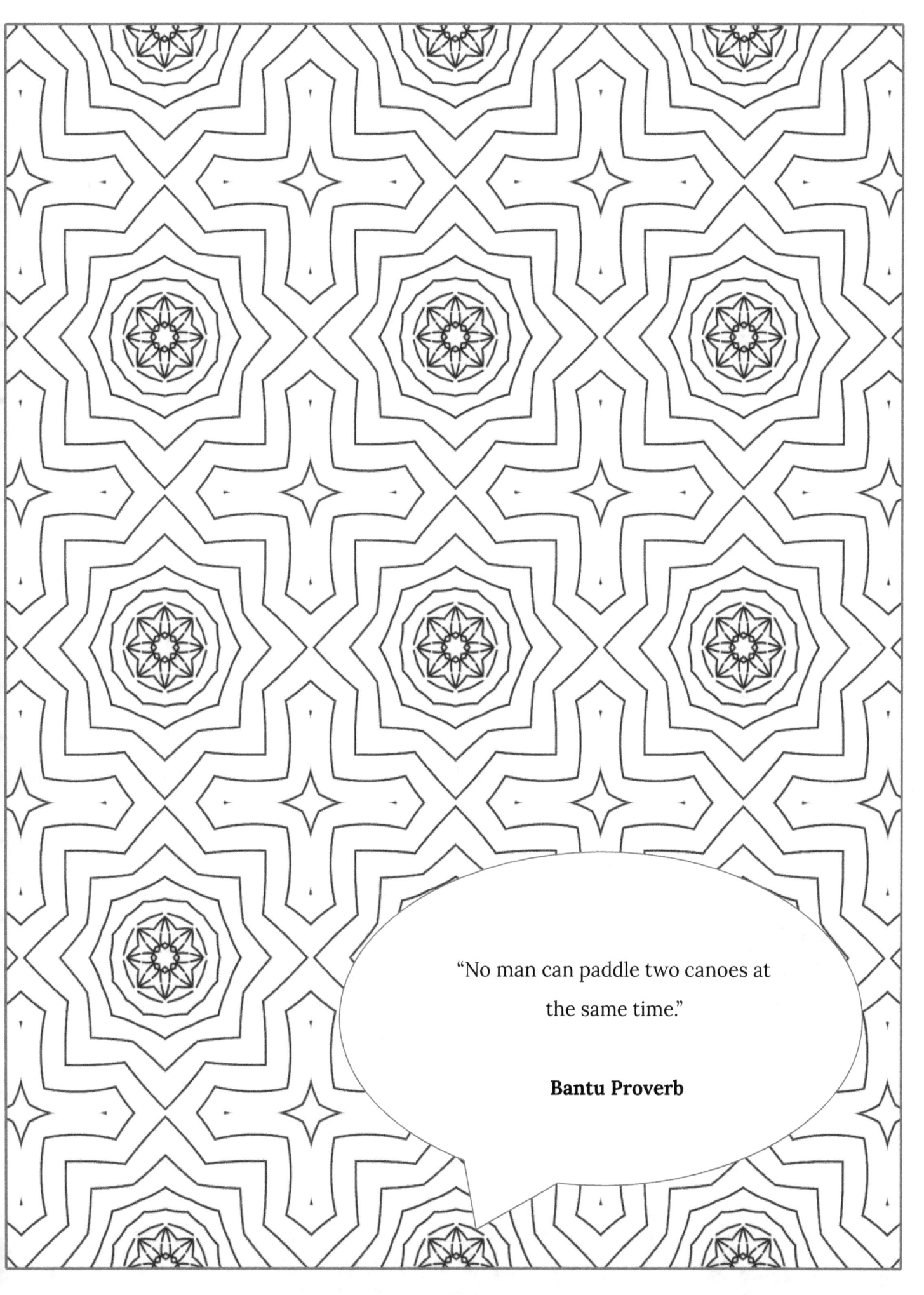

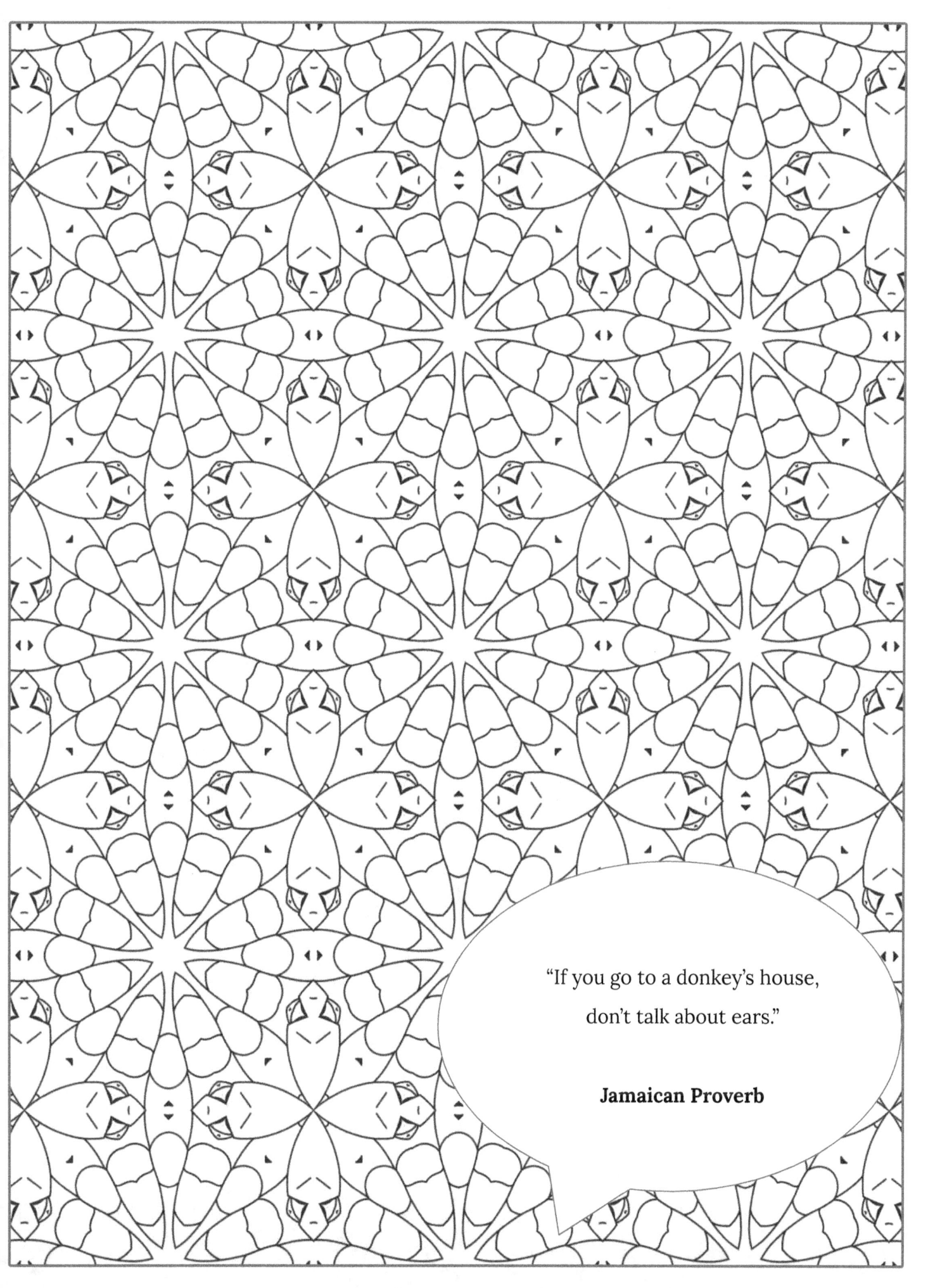

"If you go to a donkey's house, don't talk about ears."

Jamaican Proverb

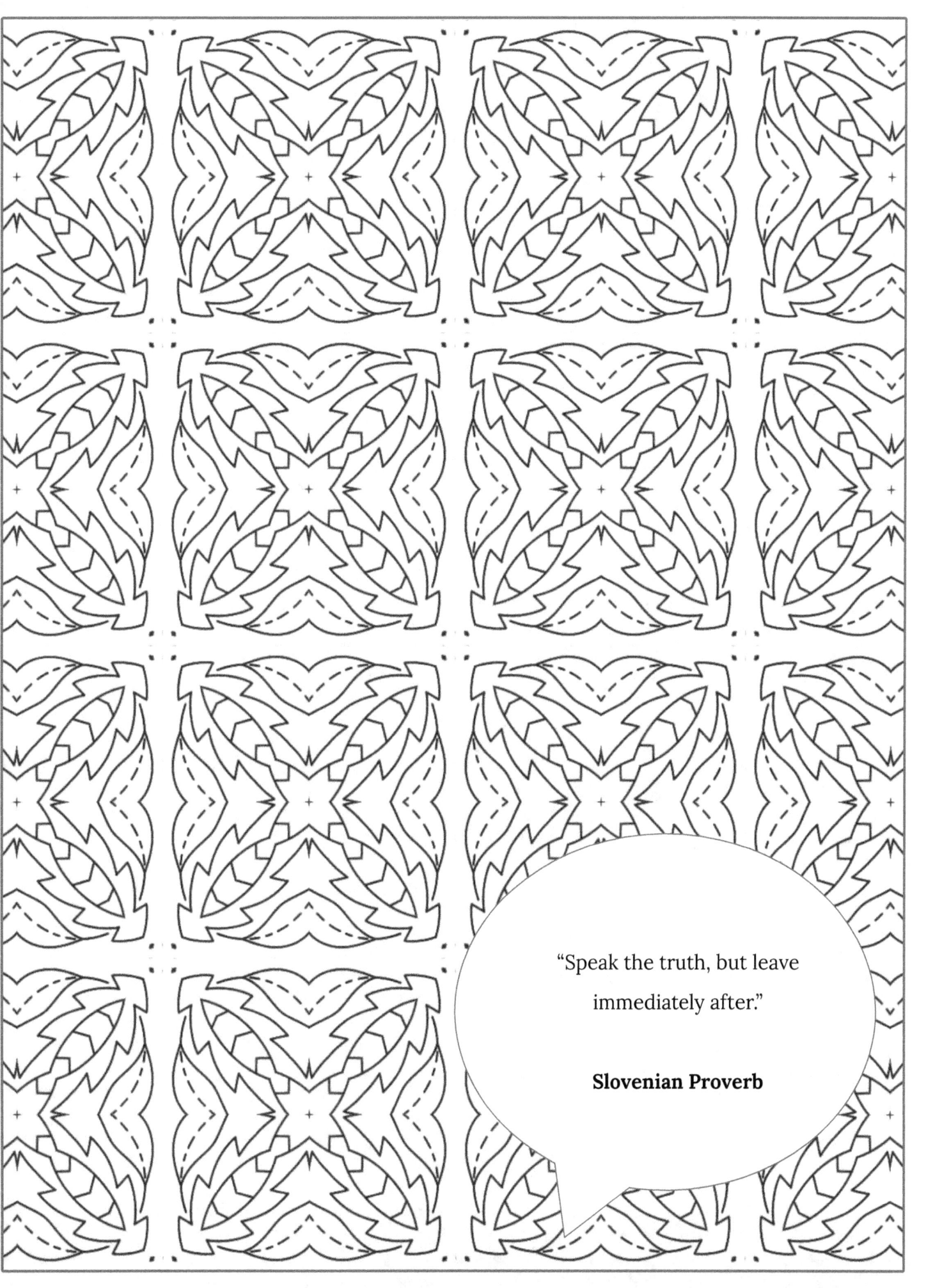

"Speak the truth, but leave immediately after."

Slovenian Proverb

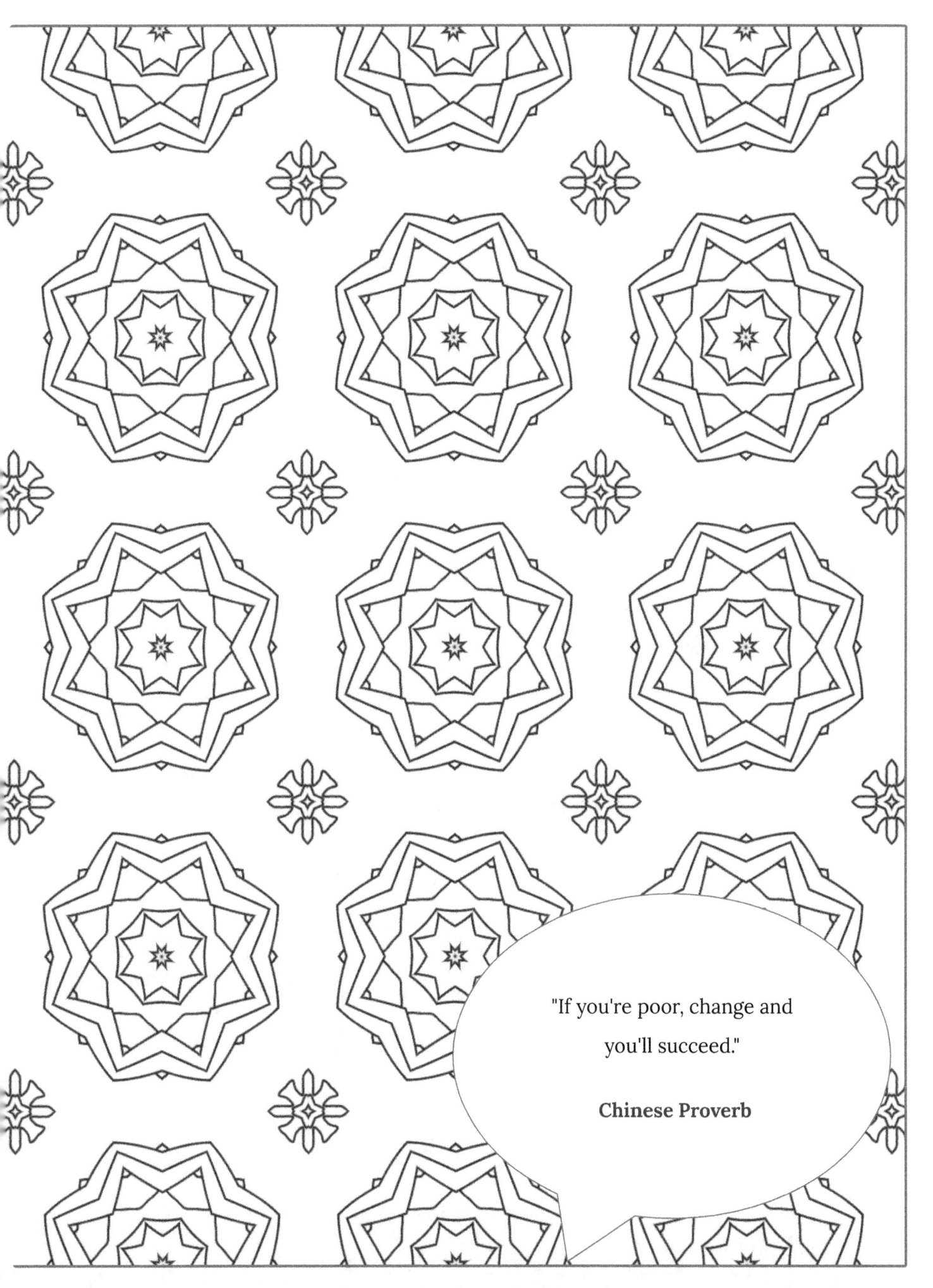

"If you're poor, change and you'll succeed."

Chinese Proverb

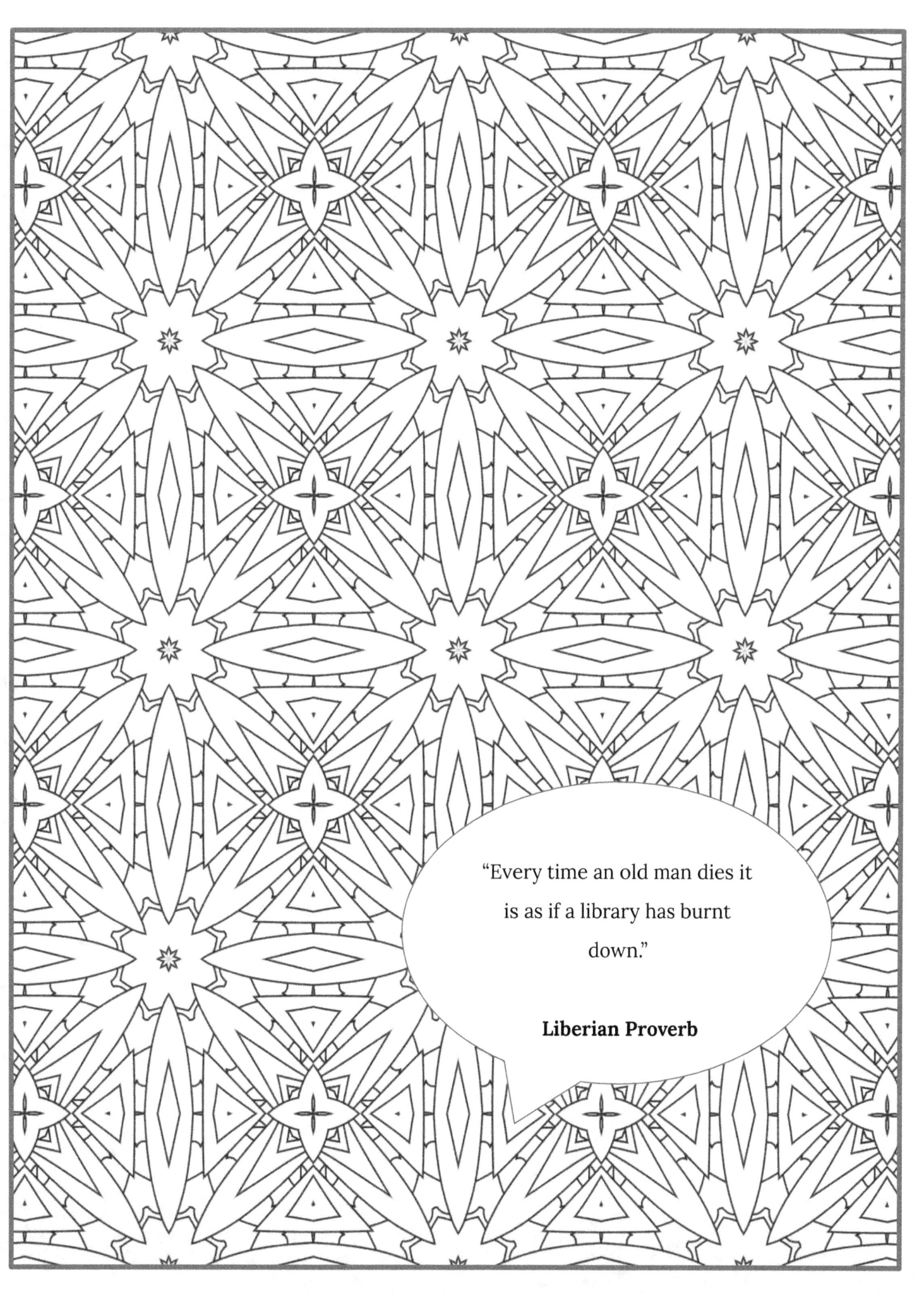

"Every time an old man dies it is as if a library has burnt down."

Liberian Proverb

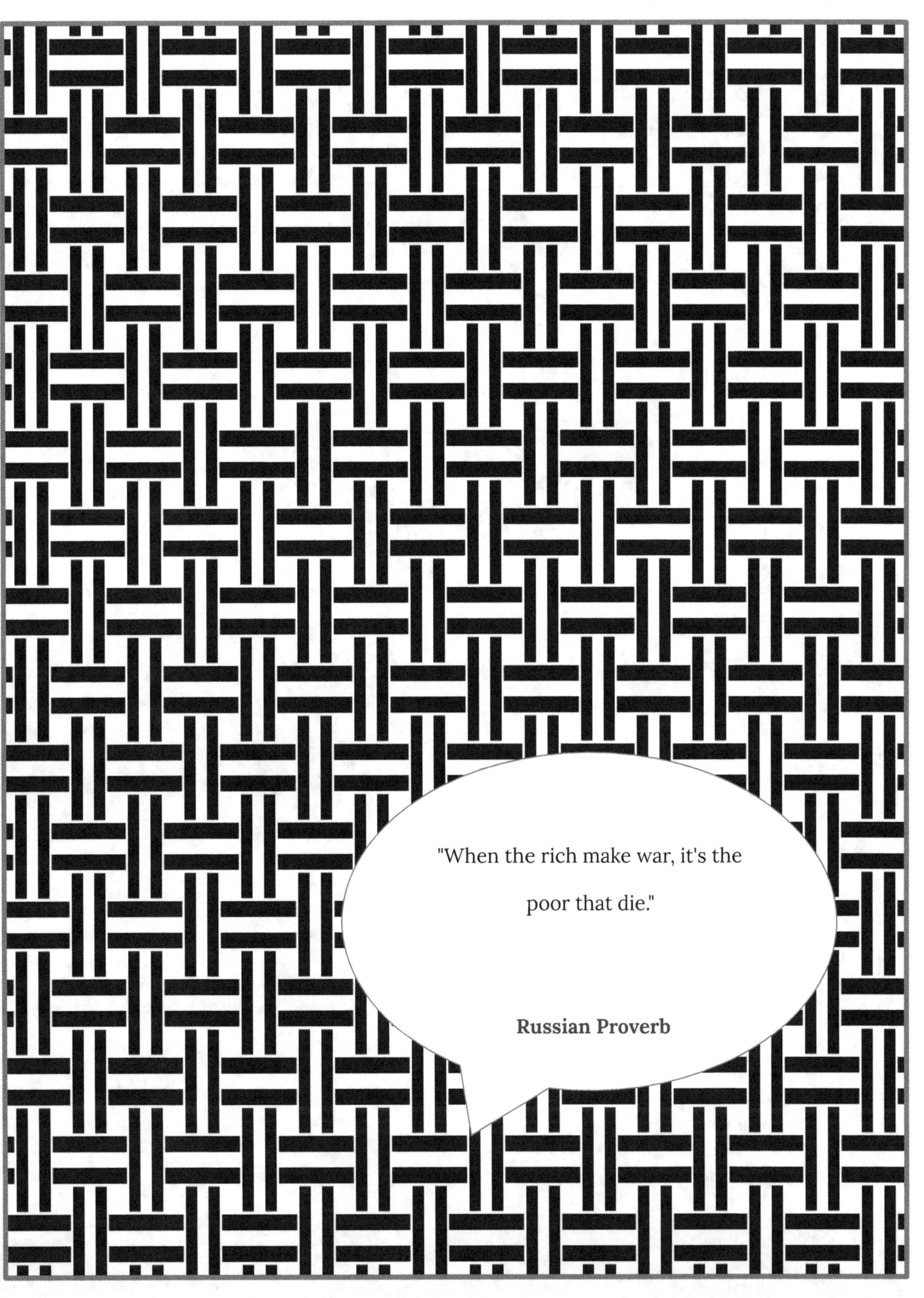
"When the rich make war, it's the poor that die."

Russian Proverb

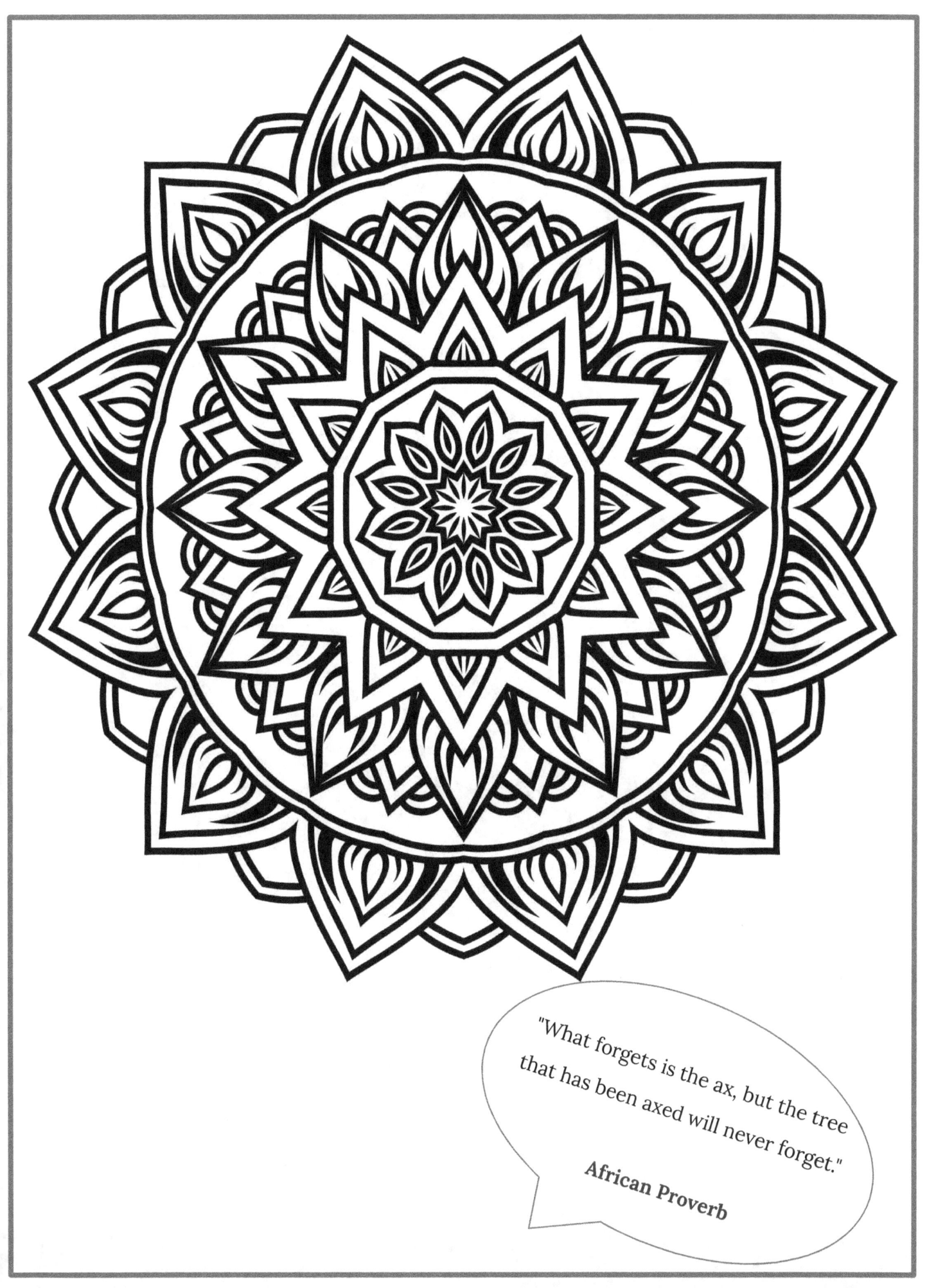

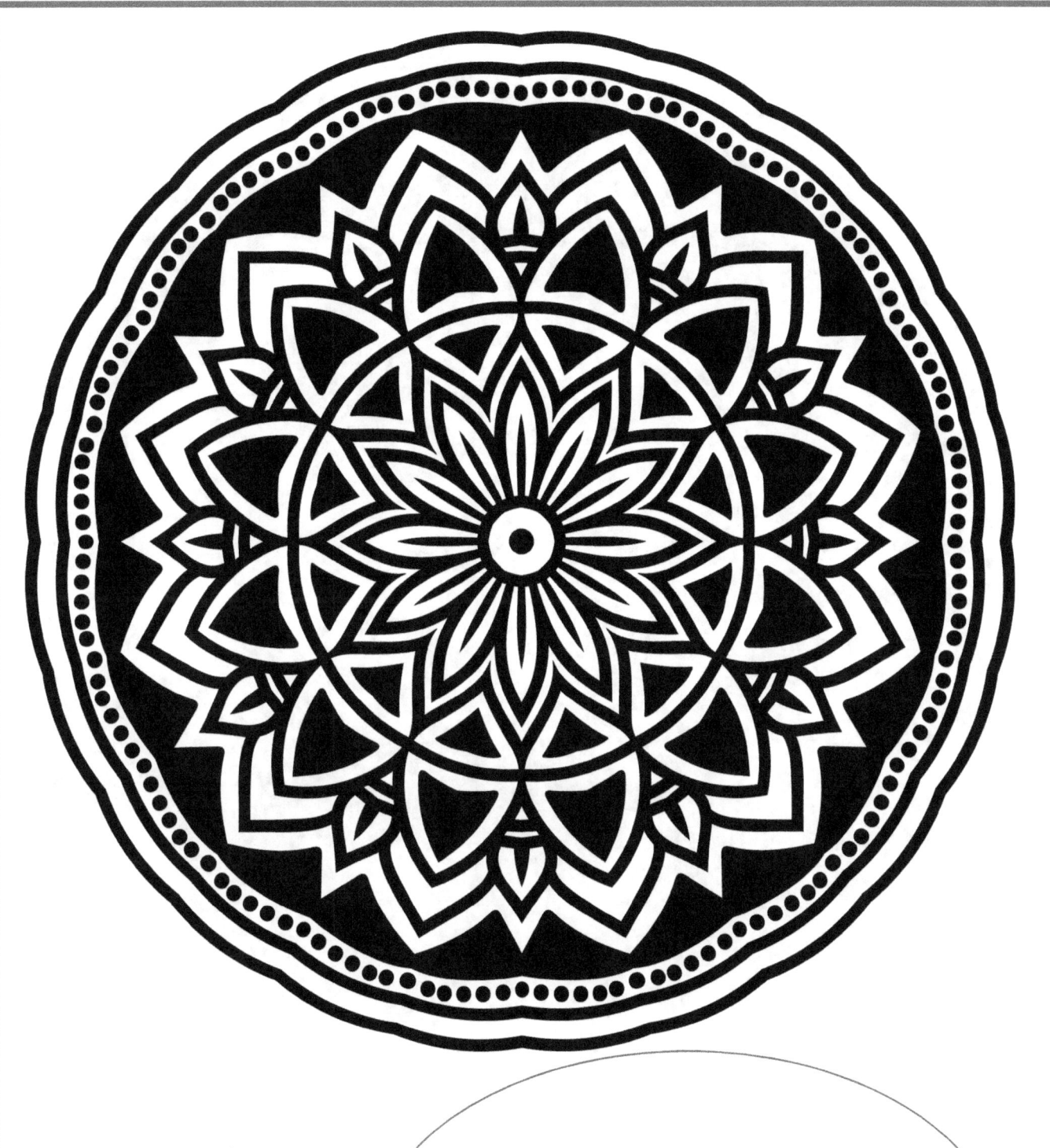

"A bad worker blames his tools."

Australian Proverb

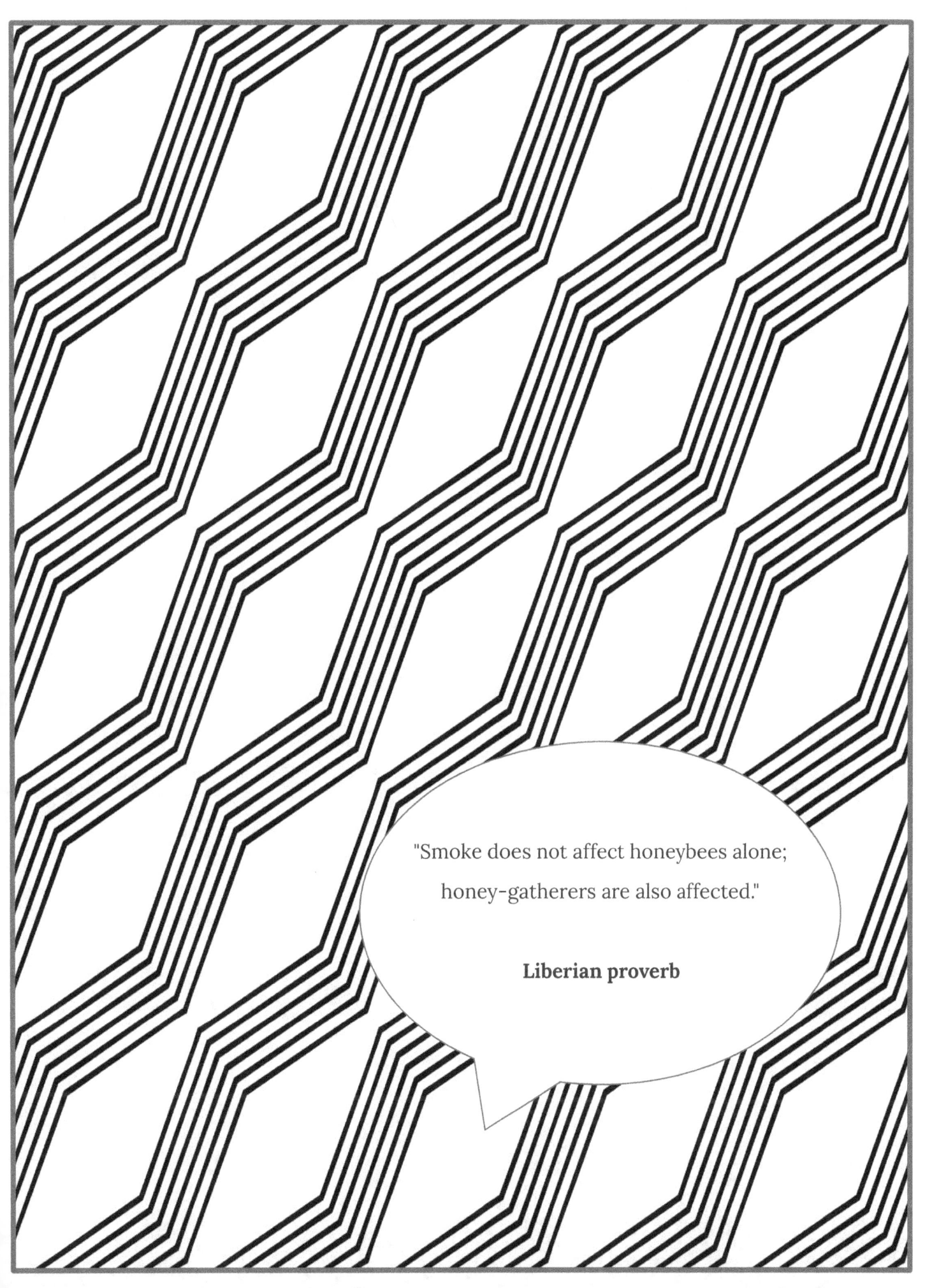

"No shame in asking questions, even to people of lower status."

Chinese Proverb

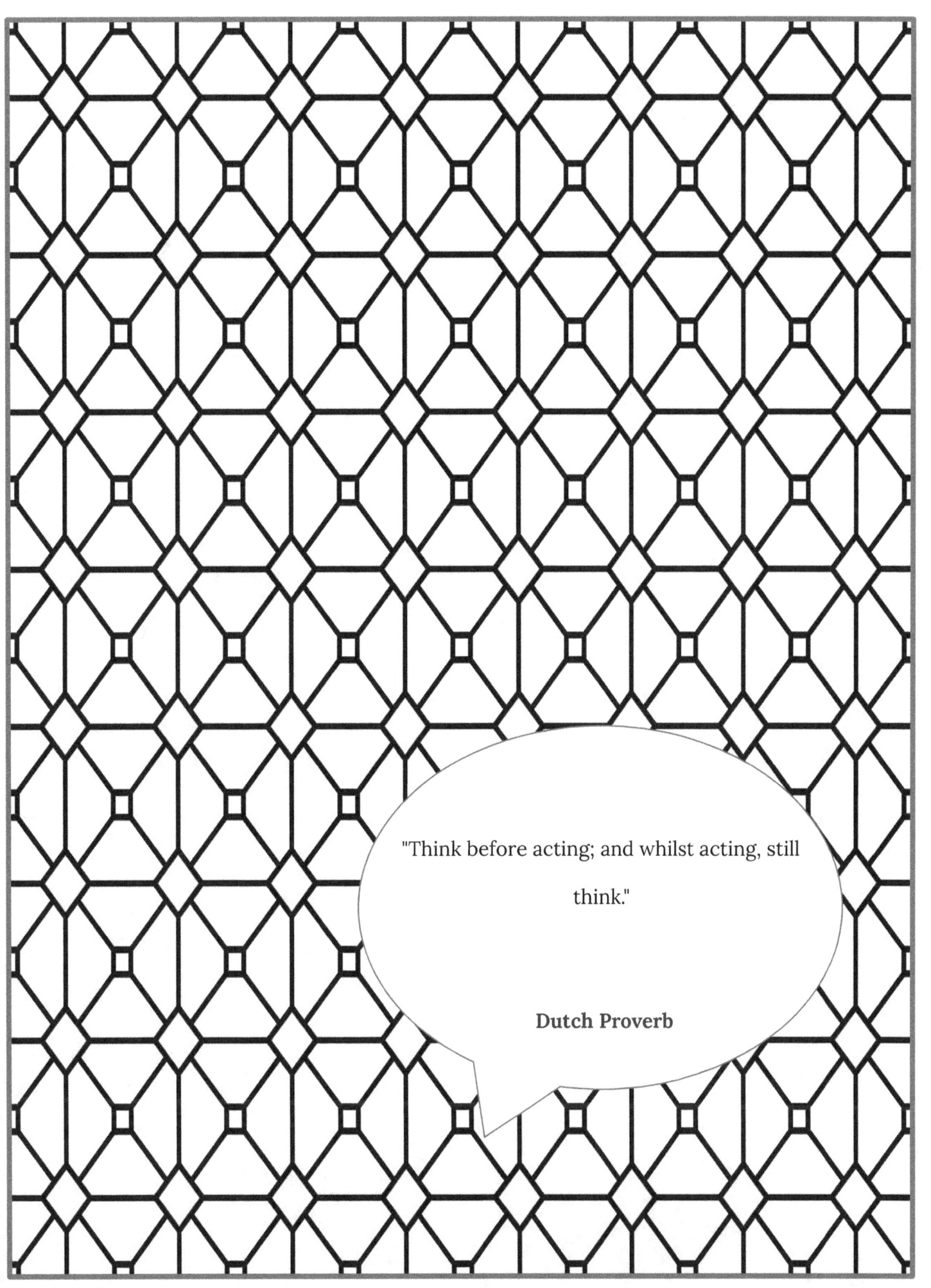

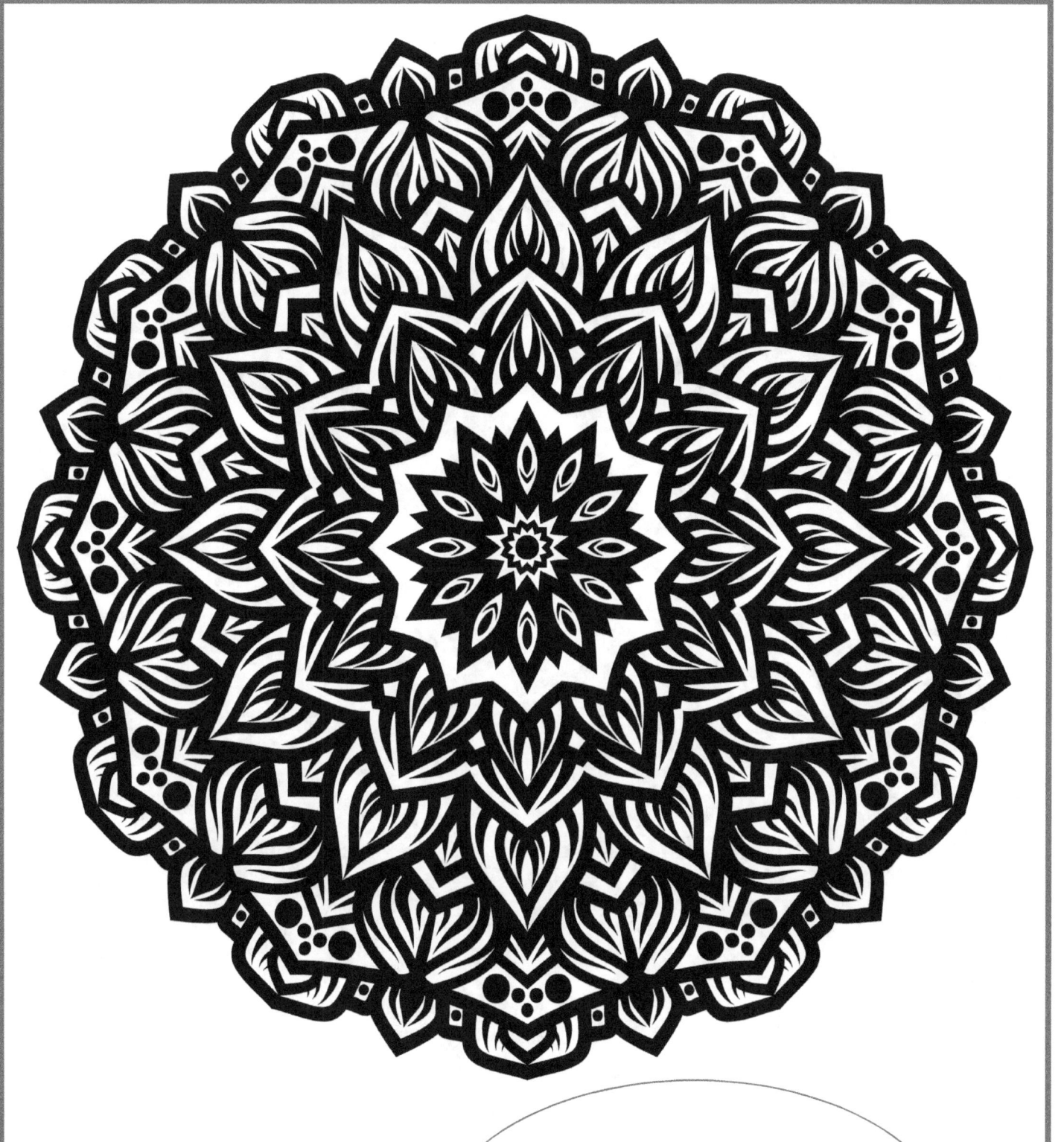

"A leader is not necessarily one who knows the way but one who thinks he knows the way."

Jewish Proverb

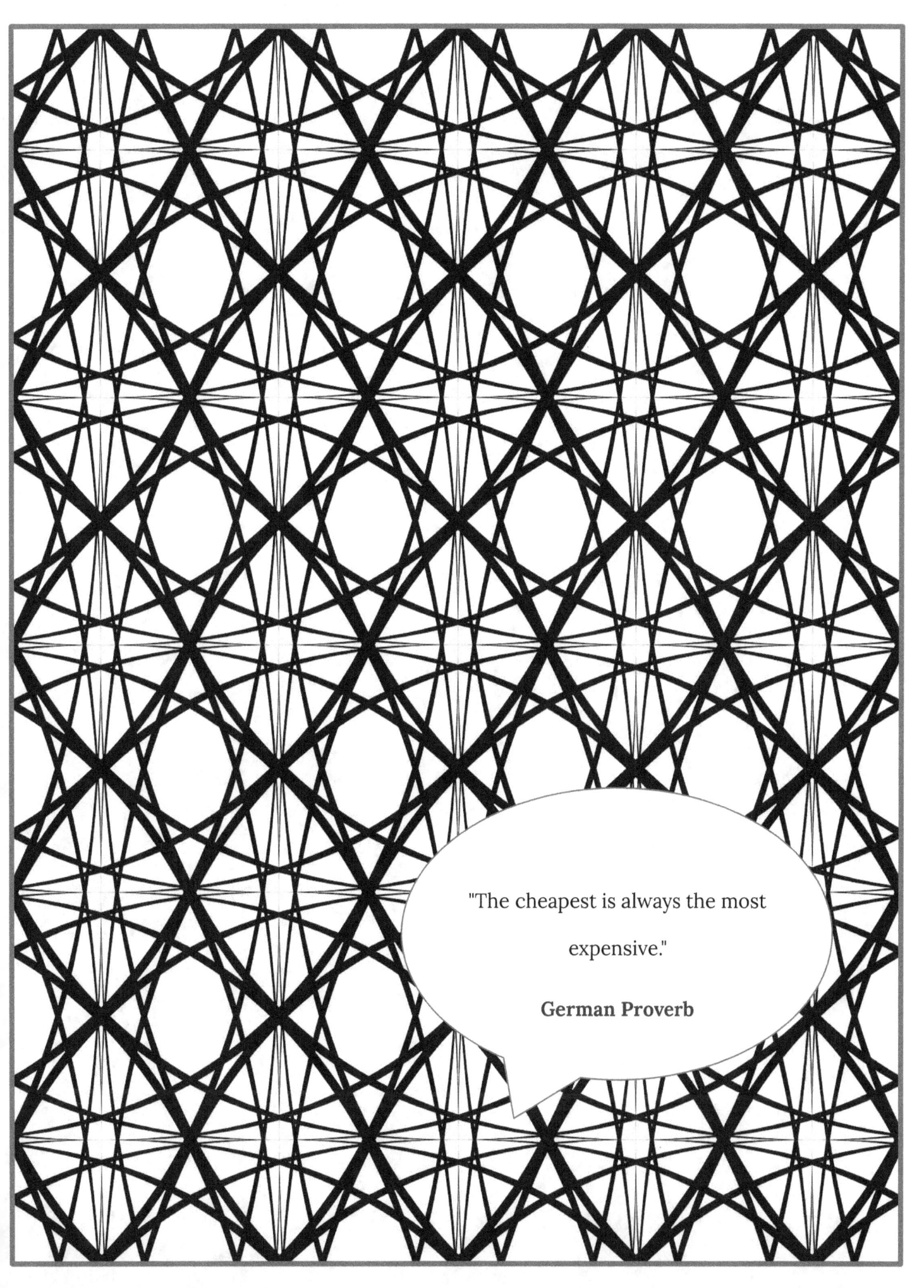

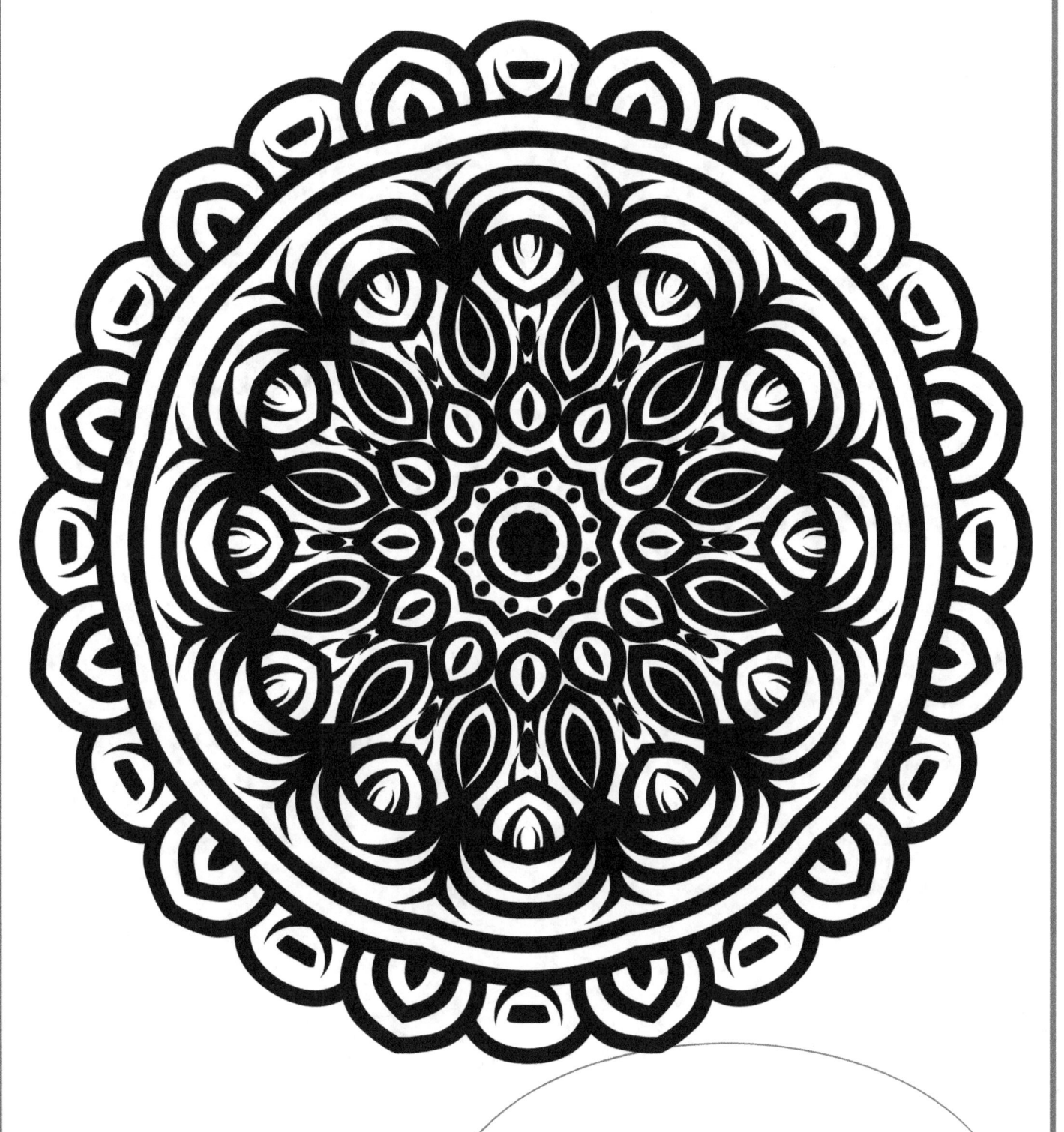

"Many hands make light work."

Russian Proverb

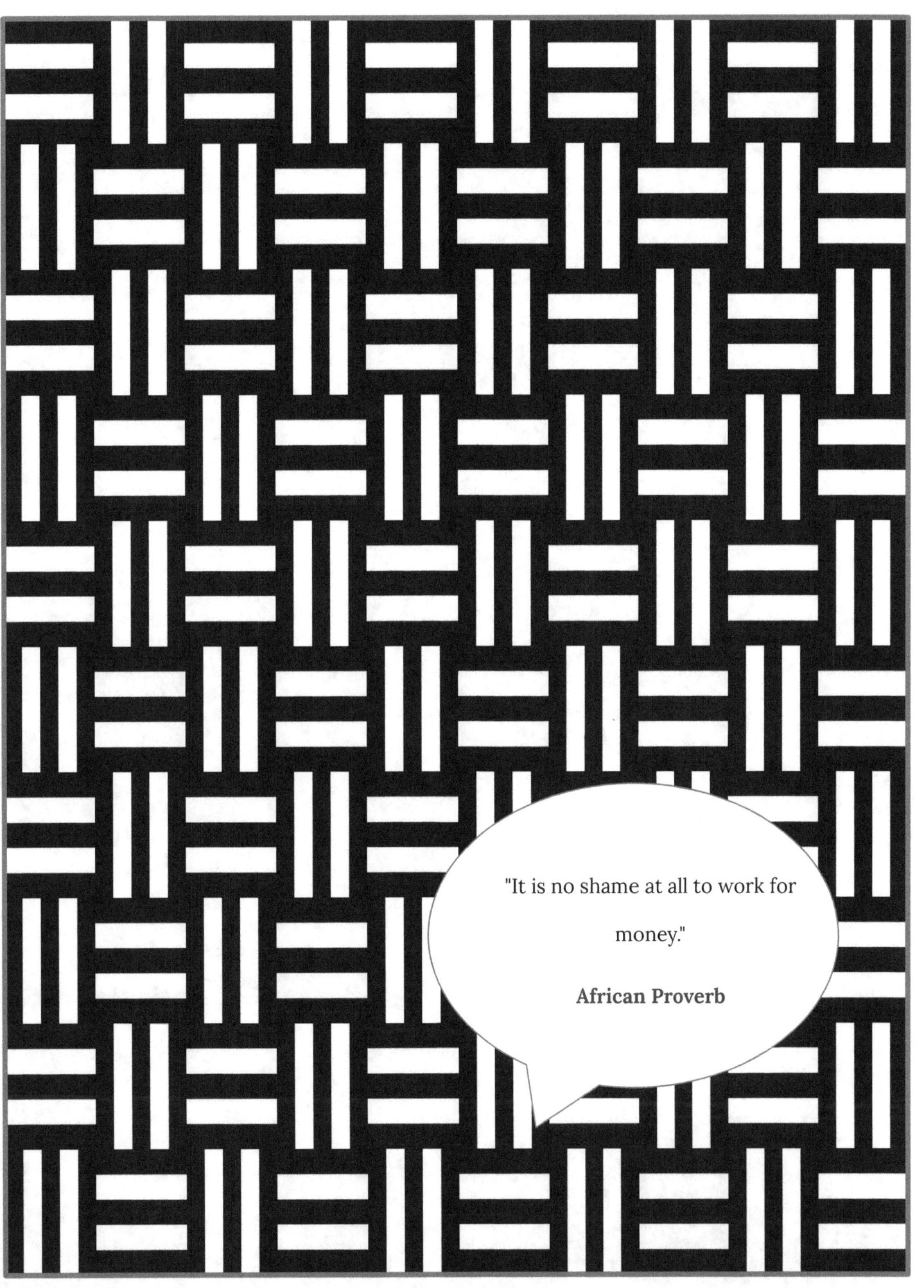

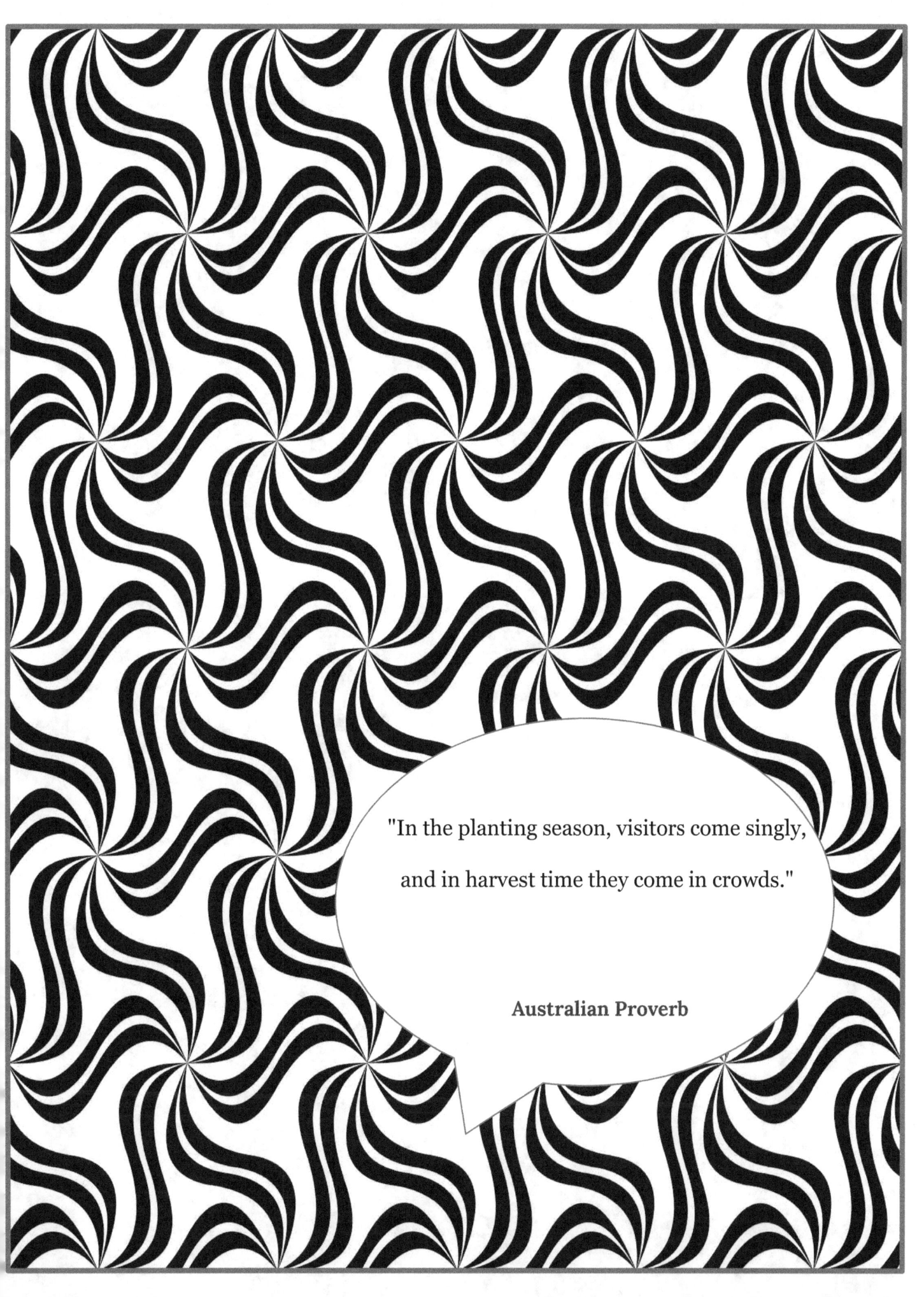

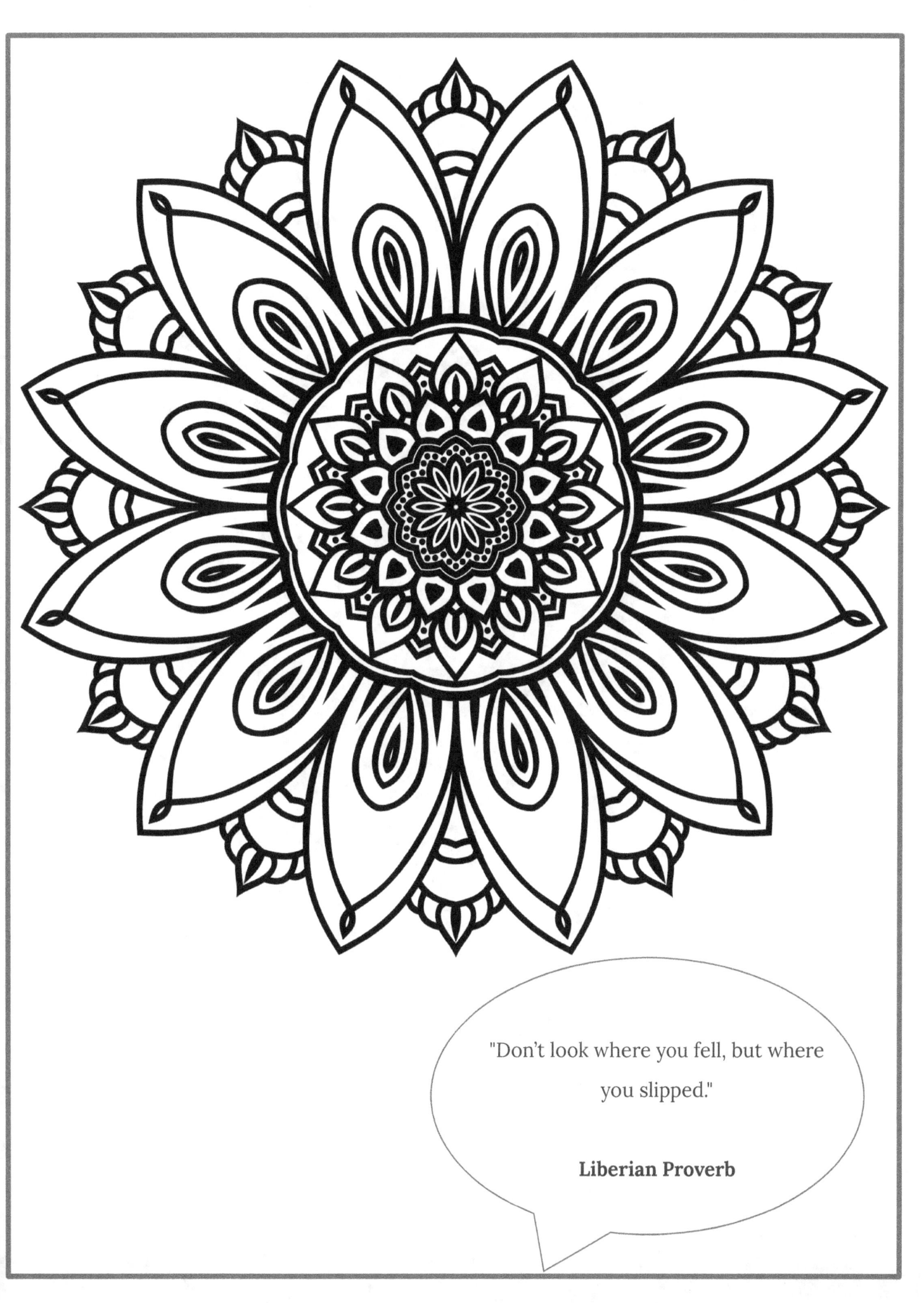

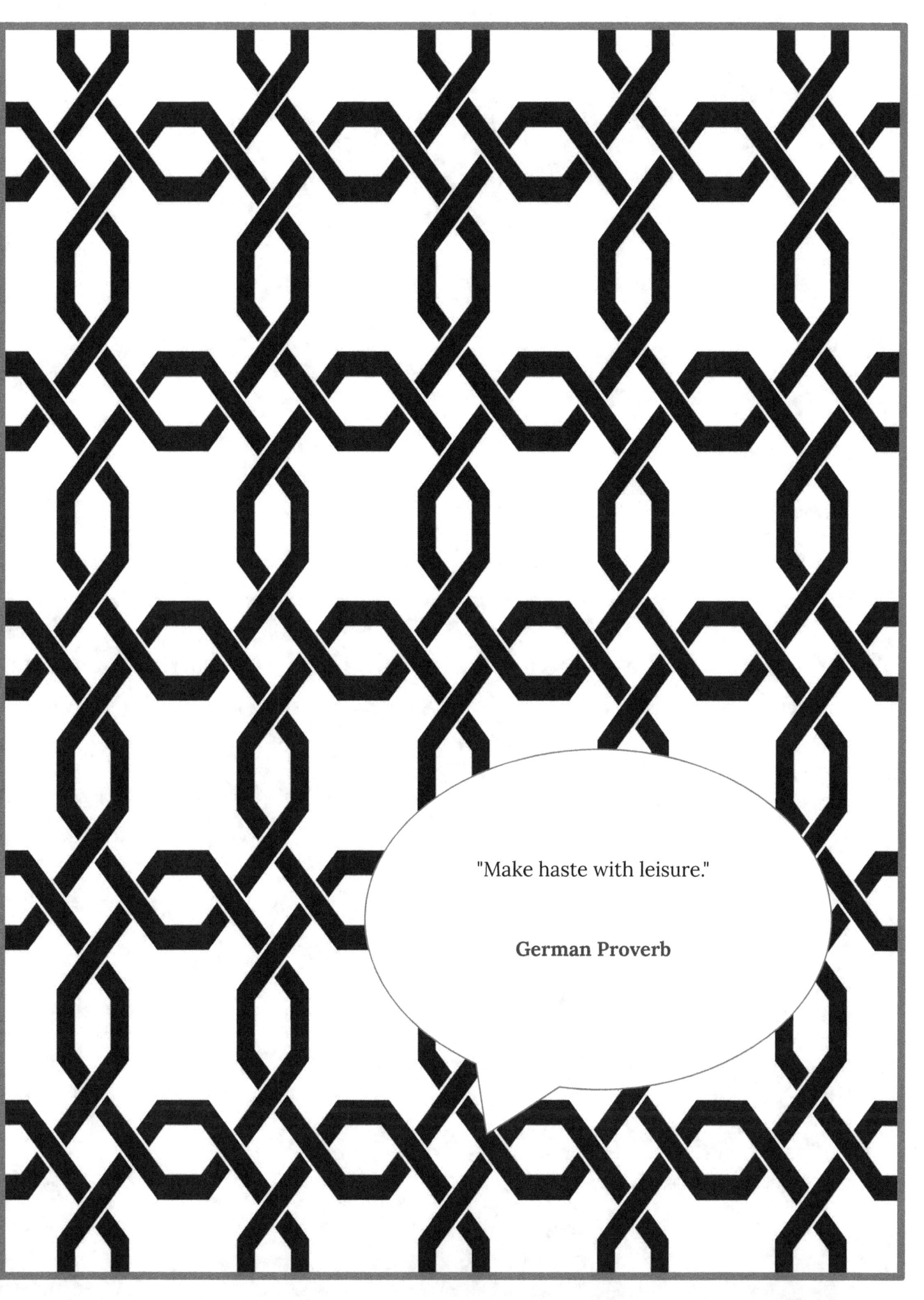

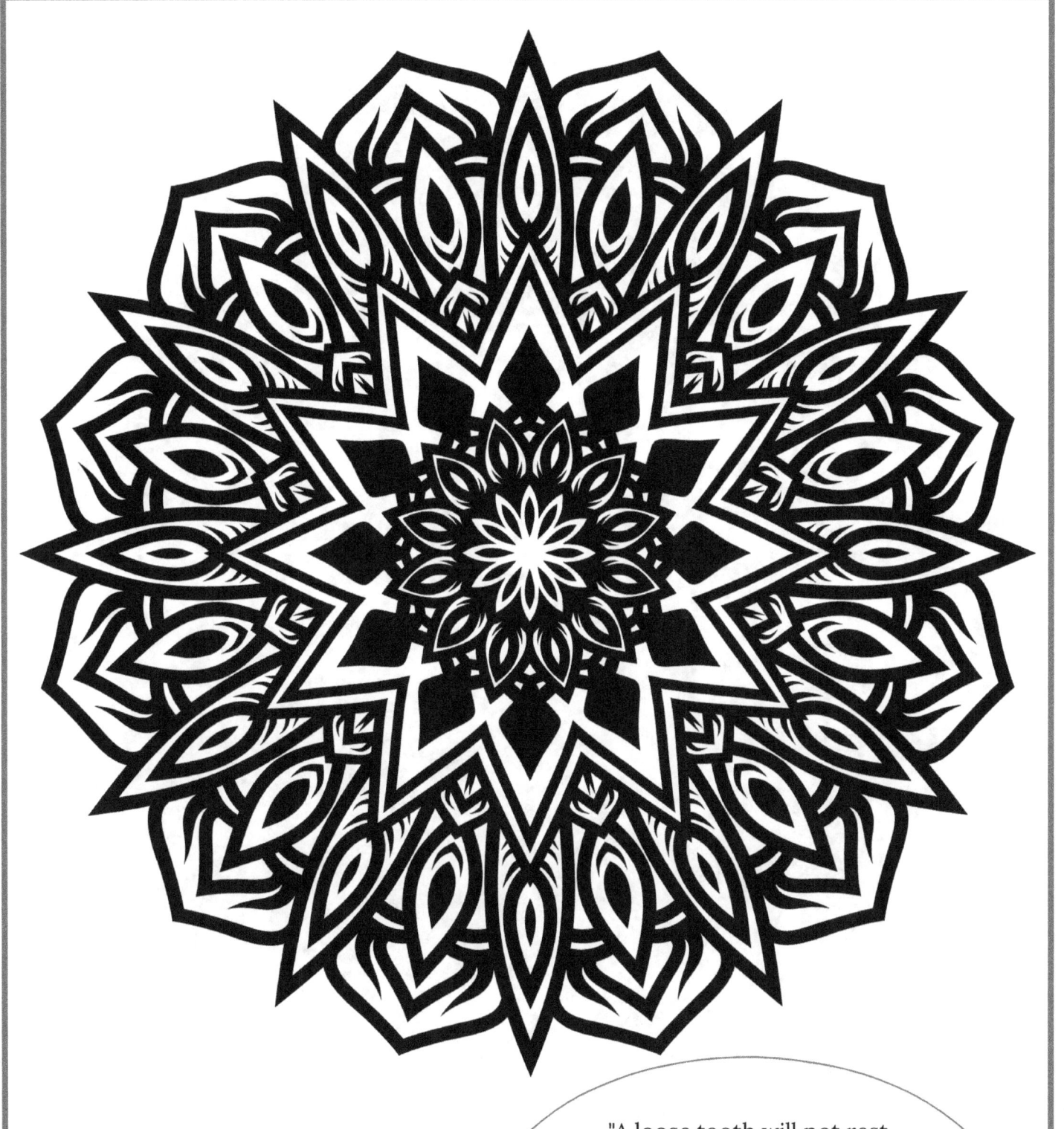

"A loose tooth will not rest until it's pulled out."

African Proverb

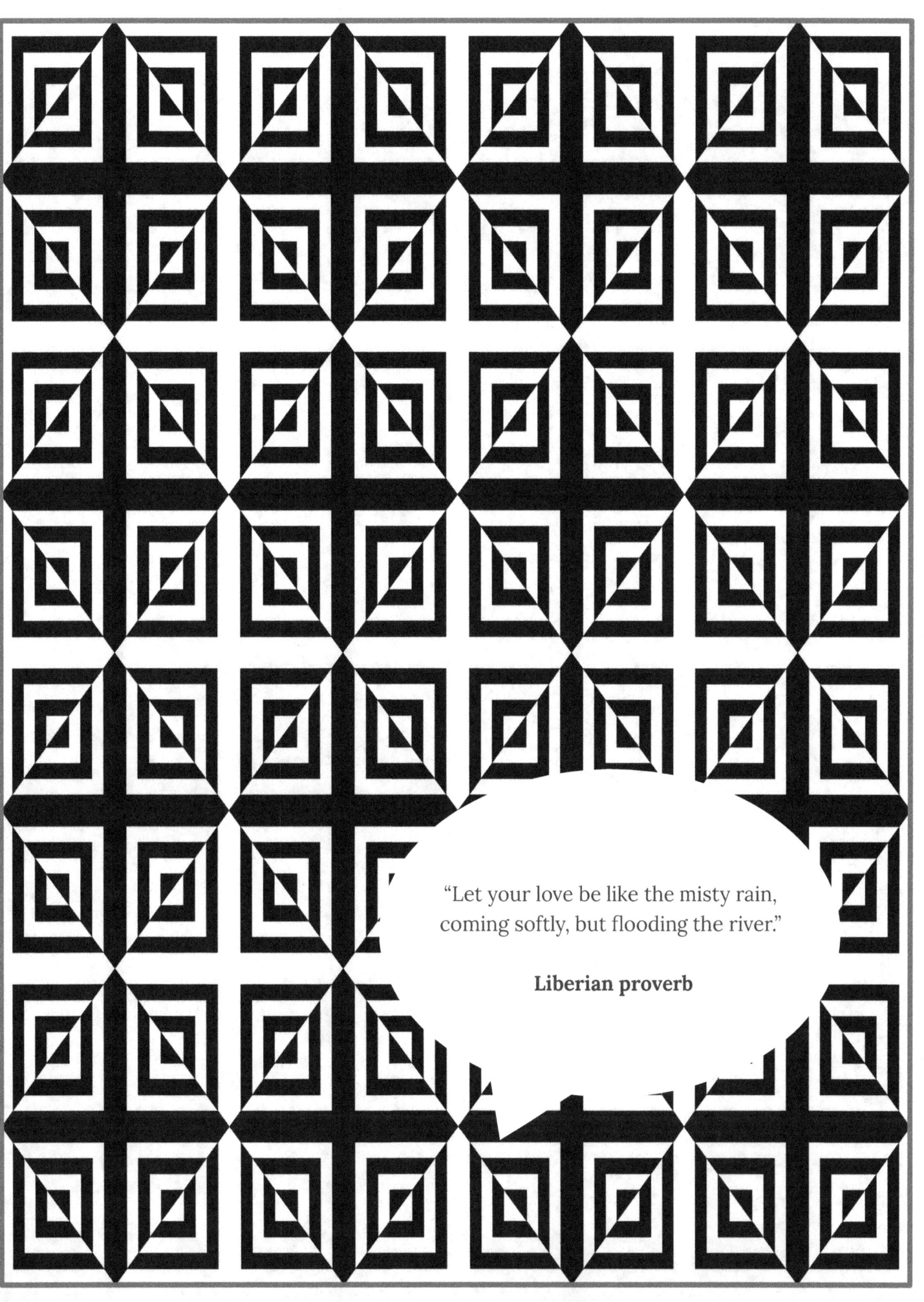

"Let your love be like the misty rain, coming softly, but flooding the river."

Liberian proverb

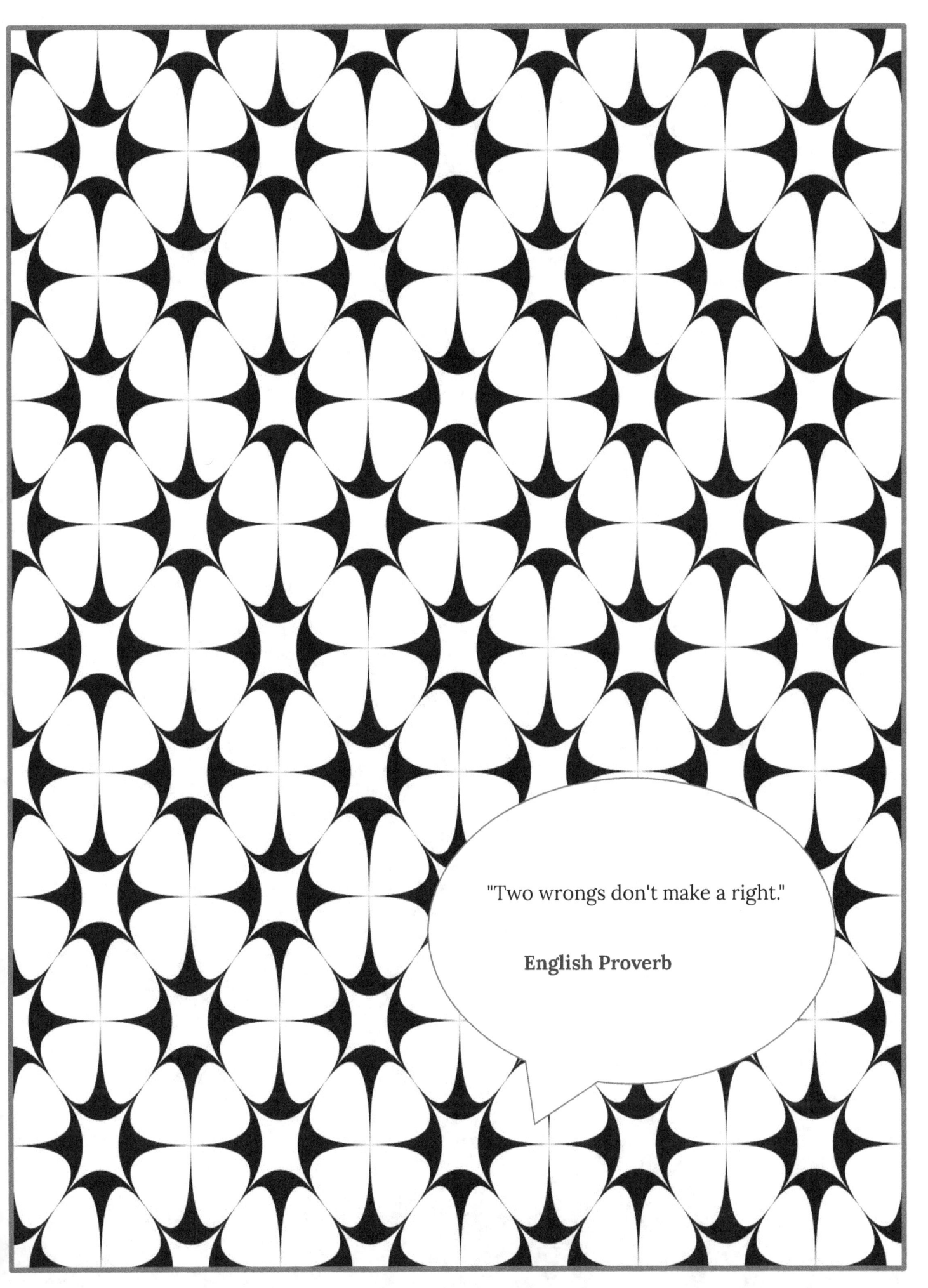

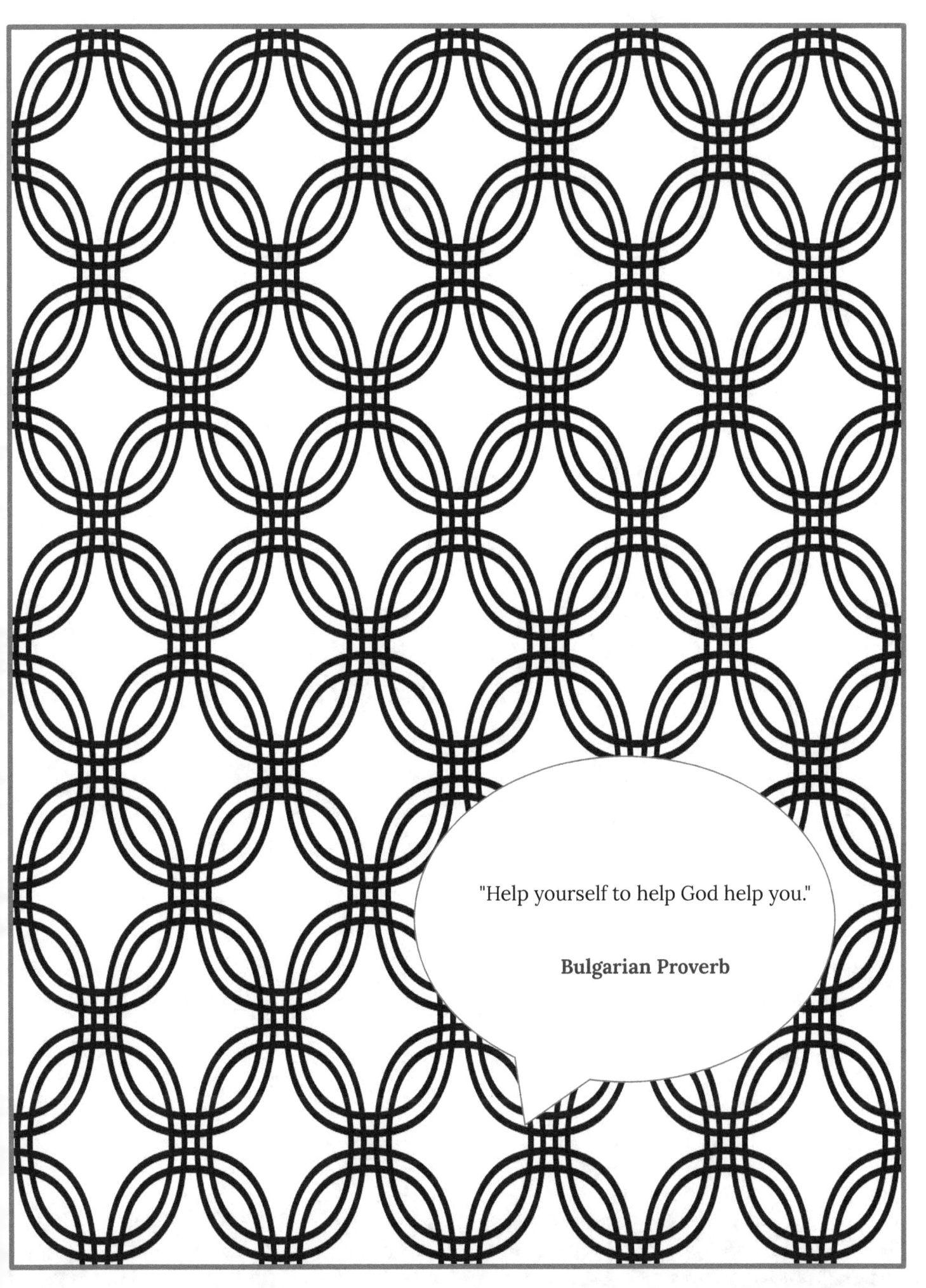

"Help yourself to help God help you."

Bulgarian Proverb

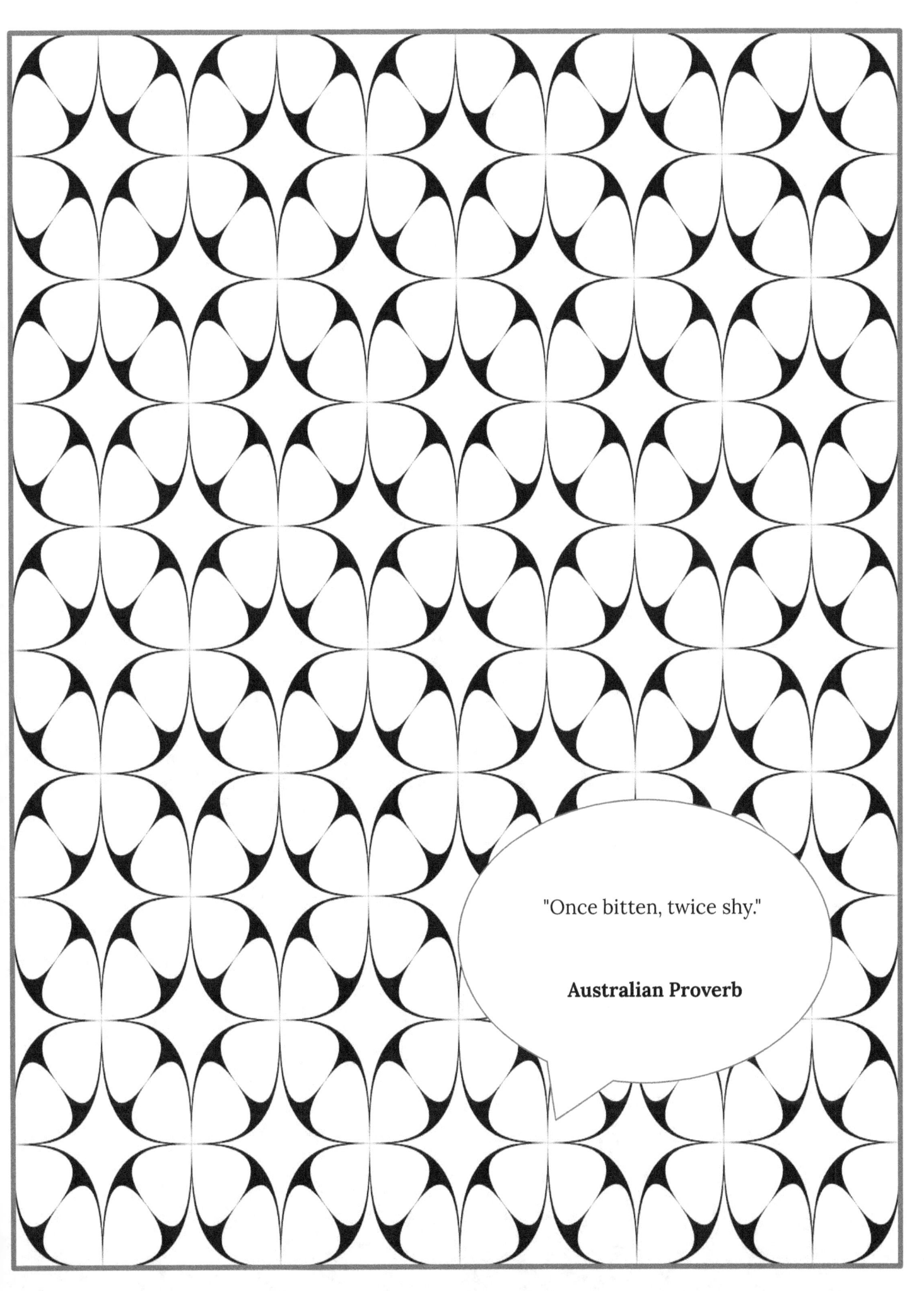

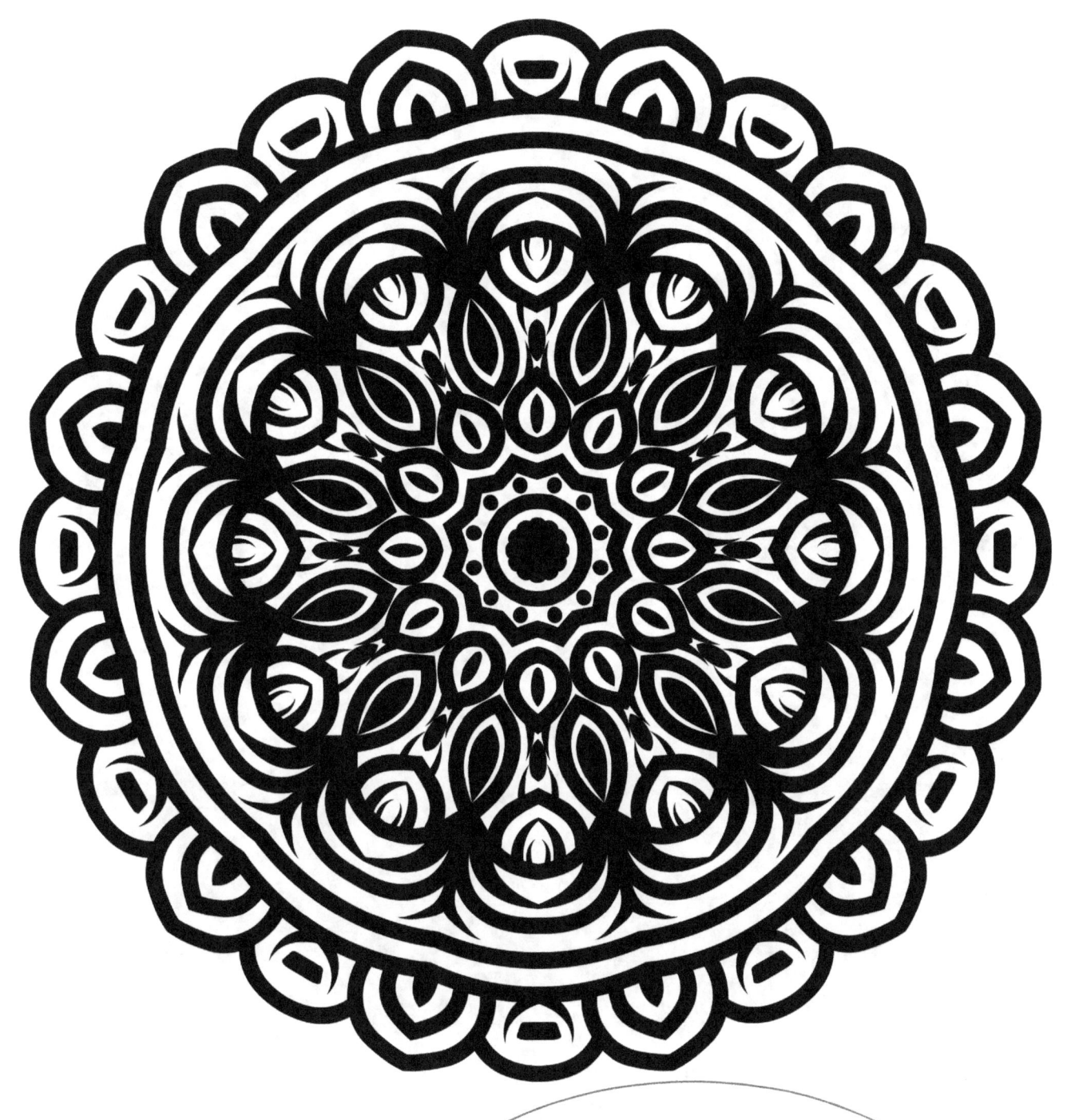

"Tell me who your friends are, so I can tell you who you are."

Bulgarian Proverb

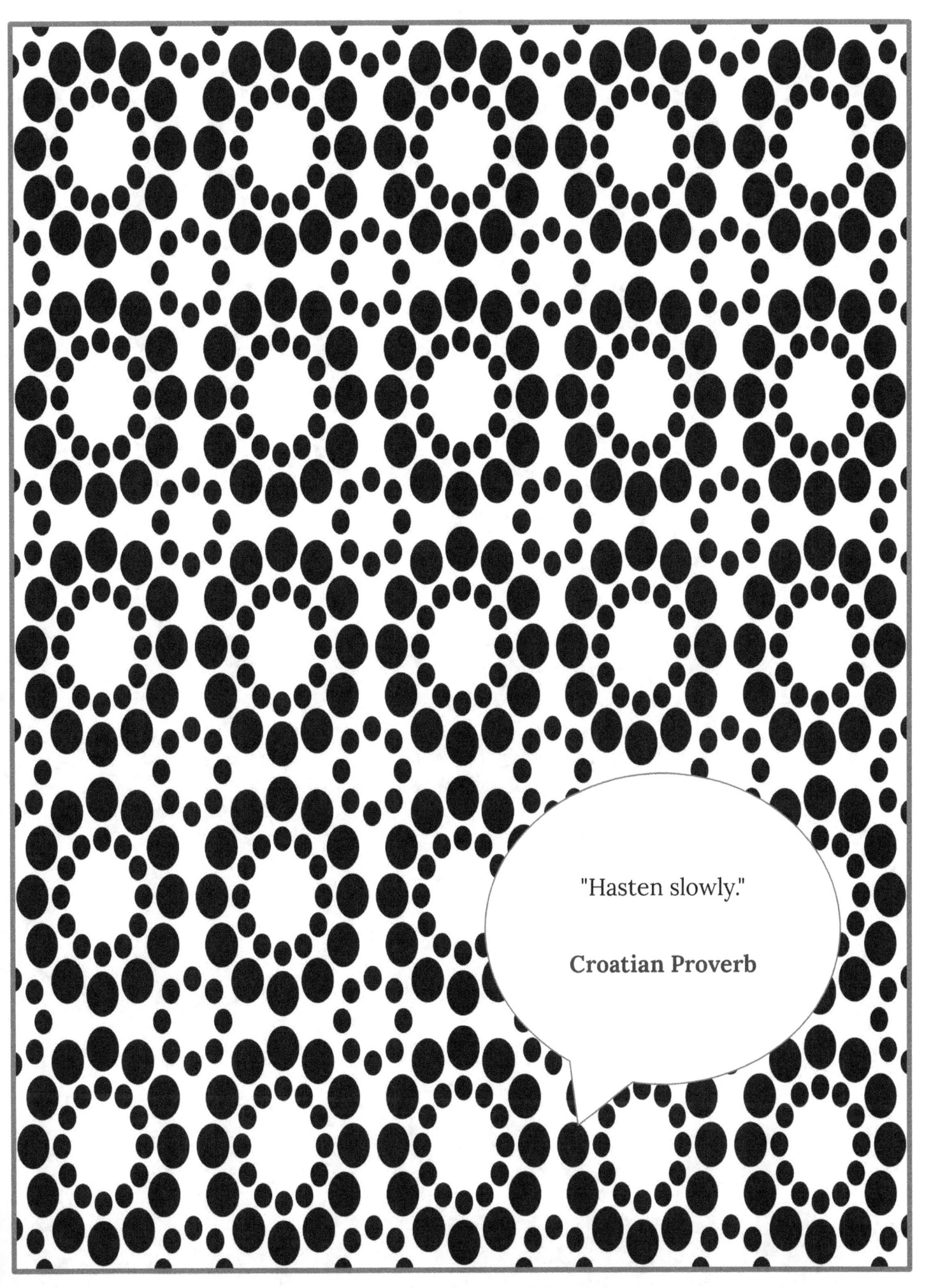

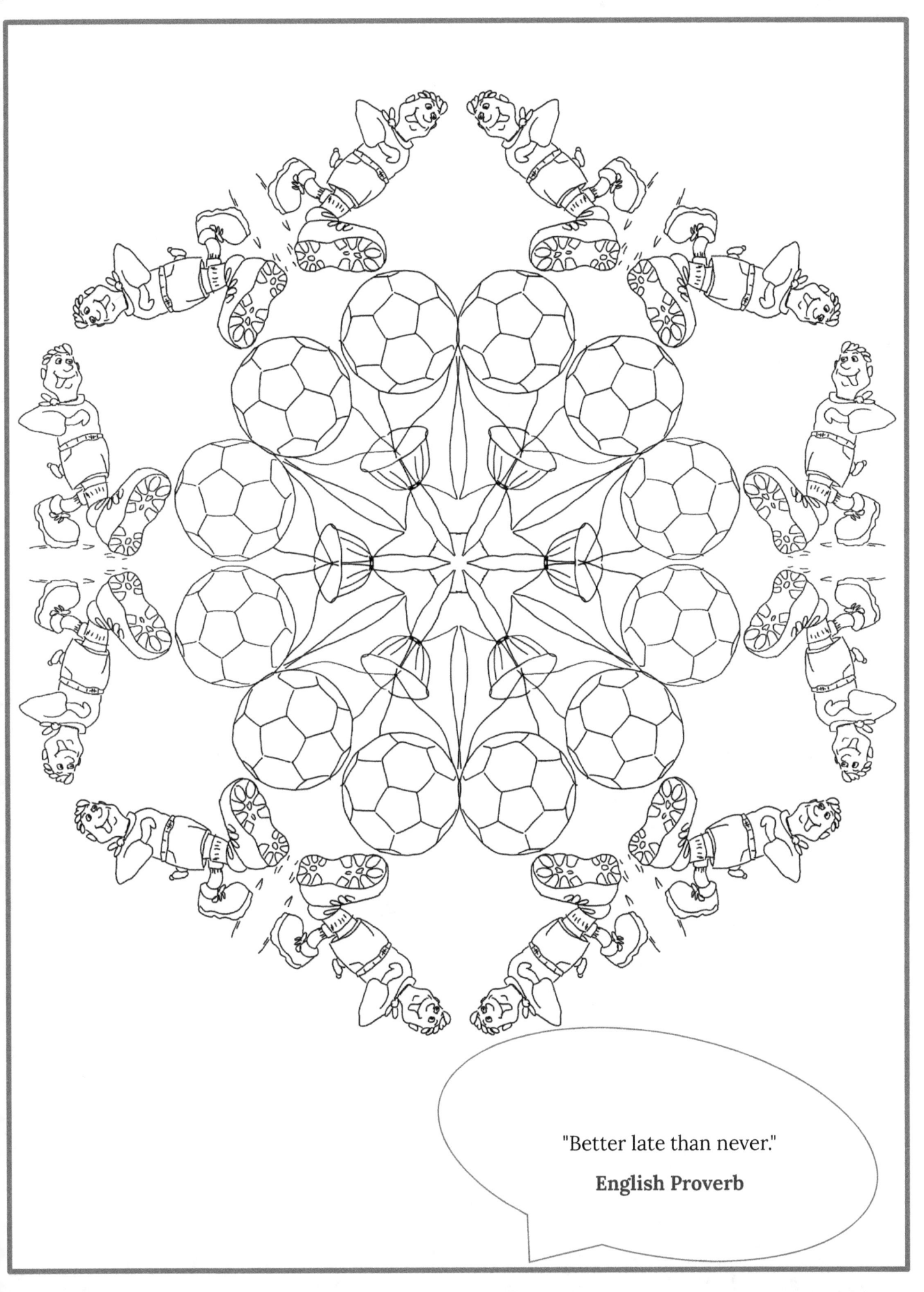

"Better late than never."

English Proverb

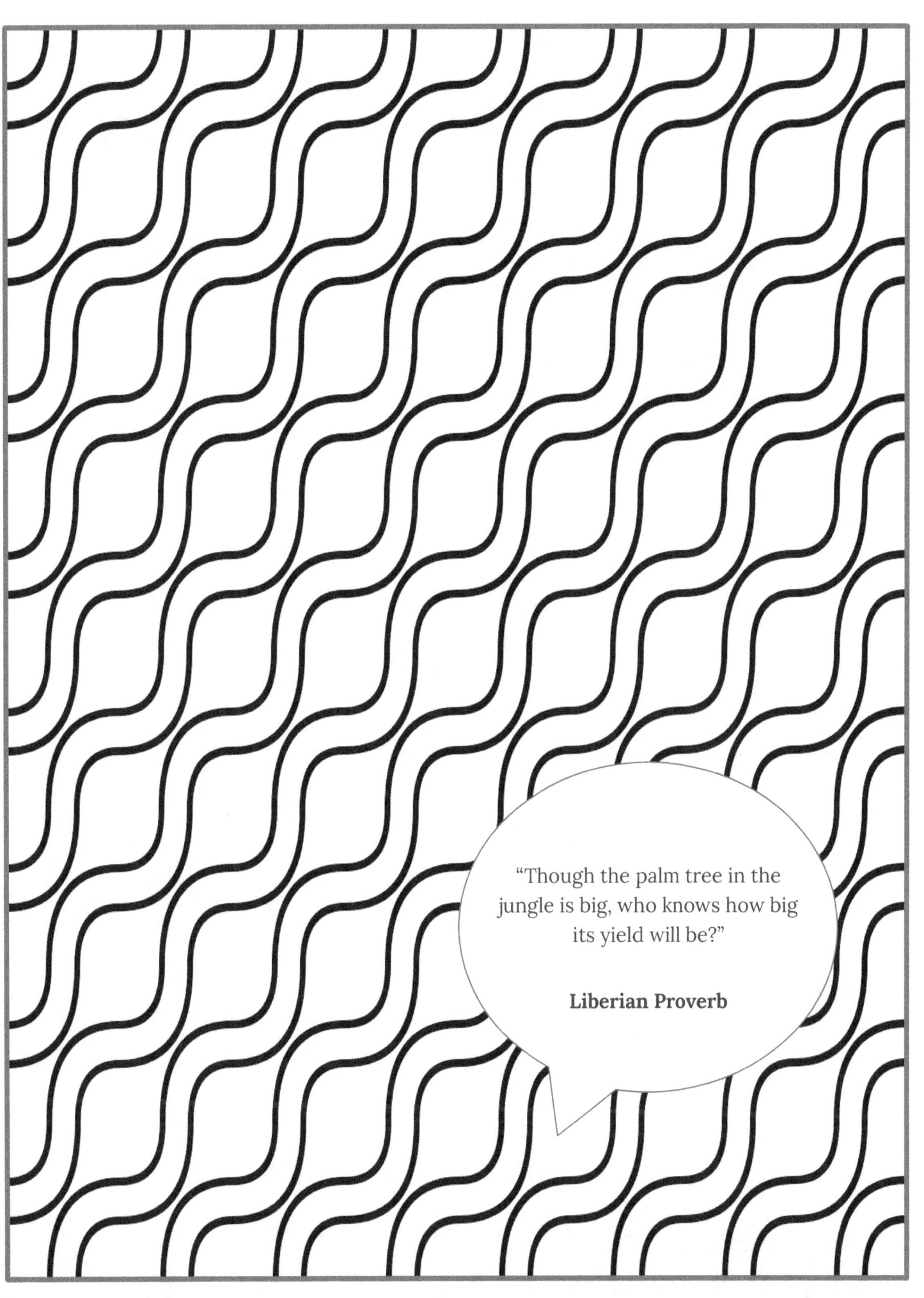

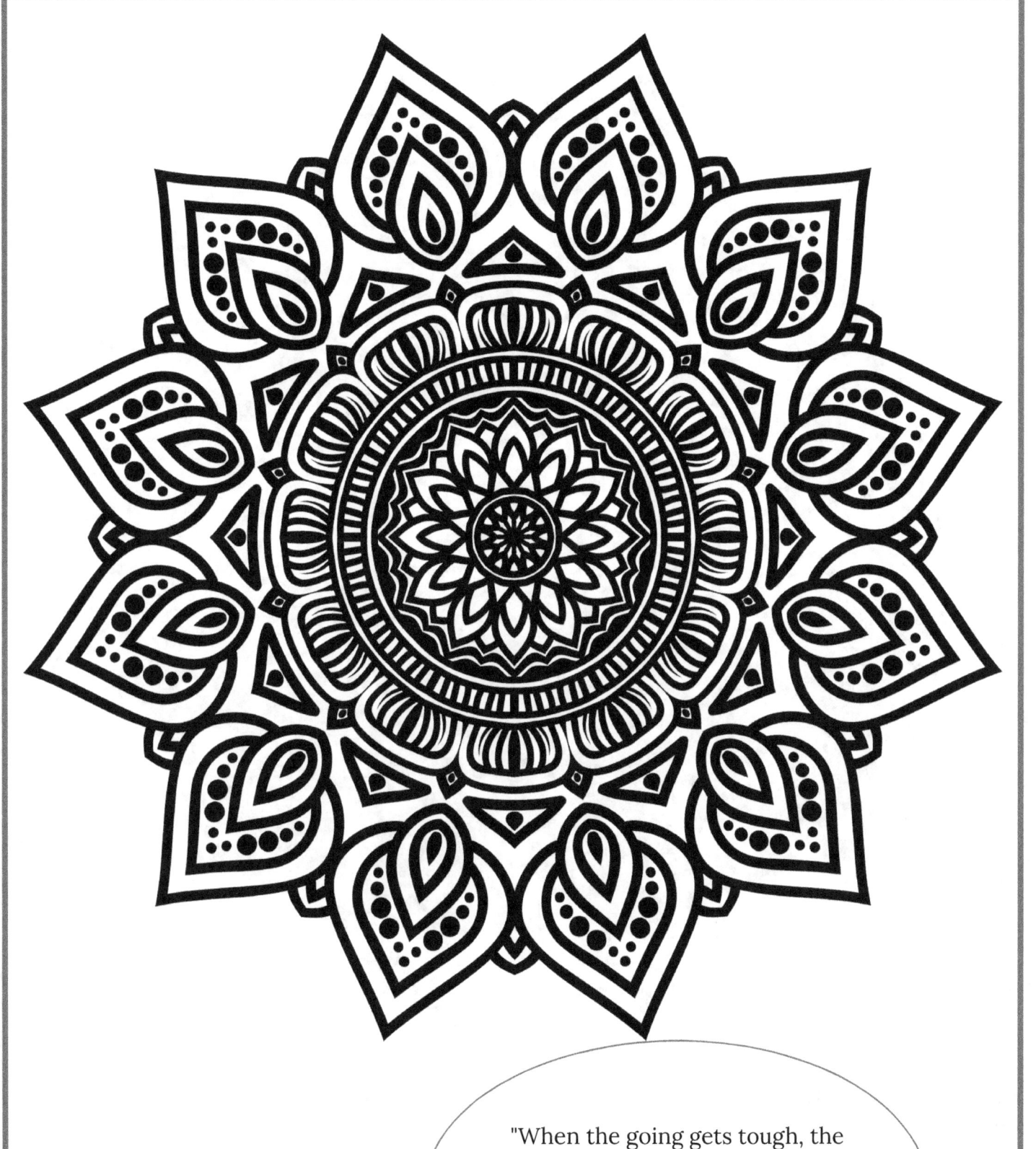

"When the going gets tough, the tough get going."

English Proverb

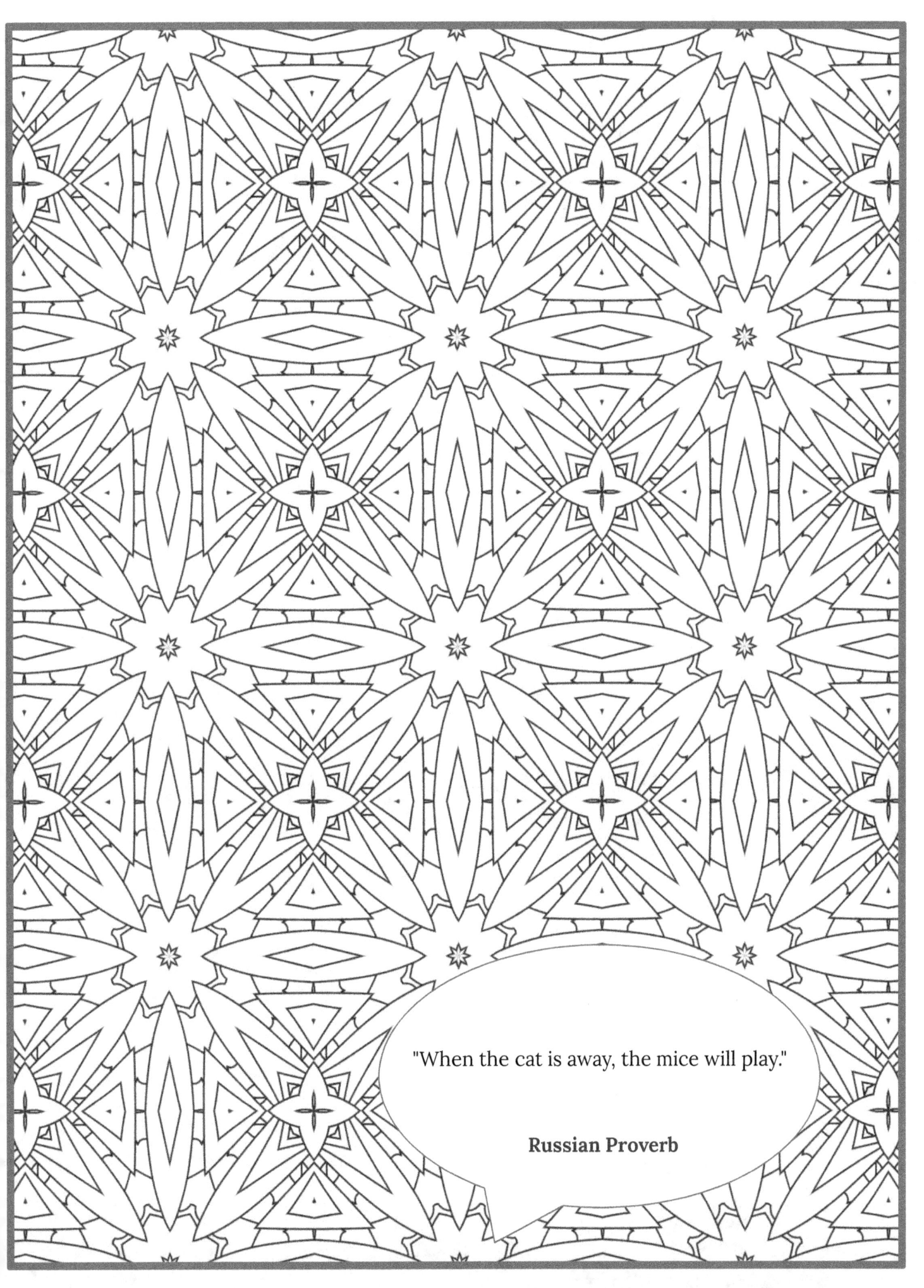

"When the cat is away, the mice will play."

Russian Proverb

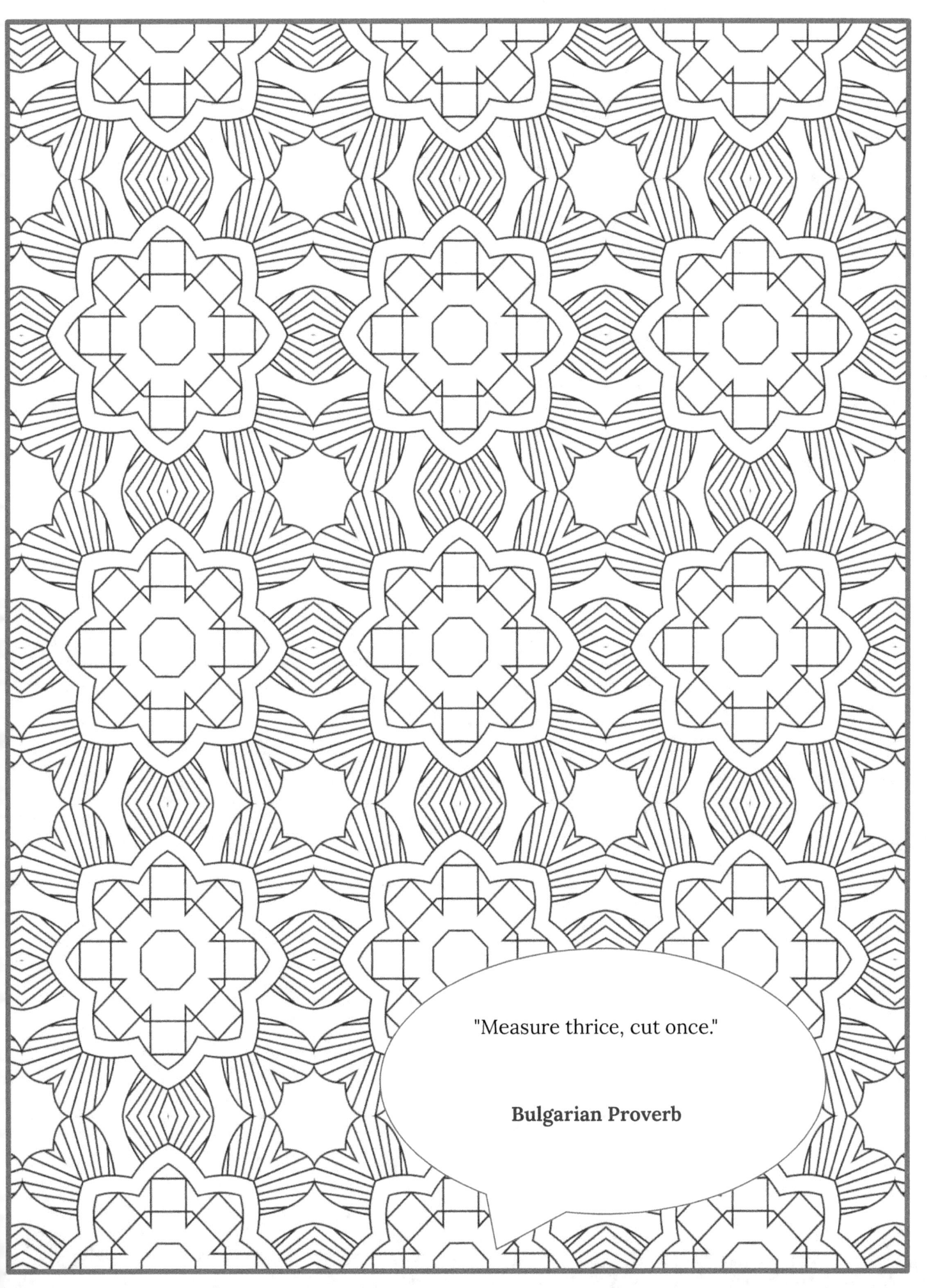

"Measure thrice, cut once."

Bulgarian Proverb

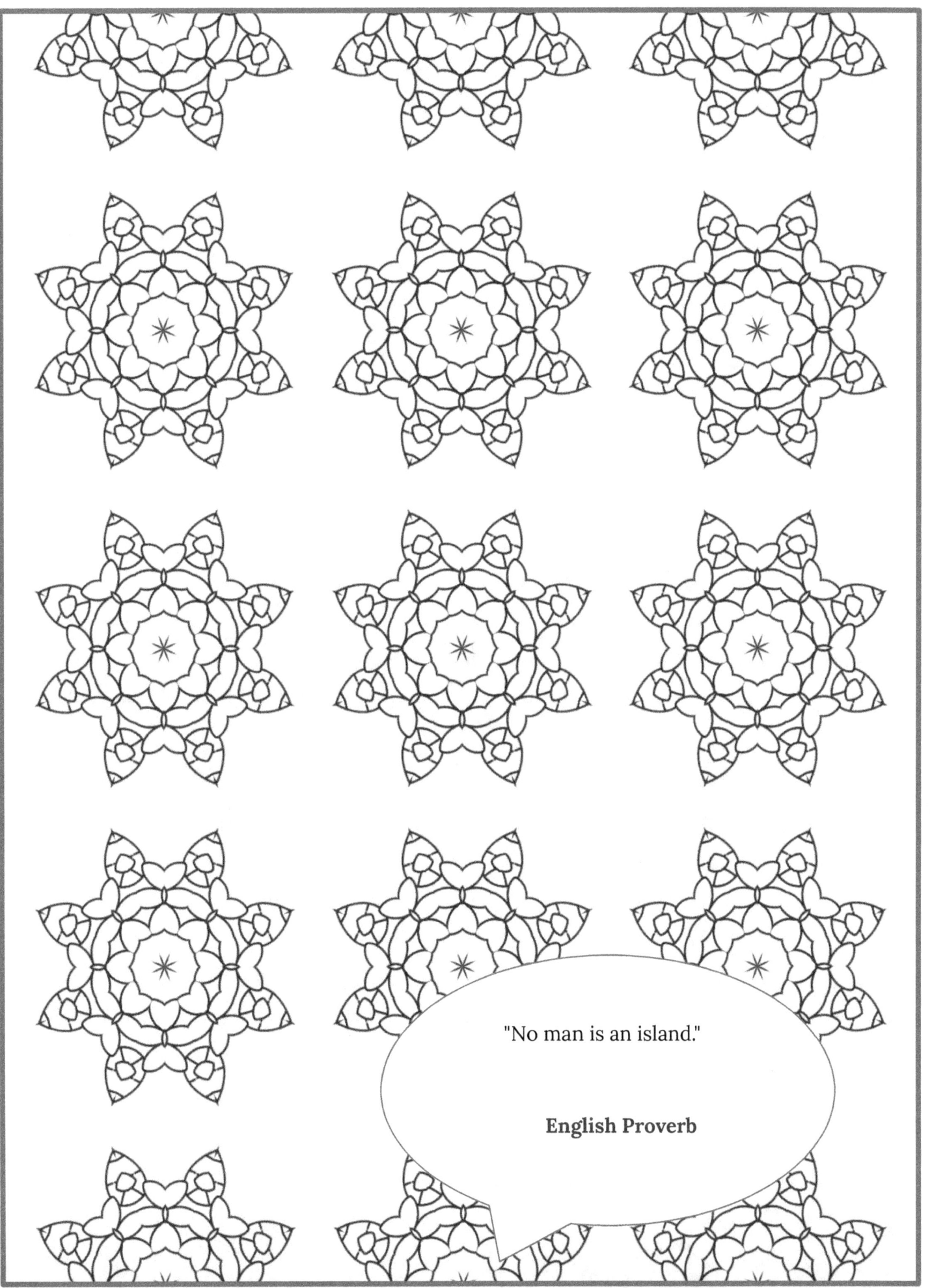

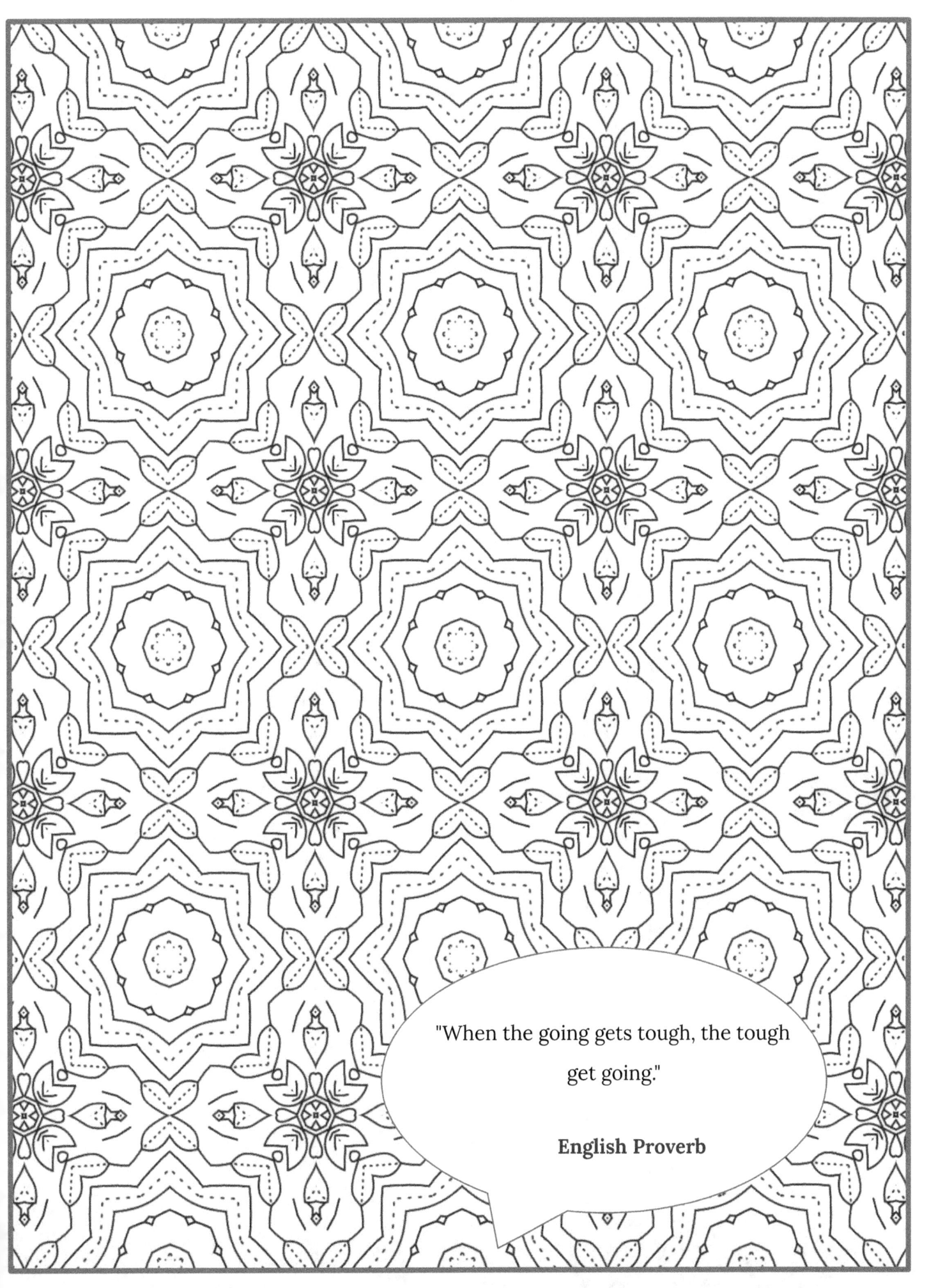

"When the going gets tough, the tough get going."

English Proverb

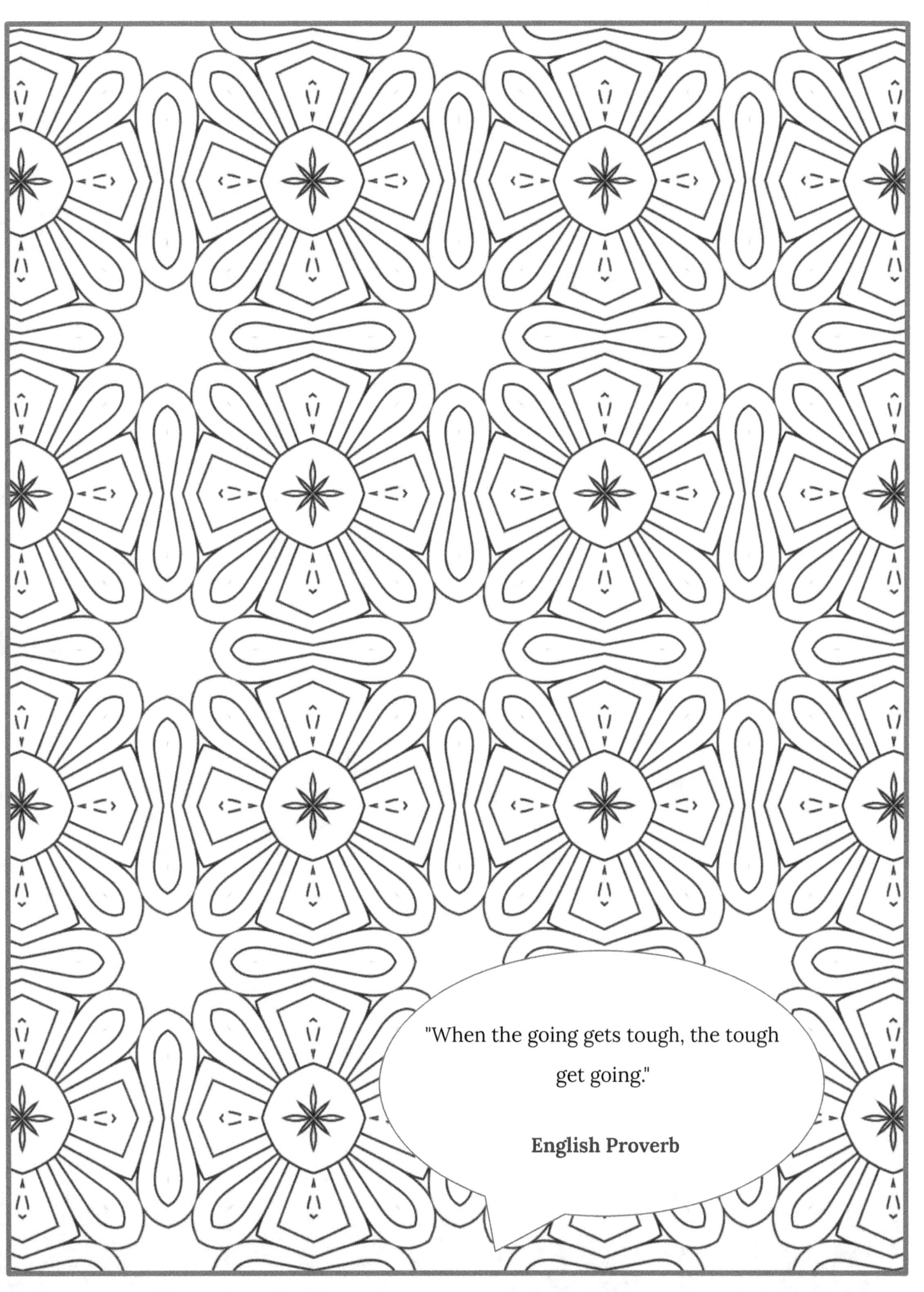

"When the going gets tough, the tough get going."

English Proverb

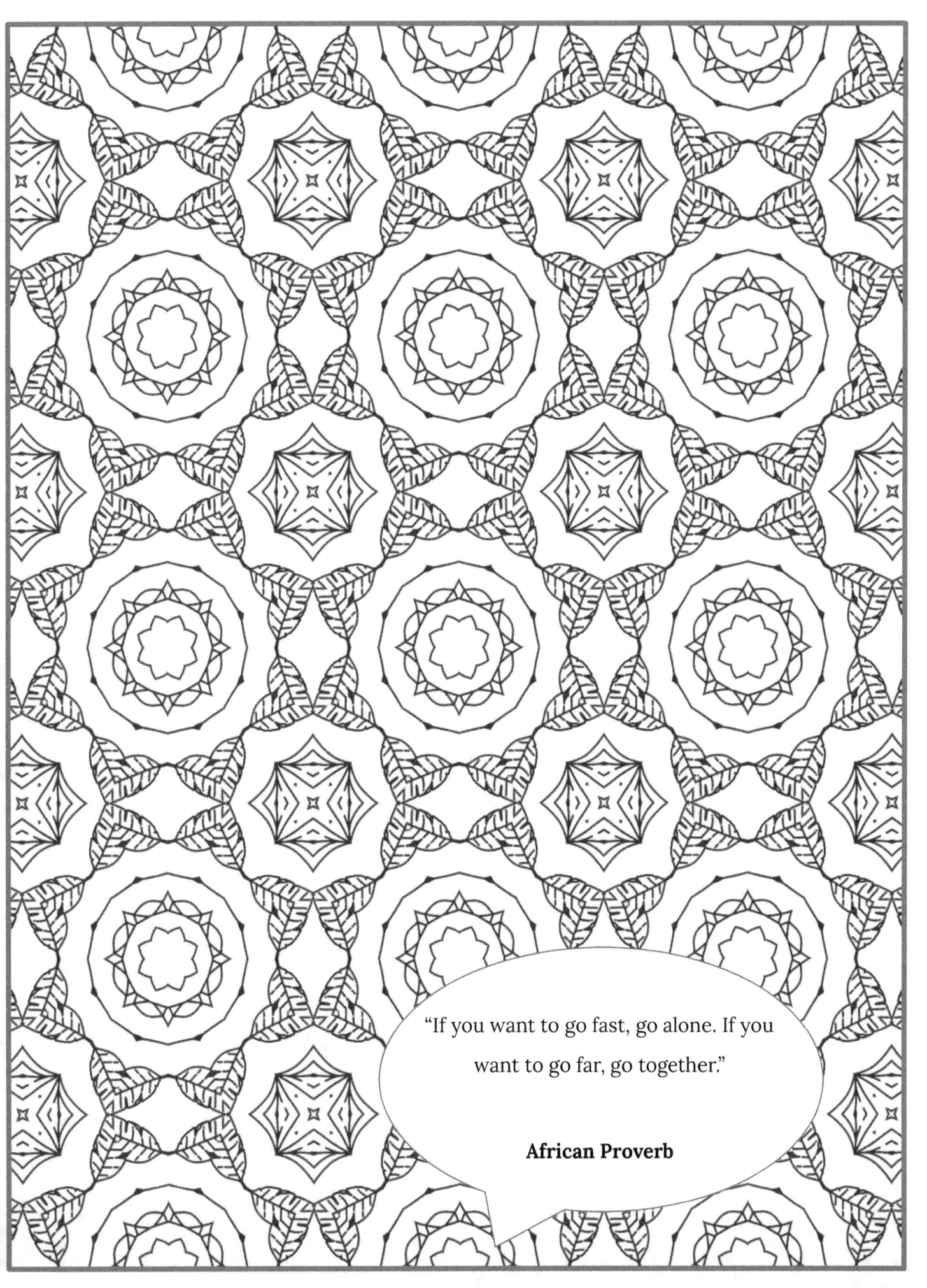

"If you want to go fast, go alone. If you want to go far, go together."

African Proverb

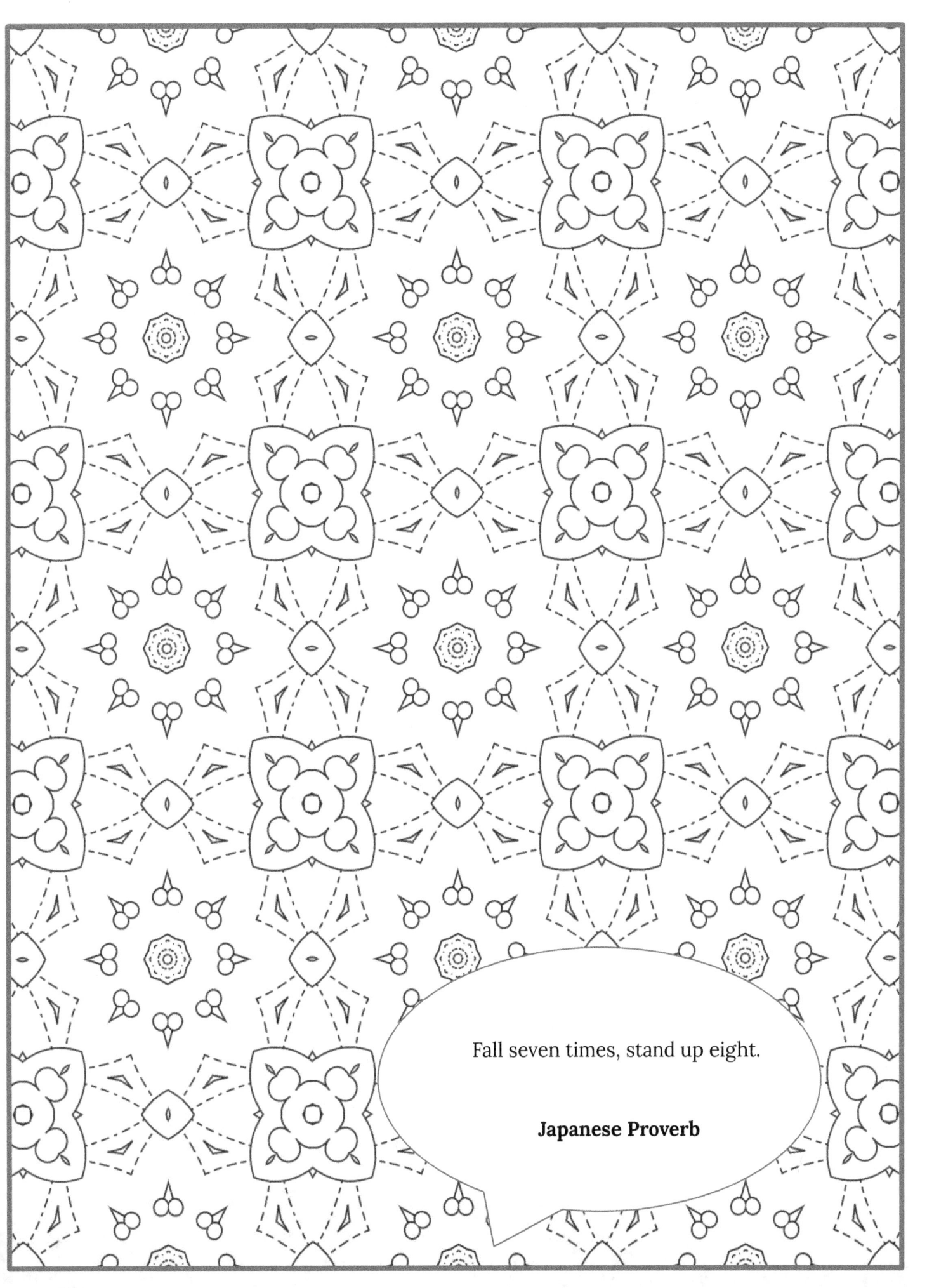

Fall seven times, stand up eight.

Japanese Proverb

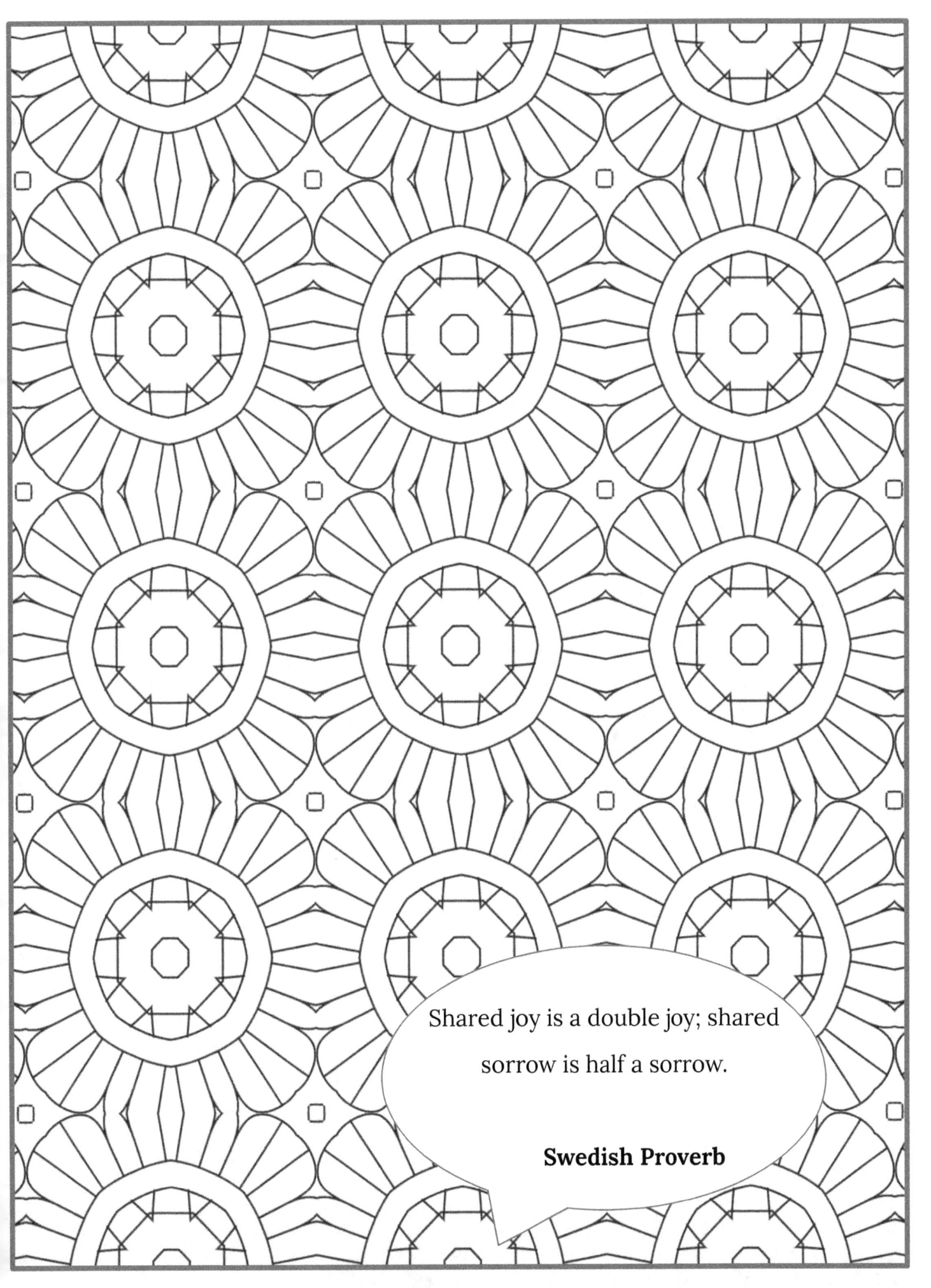

Shared joy is a double joy; shared sorrow is half a sorrow.

Swedish Proverb

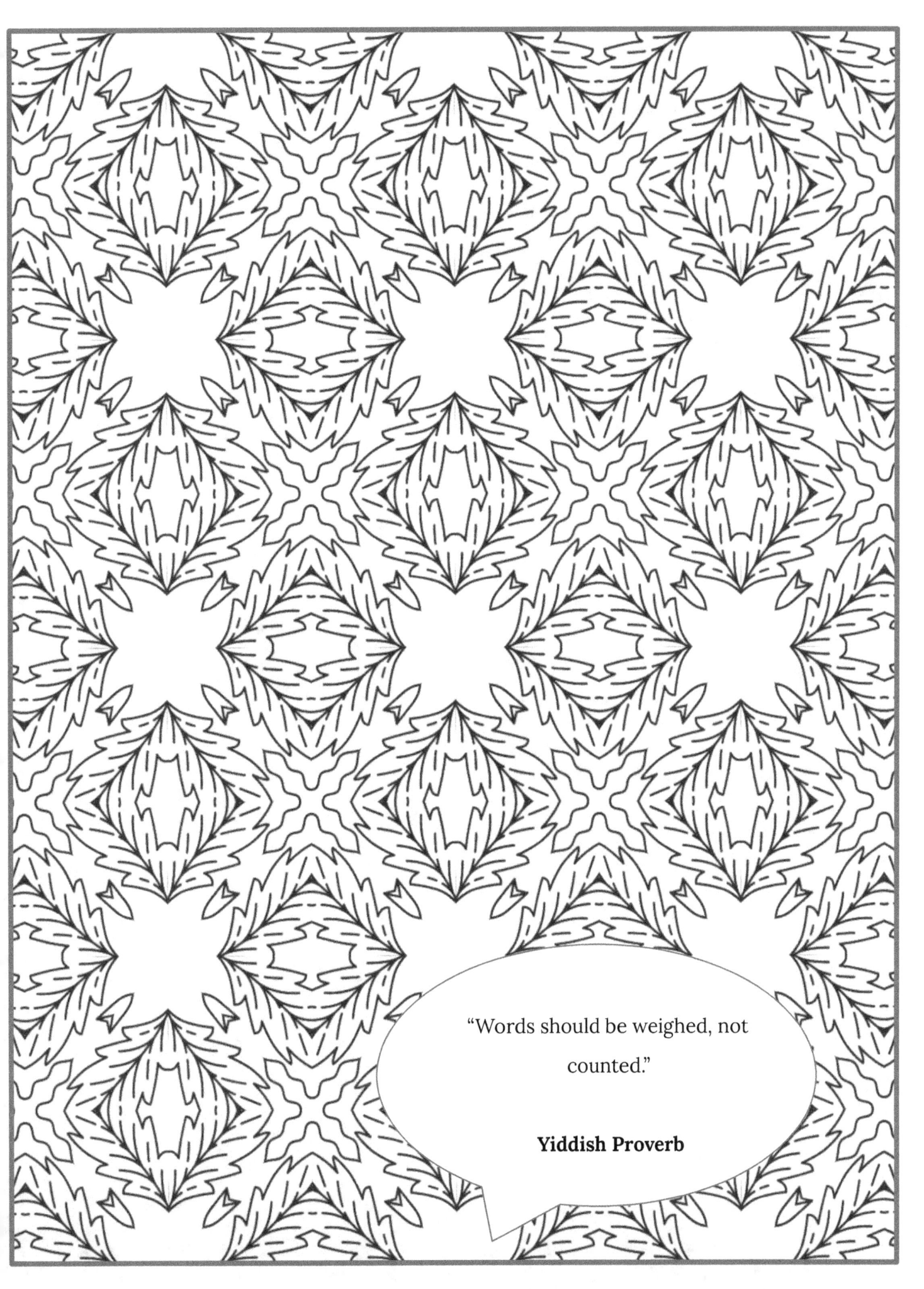

"Words should be weighed, not counted."

Yiddish Proverb

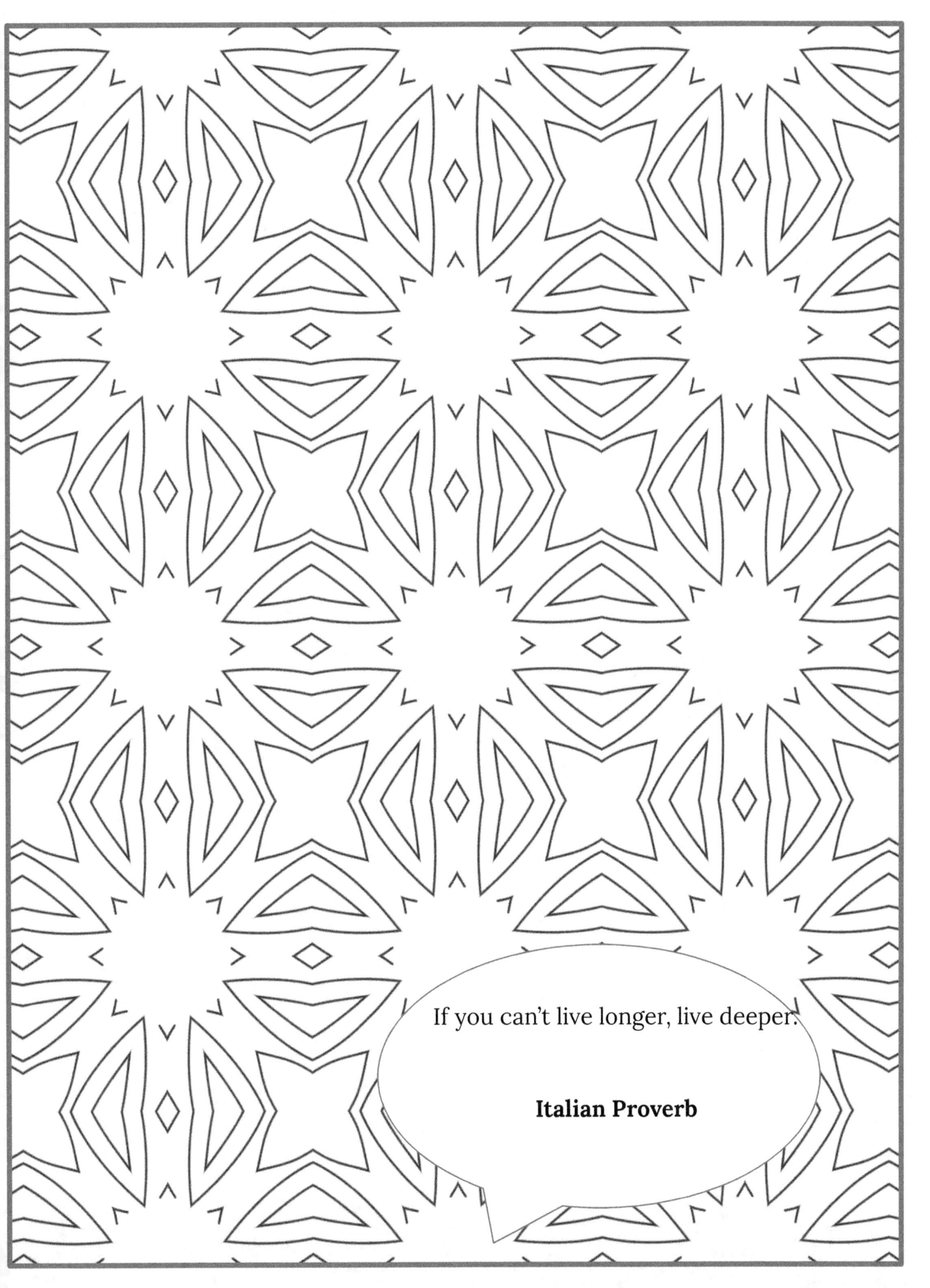

If you can't live longer, live deeper.

Italian Proverb